Black Women's Experiences of

ice

SS:

TAGE

ommentator on issues
he is an independent
at Birkbeck College,

tice soon became key
ed in 1997 (and was
extended edition, the
ater awareness of the
into contact with the

Black Women's Experiences of Criminal Justice
Race, Gender and Class: A Discourse On Disadvantage

SECOND EDITION

Published 2003 by
WATERSIDE PRESS
Domum Road
Winchester SO23 9NN

Telephone 01962 855567
Fax 01962 855567
email enquiries@watersidepress.co.uk
Online catalogue www.watersidepress.co.uk

ISBN Paperback 1 872 870 52 X

Cataloguing-in-Publication Data A catalogue record for this book can be obtained from the British Library

Cover design John Good Holbrook Ltd, Coventry/Waterside Press

Printing and binding Antony Rowe Ltd, Chippenham

First edition 1997 Paperback 1 872 870 54 6

Black Women's Experiences

of

Criminal Justice

RACE, GENDER AND CLASS:
A DISCOURSE ON DISADVANTAGE

SECOND EDITION

Ruth Chigwada-Bailey

WATERSIDE PRESS
WINCHESTER

For my late parents

Rina and John Chigwada

Black Women's Experiences of Criminal Justice

SECOND EDITION

CONTENTS

Extracts from the Foreword to the First Edition

There has been, in recent years, an encouraging increase in the attention given to issues of race as they affect the position of ethnic minorities within the criminal justice system. This focus was given impetus by section 95 Criminal Justice Act 1991. A number of influential studies, some of them mentioned in this book, act as a reminder of the need for this provision which requires the Home Secretary to publish relevant information for the information of people involved in the administration of justice. These and other data have done much to raise awareness of the way in which minority ethnic groups, in particular Afro-Caribbean people, have been disadvantaged in matters of criminal justice. There is now a growing body of evidence documenting the extent to which discrimination occurs at various stages in the process including in court proceedings, prisons, and in the work of the police and of probation services. Culture, class and a complicated nexus of factors contribute to explaining the reasons underlying unequal handling but it is now clear that skin colour provides a vital key to understanding these patterns. These factors seem to have impacted disproportionately on black people and on women and this contributes to understanding black over-representation in the prison population.

In this book, Ruth Chigwada-Bailey seeks to extend our knowledge in a fresh direction by directly retelling personal experiences which inform us about the perspectives of black women who have actually been through the criminal justice process. What these women say . . . deserves to be listened to. It is some of the best information we have about the lives of such women, who, according to the statistics, are not only currently appearing in record numbers in our prisons, but appear to be suffering proportionately higher penalties for their offences. Black women face multiple hazards of discrimination through race, gender and social class. The much trumpeted efforts in the last decade or so to address problems of black disadvantage in criminal justice agencies have not yet delivered anything like the even-handed justice which is the declared aim of equality policies. Ruth Chigwada-Bailey, in setting out these experiences drawn directly on the testimony of black women trapped in the system . . . We should listen to the women in the book and I hope it will reach many people concerned with the administration of criminal justice.

Sylivia Denman CBE
Former member of the Criminal Justice Consultative Council, April 1997

Acknowledgements

The work from which this book derives would not have been possible without the participation of the women interviewed. To them all I am more than grateful for volunteering to share their experiences with me.

I am also very grateful to Jill Radford for looking at the first draft of the original manuscript and for her constructive criticisms.

Ruth Chigwada-Bailey, March 2003

Introduction to the Second Edition

This new edition of *Black Women's Experiences of Criminal Justice* follows on from the first in examining the way in which the criminal justice system (CJS) treats black women. It looks at their position within British society and tries to demonstrate how—when they come into contact with criminal justice services—the fact that they are women as well as black people works against them. As I argue throughout the book, black people are already marginalised in terms of their social status and my purpose is to show how race, gender and class are compounding forces. Taken together they have a disproportionate potential to trigger unequal treatment.

There is still relatively little information specifically dedicated to black women and criminal justice. For most purposes, black women's experiences remain subsumed within those of black men or are homogenised with those of white women. Feminist criminology has generally left out of account the black woman's specific viewpoint. Here I echo the arguments of Rice (1990: 57) that a black feminist perspective should underlie any theoretical consideration of the experiences of black women. Rice comments that because 'black criminology' has focused on *men* while 'feminist criminology' has focused on *white women*, the unique social, cultural and economic experience of black women has been overlooked.

Prison statistics

Since 1997, a central backdrop to the issues I focus upon has deteriorated. More women are going to prison (and many more people generally). The prison population of England and Wales has reached record levels. As this book goes to press it stands at 73,231 and we now have the highest imprisonment rate in Western Europe, at 134 per 100,000 of the population. In April 2002 when I started writing this book it stood at 70,590, an eight per cent increase over April 2001. There were 66,220 male prisoners, a seven per cent rise over the year and 4,370 female prisoners,[1] a 22 per cent rise. There were 12,810 black and minority ethnic (BME) prisoners compared with 10,890 a year before, up 18 per cent. The make-up of the prison population, according to ethnicity was 78 per cent white, 15 per cent black, and three per cent South Asian, Chinese and other.[2] Women now account for around five per cent of the prison population. Some 11,000 are received into prison each year. As a result prisons have become overcrowded and conditions less than ideal when seeking to address problems of the kind that I identify. Further details of these general shifts together with information about ethnic monitoring and race relations in prison are contained in *Chapter 7*.

Reasons for the increase in the number of women in prison

A variety of explanations have emerged for the increase in the number of women in prison: changes in the nature and seriousness of crimes by women; moves towards dealing with women and men more 'equally'; changes in sentencing

---

[1] This compares with fewer than 1,000 female prisoners in 1970.

[2] Home Office, *Prison Population Brief, England and Wales,* April 2002 and see *Safer Society,* Autumn 2002, p. 33. See also, now, the *Postscript* to this work at p.140.

patterns, and in the 'type' of women sentenced to imprisonment; and a general increase in the length of sentences on women. Other possible explanations include a change in the demographic structure of the population (e.g. changes in age, sex and ethnicity).[3] But the statistics suggest that there is nothing *remarkably* different in population profiles over the last ten years.[4]

The nature of 'women's crimes'

The media tends to present women's crime as an exception to the general decline in crime and as if it is getting worse. But a relatively small proportion of women commit offences. Whereas a criminal convictions is relatively 'usual' for a man, it is still 'quite unusual' for a woman. Whilst more than a third of the men born in 1953 were convicted of an offence before the age of 45, only nine per cent of women were and in 2000 of those found guilty or cautioned for indictable offences just 20 per cent were female.[5] Women offenders also have fewer previous convictions than male offenders. For instance, 54 per cent of the women convicted in 2000 had no such convictions, and only seven per cent had been convicted on ten or more previous occasions; the comparable figures for men were 42 per cent and 17 per cent respectively.[6] Women also tend to commit less serious offences (and less repeatedly so[7]).

There are exceptional and unusual offenders such as the late moors murderer Myra Hindley and serial killer Rosemary West, and women are found in all offence groups, but they make up the majority only in relation to a very small number of offences: such those relating to prostitution, no TV licence, and summary offences under the Education Act 1996 (mainly consisting of a failure to ensure their child's attendance at school). Women also make up half of those proceeded against for cruelty or neglect of children (largely under Section 1 Children and Young Persons Act 1933). Indeed, the list of offences for which women account for 20 per cent or more of all offenders makes interesting reading. It includes stealing in a dwelling, theft from shops, false accounting, social security offences, and drug offences.[8] Collectively and notwithstanding indications of some serious offences (cruelty or neglect of children, for instance) women's convictions point to the predominantly financial and generally less serious nature of their crimes.

The number of women found guilty or cautioned for violence has fluctuated widely, e.g. comparing 1989 and 1999 it increased only slightly (by four per cent), whereas comparing 1990 and 2000 it fell (by six per cent).[9] Closer examination reveals that the bulk of violent offences by women are made up of those

---

[3] See, e.g. a paper given at the British Criminology Society Annual conference (2002) by Lorraine Gelsthorpe and Allison Morris, 'The Reason for the Increase of Women in Prison'.

[4] See Home Office (2000); Office for National Statistics (2001).

[5] para. 5.4, Home Office, 200lb.

[6] Home Office, 200lb.

[7] A research study by Chris May (Home Office, 1999) shows that reconviction goes down with increasing age and is lower for women than for men, especially below the age of 30. However, the rates of reconviction for women prisoners are higher now, and closer to men's reconviction rates, than they were ten years ago. The study shows, e.g. that 55 per cent of the men and 45 per cent of women released in 1998 were reconvicted within two years. In 1990 the comparable figures were 45 per cent for male prisoners and 36 per cent for female prisoners (Home Office, 2001a, *Table 9.1*) .

[8] Home Office, 1999a, *Table 2.4*.

[9] Home Office, 200lb, *Table 5.9*.

categorised as 'less serious' and it is here that there has been the biggest increase.[10]

The number of women found guilty or cautioned for drug offences has also increased: drug offence committed by women in 1990 accounted for just five per cent of their offences, compared with ten per cent in 2000. The comparable figures for men were nine per cent and 20 per cent respectively.[11] But again in 2000, most recorded drug offences were of low seriousness. The majority (86 per cent) related to unlawful possession rather than to more seriousness drug offences such as the sale of controlled drugs and 90 per cent of the possession offences involved class B drugs.[12] Overall, therefore, it can be surmised that generally speaking women continue to be involved in less serious crime and that this has not changed, or not a great deal, over time. The 'type' of woman imprisoned remains much the same as before: most are criminally unsophisticated and serving their first custodial sentence having been received into prison largely for property offences.

By the late 1990s nine out or ten lone parent families were headed by a woman and many women rely on benefits or on low pay from part-time work (Office for National Statistics, 1999). Indeed, Smith and Stewart (1998) suggest that the financial and other circumstances of offenders have deteriorated over the last 30 years leading to the comment that imprisonment has become an effective way of managing the unemployed. This point can be readily extended to embrace the management of women who are socially and economically marginalised.

Some further reasons for why women commit crimes

The reasons why some women commit crimes can be approached on two levels. Firstly from a description of the broad features of women's structural positions and lifestyles in society it is possible to see that many are vulnerable to financial difficulties and to the stresses and strains that go along with child care responsibilities, domestic violence and high levels of childhood victimisation. Indeed, one might refer to these vulnerabilities as 'indirect' pathways to crime. Certainly research on women offenders indicates that a high number experience a wide range of social problems (Rumgay, 1996). Research on criminogenic factors points towards the significance of poor cognitive skills, anti-social attitudes and feelings, strong ties to and identification with anti-social/criminal models, weak social ties, difficulty with self-management, dependency on drugs and alcohol, adverse social or family circumstances, unemployment and literacy problems (McGuire, 1995; Mair and May, 1997). These general claims of crime causation may be perceived as gender-neutral rather than gender specific. Elaine Player (1989) cautions that women's criminality should not be perceived as a homogenous and specialist area of criminology and that social factors and processes of interaction apply equally to men and women.[13]

---

[10] Home Office, 2001b, *Table 5.11.*
[11] Home Office, 2001b.
[12] Home Office, 2001b.
[13] This finds resonance in more recent US research (see, e.g. Simourd and Andrews 1996; Broidy and Agnew, 1997; and Steffensmeier and Haynie, 2000). Other research highlights similarities and differences in patterns of/explanations for male/female offending (Steffensmeier and Allan, 1996).

The criminogenic factors associated with men offenders are clearly relevant for women offenders too—but their level of importance and the nature of the association may differ. Additional criminogenic needs exist in female offenders, although their exact relationship to recidivism is not known. Different criminogenic factors may be relevant for adult women offenders and for juvenile female offenders.

'Equality' of treatment

Report after report has questioned the treatment of women in prison and the sentencing policy and practice which has led to them being there. What seems particularly valuable from the Wedderburn Report (Prison Reform Trust, 2000) is the way in which it recognises that criminal justice policy 'should be consistent with the whole spectrum of criminal justice and social policy objectives' (*ibid*, 78, para. 7.3) thus ensuring that sentencing policy does not militate against attempts to reduce social exclusion. Recommendations for increased diversion from court on the grounds that women generally commit offences of relatively low seriousness and for a co-ordinated network of women's supervision, rehabilitation and support centres (Recommendation 4(ii)) which would facilitate a reduction in the use of imprisonment and which at the same time would serve to address women's needs for support and social integration go some way to direct attention away from the 'prisoncentricity', which has come to dominate sentencing policy. Other recommendations include the setting up of a national system of geographically dispersed custodial units to replace the present arrangements, the repeal of provisions for minimum sentences for certain offences, the reintroduction of unit fines (so as to reflect the fact that women, as a group, are relatively poor and that fines should be imposed more directly according to means) and a requirement that sentencers take into account the distinctive position of women offenders (for instance their economic position, mental health, childhood or recent experiences of physical or sexual abuse and responsibilities towards children, partners, parents or other family or household members). In combination, these recommendations (and others) stem from an understanding of the lesser seriousness of women's offending, their comparatively lower likelihood of re-offending and the strong evidence that the lives of women offenders are characterised by individual and social problems.

Conversely, in a different sense, it is possible that men and women offenders are dealt with nowadays in a more 'equal' way by police, prosecutors and sentencers than, say, ten years ago. Such ideas are grounded in a belief that women were traditionally dealt with preferentially just because they were women (and when most decision-makers were men). Commentators have suggested that a shift to more 'equal' sentencing is one powerful explanatory factor for increases in women's imprisonment (Immarigeon and Chesney-Lind, 1992; Chesney-Lind, 1997).

Hood (1992) conducted a large and systematic analysis of the effects of race on sentencing in the Crown Court (the court most likely to impose prison sentences) and although he is clear in his conclusion that the courts sentenced black men more severely than white men, he did not find any evidence of discrimination against black women or punitiveness towards women generally. Dowds and Hedderman (1997) found that, overall, women received more lenient sentences than men but that this picture was not straightforward.[14] These findings were broadly confirmed by Flood-Page and Mackie (1998). Based on an analysis of sentencing in both the magistrates' courts and the Crown Court in the mid 1990s, Flood-Page and Mackie found that women were less likely than men to receive a prison sentence when other factors were taken into account.[15]

There has been a significant increase in the proportion of men and women sentenced to immediate imprisonment and in the use of community sentences, but there has been a marked reduction in the use of fines.[16] The decline in the use of fines may be due to increases in unemployment[17] or to a preference for higher tariff penalties. Thomas (1998), however, has suggested that a major reason for the increase in the prison population concerns changes in sentencing practice brought about by the Criminal Justice Act 1991.[18] Since 1991, courts have only been able to suspend prison sentences in 'exceptional circumstances'.[19] Thus, according to Thomas what seems to have happened is that roughly the same proportion of those sentenced received 'sentences of imprisonment', but that the balance between suspended imprisonment and immediate imprisonment shifted radically. In total, 13 per cent of women in 1990, and 18 per cent in 2000 received sentences of imprisonment, but in 1990 eight per cent of these were fully suspended whereas, in 2000 only two per cent were.[20] The same is true for male offenders. Thus there is support for Thomas' claim, but it does not satisfactorily explain all the increase in the population of women (and men) sentenced to imprisonment

Black people and the criminal justice system

In mid-2000, BME males made up 19 per cent of the male prison population of England and Wales—between two and three times the proportion in the general population. BME women account for 25 per cent of the female prison population—over three times that proportion (Social Exclusion Unit Report, July 2002). BME now make up eight per cent of the total population of England and Wales (See *Labour Market Trends*, December, p.660).

---

[14] Based on an analysis of more than 13,000 cases, e.g. female shoplifters were less likely than comparable men to receive a prison sentence and although women and men had an equal chance of being sentences to imprisonment for a first violent offence, women who were repeat violent offenders were less likely to receive a custodial sentence. Also, although recidivist women and men sentenced for drug offences were equally likely to be sentenced to imprisonment, women first time drug offenders were significantly less likely to receive a prison sentence than comparable men. However, although this analysis took account of offence type, it did not closely examine potential differences within offence groups.

[15] For example, men with previous convictions sentenced in the magistrates' courts were four times more likely to receive a custodial sentence than women who were repeat offenders and men with previous convictions sentenced in the Crown Court were one-and-a-half times more likely to receive custodial sentences than women with previous convictions. However, again, differences within offences with respect to seriousness were not closely examined and we know that the levels of seriousness of men's and women's offences are different.

[16] Closer examination of sentencing trends suggests that major changes with regard to community sentences began between 1992 and 1993 for men and between 1993 and 1994 for women

[17] Office for National Statistics, 2001.

[18] See now, principally, the Powers of Criminal Courts (Sentences) Act 2000.

[19] The Court of Appeal has interpreted this narrowly and excluded factors such as previous good character. Such factors are seen as relevant in determining whether the threshold for custody has been reached and not in determining whether or not to suspend a prison sentence (Thomas, 1998).

[20] Home Office, 200lb, *Table 7.10*.

Black people (Africans and Caribbeans) who make up two per cent of the population of England and Wales account for 15 per cent of the total number of prisoners (Prison Reform Trust, October 2002). Nineteen per cent of women prisoners are black in comparison to 12 per cent of men prisoners.

The over-representation of black young people within the youth justice system, at almost every level, also continues to be a cause for concern. Whilst estimates put the proportion of the population in England and Wales of black ethnic origin at two per cent, black young people account for 6.1 per cent of the population sentenced through the youth justice system. More worryingly the over-representation is particularly marked at the level of custody with 8.5 per cent of those subject to a detention and training order and 21.8 per cent of those sentenced to long-term detention under section 91, recorded as black or black British (See Nacro, *Youth Crime Briefing*, March 2002, p.4)

The disproportionate number of black people in prison is certainly striking, perhaps fuelling the myth that those from the black community are in fact more dangerous than their white counterparts. Research (outlined in later chapters) has shown that, generally speaking, people from racial minorities are treated more harshly by sentencers than white offenders—but, this is not because they have committed more serious crimes. Indeed, there is no evidence to suggest that black people are more likely to commit more offences or more serious crimes than are white people. In some quarters there is a widely held perception that people from the black community and other ethnic minorities are not treated fairly, and that this is caused by direct, indirect or institutional racism. This is exacerbated by problems of stereotyping as described in *Chapter 1.*

Since the Criminal Justice Act 1991, aggravating and mitigating factors have focused primarily on the *offence* not the *offender* (what is called 'just deserts', 'commensurate' or 'proportionate' sentencing). This led to an increasing number of women with children being imprisoned; and an increasing number of women with addictions, mental illness and/or histories of physical and sexual abuse. It meant also that women committing crime out of need could be as readily imprisoned as those offending out of greed or from other motives.

This insensitivity which values formal justice (treating like offenders alike) above substantive justice (doing what is appropriate in an individual case) affects men as well as women, but because of the circumstances typically surrounding women's criminality, the latter have been disproportionately affected and their imprisonment has grown at a faster rate.[21] Cherie Booth QC, addressing the Fawcett Society (which campaigns for equality for women), condemned the 'warehousing of women in prison' saying that a '155 per cent increase . . . between 1993 and 2000 was a cause for concern'. Talking of her visits to women's prisons, she sensed 'a terrible shame of depression and grief'. She accused the judiciary of 'warehousing the problems rather than dealing with the root causes'.[22]

---

[21]   The sharp increase in the black prison population overall may be due in part to similar factors (being female apart), but the fact that it is increasing at such a rapid rate still raises questions. The younger age structure of black people in England and Wales may provide part of the answer, as those entering the risk period for offending behaviour are more likely to be from ethnic minorities (see Bowling and Phillips, 2002). All the minority groups tend to be younger and this is especially true of 'other' groups (many of whom are of mixed ethnic groups) and Bangladeshis.

[22]   See *Safer City*, Winter 2002, p.13.

Black people as victims of crime

Black people continue to be victims of racial violence and the *British Crime Survey* shows that ethnic minorities are more likely to be victims of crime than white people. Pakistanis and Bangladeshis are at greater risk of suffering almost every category of crime. Socio-economic factors play a significant part in this increased risk: ethnic minorities tend to be younger, poorer, and live in high crime areas.

Race hate crimes rose 20 per cent in one year according to figures released in February, 2003 by the Attorney General. The news report showed that the Crown Prosecution Service dealt with 3,728 cases over the previous 12 months-mainly involving racist attacks or vandalism. Lord Goldsmith said: 'Persecuting a person for the colour of their skin, their ethnicity or their religion is not just an attack on their identity, their community and their democratic freedoms', adding that 'The level of retractions by witnesses is very high because of intimidation or the fear of reprisals' (*Mirror*, 6 February 2003). He also stated that the figures (which covered England and Wales) can also be seen as a demonstration of the increased tendency within BME circles to report such crimes.

The *Daily Mail* (14 October 2002) reported a case of a black teenager stabbed in September, 2002 in a racist attack near the scene of Stephen Lawrence's murder. Other passengers watched as two white thugs attacked the 15-year-old on the top deck of a London bus. 'The boy tried to get off the vehicle with friends after the men—aged between 18 and 25—shouted racist abuse. But he was knocked to the floor and kicked and punched before what appeared to be a Swiss army knife was plunged into his heart. He staggered off the bus and collapsed in a shop, where his friends phoned for an ambulance. Police said it was 'miraculous' he survived. The boy was set upon after getting on to the bus in Brockley, South East London, with three friends'.

Detective Inspector, Tim Carter, who was investigating the attack, said 'the boy survived 'by the skin of his teeth'. He added: 'It is little less than a miracle' Brockley is three miles from Eltham, where Stephen Lawrence, aged 18, was fatally stabbed by a gang of white youths while waiting for a bus in 1993. Stephen's killers have never been brought to justice. 'It is feared a racist gang may be responsible for a spate of vicious attacks in South East London. In August 2002, a 14-year-old black boy suffered a fractured jaw after he was punched in the face by a white man in an unprovoked attack. Two weeks earlier, a black man was beaten by a white gang carrying a knife, baton and spray can. There were three other attacks in July (*Daily Mail*, 1 October 2002).

The *Voice* (February, 2003) reports the case of Norris, 27 and Acourt, 26 who were sent to prison for 18 months for racially abusing an off-duty black police officer (something which does not encourage black people to join the police force). They were two of the five suspects in the Stephen Lawrence murder case.[23]

Foreign nationals

In September 2001, there were 14,480 prisoners from ethnic communities, of whom 5,130 were foreign nationals. It is sometimes confusing and difficult to understand how someone becomes classified as a 'foreign national'. During my research for the first edition of this book, I learned from a British born woman of

---

[23] The Crime and Disorder Act 1998 makes racial motivation and (as later amended) religious motivation a mandatory aggravating factor in relation to any offence.

Jamaican heritage about a duty solicitor who came to see her and told her that she had been asked to see 'a Jamaican woman'. The woman found this difficult to understand as she had a British passport (which had been taken from her by a customs officer). Other women I talked to who had been living in the UK for over six years—with permission to stay indefinitely—were deported at the end of their sentences as they were then classified as foreign nationals. More information is contained in *Chapter 7.*

Criminology

As emphasised in the first edition, mainstream criminology has historically been largely concerned with the study of working-class men and boys. Within the critical criminology literature, class, race and gender have each been given independent and largely separate attention. What has been conspicuously absent has been investigation of their various intersections.

Race, class and gender, each on its own or in combination, shapes or structures the life course of an individual. In other words, they function to enhance or to limit access to economic and political power, which in turn, shapes life choices (see Groves and Frank, 1993). In general, e.g. men have more choices than women do, white people have more choices than people from the ethnic minorities; and wealthy people have more choices than poor people. Combining such factors one can see that wealthy, white males have access to the greatest number of choices in the course of their lives, while poor, black and other minority women would appear to have the fewest.

Within criminology, the intersection of race, class and gender and the effects of these factors upon the life courses and choices of people have rarely been examined. Groves and Franks (1993) argue that class and race affect the type of choices an individual has at his or her disposal. From this, they argue that those with a greater number of choices should be held more accountable for their behaviours. Their argument is compelling, and stands in direct contrast to actual criminal justice and legal practices which tend to hold the relatively powerless more accountable (i.e. sentences, measured by length or type, are more severe for powerless people compared to powerful people).

Race, class and gender affect what people do, how they do it, how they are perceived by other people, and other people's reactions. Taken as status or structure, race, class and gender act as 'codes', repositories of behavioural cues, possibilities and choices (Thomas, 1991). The socialisation process a person passes through as they grow up, from cradle to school classroom, teaches them how to behave so that they conform to their own status, and react to the statuses of other people. For example, black British men react to white men differently than they react to other black British/foreign black nationals; upper-class women react to upper-class women differently to how they react to women they perceive to be from classes below them, and so on. These socialised reactions differ from person to person because people from different structural locations (defined by race, class and gender) are taught different lessons.

Radical criminologists understand race and gender along with class as structuring forces that affect how people behave, how others react to and define that behaviour, who has the power to define and label behaviours, and how law and law enforcement are organized and focused to control behaviour.

'Traditional' criminology does not wholly address the many ways in which class, race and gender affect the life course of an individual, his or her access to crime, the criminal justice response to people, and the chances that someone will be labelled as a criminal. As intimated at the start of this introduction, a key to understanding this book lies in the proposition that the effects of race, class and gender are not simply additive forces (see also Anderson and Collins, 1995). If someone is a lower-class, black woman she will not experience the simple negative additive effects of being 'female', 'black' and 'lower class'. Rather, her experience will result from how these forces intersect and interact with each other through the social and economic structure. The effect is contextual, not mathematical (*ibid.*).

Looking to the future

According to Home Office research published in November 2002, discrimination is still apparent at all points in the criminal justice system (CJS). The research shows that people from black and minority ethnic groups are more likely to have worse experiences in the CJS and that they are over-represented in all stages of the penal system. In their foreword the Lord Chancellor, Home Secretary and Attorney General state:

> The statistics we are publishing today showed that people from black and minority ethnic groups are more likely than the rest of population to believe that the CJS as a whole is doing a good job but continue disproportionately to run foul of the CJS . . . A modern, fair, effective CJS is not possible whilst significant sections of the population perceive it as discriminatory and lack confidence in it delivering the service. Though some of the disparities the statistics show are unacceptable by any standards, some of the others may be more complex. The statistics fail to answer the question whether the differences in arrest rates, cautioning and sentencing reflect underlying differences in type of offence or whether they reflect discrimination by the system. We need to get behind the numbers to understand the process through which discrimination may be occurring in the CJS. We need to ensure that the CJS bases its decisions and actions on effective law enforcement. In doing this it must not be influenced by prejudice or political correctness. This is an admission to the fact that racism does play a part in the number of black people who find themselves in prison. (Foreword, *Race and the Criminal Justice System*, a Home Office publication under Section 95 Criminal Justice Act 1991, 2002).

A Social Exclusion Unit report published in July 2002, *Reducing Re-offending by Ex-Prisoners* also states that the reasons behind the over-representation of black people are complex. It explains that several indicators can be found in the profile of the black population generally that suggest why contact with the criminal justice system is much higher. People from the black community are disproportionately likely to suffer from a range of aspects of social exclusion. For example the 1998, 56 per cent lived in the most deprived local authority areas. These contained proportionately four times as many people from ethnic minority groups as other areas (SEU, 2002, p.148).

At the time of writing there is yet another Criminal Justice Bill before Parliament (and this time one which is likely to affect the entire sentencing structure). The White Paper upon which the Bill is based, *Justice for All* (2002), reveals the challenge the government faces to honour its commitment to create a fair and just system in which the public can feel confident. It states that black people are: 'More likely to be arrested, more likely to be victims of crime, less likely to be cautioned, more likely to plead not guilty, to have their case continued, and to be acquitted, more likely to receive longer custodial sentences and less likely as court users to be satisfied with the court'.

As already noted, black people are disproportionately represented at all stages of the CJS. Proposed legislation (see principally *Chapter 5*) will do little to redress this imbalance, e.g. those to disclose previous convictions in court during someone's trial, greater use of hearsay evidence, changes to the double jeopardy law, the introduction of a new 'custody plus' sentence for short-term prisoners, and tougher sentences for certain offenders. Similarly, legislation aimed at curbing anti-social behaviour, or to revive plans to cut the social security benefits of the parents of tearaway children, or to deal with so-called 'nuisance' tenants are likely to be discriminatory in their application if the experiences described in this book are anything to go on.

THE INTERVIEWS

The original research for this book was based on lengthy and searching interviews carried out with black women living in Britain who had become involved with the criminal justice process, and they had generally ended up in prison. I asked the women about the treatment they had received and their personal *perception* of events, which—whatever the actuality—was reality to them. The important thing was to listen to them to see whether anything might be learnt from overlapping comments or the fact that a point of view coincided with or was supported by other information.

I wrote to various organizations, working with women inside prison and after release, including area Probation Services.[24] My letters explained that I was interested in talking to black women who had been in prison. Once I was in touch with one black female prisoner word spread. Various women telephoned or wrote from prison saying that they would be interested in taking part, creating a 'snowball' sample, in effect self-selected and voluntary. This had the advantage that the participants were both willing to talk and interested in the project. In fact, all the women demonstrated enthusiasm.

The black women in the sample
The profile of the 20 women in my final sample was as follows:

- sixteen were black British, i.e. born in Britain
- four were born outside Britain but had been living in this country for at least five years
- all were of African-Caribbean background
- their ages ranged from 21 years to 38 years
- for sixteen of the women it was their first time in trouble with the law and thus their first time in prison (where applicable)
- the other four had been in trouble with the law from the age of 12 or 13

---

[24] The National Probation Service was created in 2001.

- their offences ranged from fraud, shoplifting, handling stolen goods and drugs offences to robbery
- sixteen were unemployed at the time of arrest, one worked in the post office, one as a child minder and for the tourist board, one was a qualified secretary and another had an import and export business
- three possessed GCSE 'O' levels; the rest had left school without any qualifications
- two were in private rented accommodation; the rest lived in council properties (usually flats)
- eighteen were still in prison; the remaining two were on probation (but had previously been to prison)
- those women who *were* in prison were serving sentences of between 18 months and eight years
- eighteen were single, one was married and one divorced
- all the women had children and five of them had their children with them in prison.

Interview method

I conducted the interviews informally using a few headings to stimulate discussion. I allowed the women ten to 15 minutes after each interview to ask me questions (unrelated to the interview if they so wished). In fact they asked a great many questions giving a degree of insight which bolstered understanding of their attitudes and reactions to the criminal justice process, for example, some of them wanted guidance with further education and some to talk about problems concerning accommodation after release: see, e.g. *Chapter 8*.

Issues explored

I interviewed them about their experiences with the police, customs officers, solicitors, prison officers, barristers, probation officers, magistrates and judges. I asked them to think back to the time when they were arrested and what had transpired between then and the present time. I was particularly interested in exploring the women's perceptions of the following issues:

- How were they, as black women, treated by people within the criminal justice process?
- Were they seen as potential suspects or deserving of a particular kind of treatment?
- When arrested, were they accorded fair treatment and, for example, access to a lawyer?
- Did they think that they had received their 'just deserts' or were they aggrieved at their punishment?
- How did the stereotype image of the black woman fit with the dominant white ideology of a 'good' woman—that is, did their lifestyle meet expectations about the way women should behave?
- What part did their culture and race play from arrest to sentence?
- Did their cultural background have any bearing on decisions, e.g. to bring charges, on the risk that they might re-offend, on the jury's decision as to guilt or innocence, or the judge's or magistrates' decision about sentence?
- Did 'chivalrous treatment' play any part in the way they were treated?

I pointed out that I was unlikely to be shocked or offended by anything they said, and encouraged them to talk freely about their experiences.

It may not be generally understood that many black women in prison are worried about their families and friends finding out about this because so much stigma can attach in a black community to being an ex-prisoner. I had to convince one woman from Nigeria that I was not Nigerian before she would agree to be interviewed so worried was she that the news might carry back home. Whilst there is no way of knowing, I have no special reason to believe that any of the women tried to mislead me or did not tell the truth concerning their *perceptions* (it is accepted that this is not quite the same thing as saying that the 'facts' they related or, in some cases, the allegations they made, are true or valid).

I was concerned to explore whether any differences in treatment accorded to women of different races might be attributed to rules, policies or directives within organizations, or to institutional or individual racism? In the following chapters, these questions are addressed by looking at what the women said and at some of the other information which is available about black people, women, crime and the criminal justice process.

STRUCTURE OF THIS NEW EDITION

The chapters which follow have all been revised to remove redundant material and to insert new information and data. Hopefully, the considerable support I have already received for the views expressed will gather further momentum, with a view to 'making things happen'. The opening chapters emphasise the need to hear the voice of black women when considering the causes of crime and administration of justice and the absence of black women's voices and experiences in this debate. *Chapter 3* examines the policing of black women and *Chapter 4* their involvement with the National Probation Service. *Chapter 5* concentrates on the courts and sentencing and *Chapter 7* deals with black women's experiences of prison (and the system which brought them there). The closing chapter deals with points made by the women interviewed which I have drawn together under the title *Hopes and Ambitions*.

Beatrice's Case

One woman who was unhappy with the way she had been treated by customs officers, the police and the courts asked me to attend the second hearing of her case. I also attended the third trial, as on the second hearing the jury could not reach a verdict. *Beatrice's Case* is described in some detail in *Chapter 6*. It deals with white perceptions of black women's 'inferior' culture, looking at how race, gender and class are articulated from arrest to sentence. In a convenient form, it serves to illustrate how the criminal justice process can be perceived by black women—and possibly how it can go astray.

Ruth Chigwada-Bailey
March 2003

CHAPTER 1

A Combination of Forces

This book considers ways in which disadvantage may be aggravated in the case of African-Caribbean women who find themselves on the wrong side of the criminal law. When this happens, the various stages that make up the criminal justice process of England and Wales[1] may be driven by one (or more) of several forces—each constituting a hazard in itself—but which, *in combination*, create a greater potential for unequal treatment. These forces are:

- those which affect black[2] people in general, whatever their gender, living in a society where the dominant values, culture, institutions and sense of history are those of white people;
- those which affect women, whatever the colour of their skin, living in a society devised, organized and run primarily by men; and
- those which affect people, whatever their gender or the colour of their skin, who are at the lower end of the economic or social scale. It can be noted that a person's status in this regard may be partly influenced by either of the first two considerations.

The three strands are referred to throughout this book as 'race', 'gender' and 'class'. It is not simply a question of adding together the effects of these various aspects of disadvantage, rather of considering ways in which, when they intersect and interact, they compound one another—the argument being that the whole is greater than the sum of the parts. As will be emphasised throughout this work, black *women* are a further marginalised group. They are poorly represented in education, the professions, commerce, industry and politics. They suffer higher levels of unemployment than most other groups.

SOME INDICATORS

In July 2002, the Social Exclusion Unit (SEU) published a report, *Reducing Re-offending by Ex-prisoners* which highlights the fact that prisoners tend to come from, and return to, socially excluded backgrounds. Thus, e.g. prisoners are 13 times more likely than the general population to have been in care as children and 14 times more likely to be unemployed. Some 60-70 per cent were using drugs before imprisonment; more than 70 per cent suffer from at least two mental disorders; and over 50 per cent of men prisoners and more than 70 per cent of women prisoners have no educational or other qualifications at all.

Women's offending is often directly linked to social exclusion. The SEU report argues that women who commit crimes are commonly products of an

---

[1] For a description of that process, its personnel and their roles and responsibilities, see *Introduction to the Criminal Justice Process* (2002), Gibson B and Cavadino P, Waterside Press.

[2] The term 'black' is used in this work to refer to people of *African* descent. Except where the context clearly implies otherwise, the term 'ethnic minority' is reserved for other *non-white* groups such as people of Asian descent.

environment that fails to provide them with the necessary confidence, values, skills and opportunities to lead law-abiding lives. It goes on to say that various factors are involved: poverty, negative experiences of education, experience of abuse, violence, sexual abuse within the family and in relationships, a history of being in care, drug or alcohol misuse, an environment where law-breaking is considered the norm, homelessness or inadequate housing, sexual activity and pregnancy at a young age, sexual exploitation, racism, poor health (both physical and emotional) and mental illness. Black women who come into contact with the criminal process also have racism to contend with on top of the disadvantages faced by women in general.

The SEU report highlights the extent of disadvantage amongst short-term prisoners (those serving under 12 months) and recommends action to reduce poverty and promote access to employment. Women are recognized as a disadvantaged minority with very specific needs. HM Prison Service (HMPS) is currently implementing policies to address the resettlement needs of women prisoners, the majority of whom are serving short sentences and who are discharged into the community without supervision or support from the National Probation Service (NPS). Constructive work undertaken in prison to address issues such as homelessness, poverty, substance misuse and unemployment may not be continued after release and many women simply return to a cycle of social exclusion and re-offending.[3]

Indeed, women offenders are a disadvantaged minority within the criminal justice system as a whole. Statutory services are designed with the majority male offender population in mind and often fail to confront the particular needs of women. Black women, disproportionately represented within the female prison population, have very specific needs. The research indicates that poverty is a clear factor in women's law breaking more frequently than in men's. Women's responsibilities as primary carers of children and other dependents mean that a prison sentence can have a significant impact on a whole family. It is estimated that two-thirds of women in prison are mothers. A history of childhood neglect and abuse, experience of sexual trauma and sexual violence, and problems associated with poor physical and mental health are common to women offenders. The research shows that experience of violence and coercion within relationships is experienced by up to 80 per cent women offenders. Over 50 per cent of sentenced women have used drugs in the year before their imprisonment. Drug offenders account for 50 per cent of the prison population increase between 1993 and 1997.

Income and class

Black women experience high levels of poverty, it being a feature of women in prison that they suffer this particular disadvantage. However, not all poor people commit crimes or end up in prison. For example, Bangladeshis, the group with the highest unemployment rate, are under-represented in prison. It does seem to follow, however, that if a woman belongs to a group which is both black (and therefore at extra risk of imprisonment) and poor (thus fitting a description which accords with that of other women in prison) then there is a greater, rather

---

[3] There are now extensive moves towards accredited and compatible programmes across HMPS and the NPS and a promise of a more 'joined-up' approach generally.

than a lesser, chance that she will end up in prison through a combination of factors within which poverty is subsumed.

A study of income distribution in London demonstrates the stark difference between ethnic minority groups with, e.g. 76 per cent of the Bangladeshi population being amongst the lowest one-fifth of earners in the capital (*Runnymede Bulletin*, December 2001). Black and ethnic minority communities also tend to have lower average incomes and higher unemployment. The London Health Observatory (1998) found unemployment amongst the white population to be 6.5 per cent, whilst the rate for Indians was 7.4 per cent, for black groups 20.5 per cent and Pakistanis and Bangladeshis 15.9 per cent. A 1995 Policy Studies Institute survey showed that the mean weekly earnings of people from all ethnic minorities was £296 compared to £336 for white people. Bangladeshi people had the lowest weekly income of £191 and Bangladeshis and Pakistanis are also the poorest groups, with 60 per cent living in low-income households (Pathak, 2000). Bangladeshi and black-Caribbean heads of household are also most likely to be in social housing (DETR, 2000).

According to the Office for National Statistics,[4] 30 years after the Equal Pay Act women in the UK still earn substantially less than men. In the year 2000, women who worked full time earned 81.6 per cent of the average gross hourly earnings of male full-time workers. The subsequent introduction of a minimum wage gave over a million women an immediate pay rise. This helped to raise the minimum rate to £4.10 by October 2001. If women generally are earning substantially less than men where does this leave black women?

Lone parents

The number of one-parent families has trebled in the last 30 years, the most rapid increase being since the mid-1980s—although this has now slowed[5]. Eleven per cent of lone parents are from black or ethnic minority communities. Forty-nine per cent of black families are headed by a lone parent, compared to eight per cent of Indian, 15 per cent of Pakistani and Bangladeshi families, 21 per cent of white families and 29 per cent of mixed race and other ethnic groups. Research shows that ethnic minority groups experience much higher levels of unemployment and economic disadvantage (Phatt and Nobble, 1999). However, black-Caribbean lone parents are significantly more likely to be working and working full time than any other group and they are less likely to be getting benefits. Bangladeshi and Pakistani lone parents tend to be older on average than other lone parents. Lone parents have overtaken pensioners as the poorest group. Three in five children (62 per cent) in one-parent families are poor, compared to one in four children (25 per cent) with two resident parents. Nearly half of all poor children now live in one parent families—45 per cent.[6]

According to more recent findings (Nacro, *Safer City*, 2002), as announced at a conference of the British Psychological Society's Division of Forensic Psychology in April 2001, boys who have a father figure are at lower risk of committing crimes. Of the boys with a criminal record, 45 per cent said they had

---

[4] *New Earnings Survey 2000*, revised figures January 2002.
[5] See *One-Parent Families Today: The Facts*, Sept 2001, p. 2.
[6] DSS, 2001, *Households Below Average Income 1994/95-1999/2000*.

no father figure, 30 per cent had a step-father and 22 per cent had a biological father not living at home. The research is based on a study of 68 boys aged 12-26 years, half of whom were in young offender institutions.

The sample is too small to reach a conclusive finding but such reports serve to criminalise black people, and thus black women and to reinforce beliefs that the home environment they provide—especially their style of parenting and mothering—is to blame, an attitude which may also be coloured by impressions of loose sexual practices (see further under *Stereotyping etc.*, below).

We are now in a climate where single parents are being blamed for the misbehaviour of their children. Jailings of single parent women in 2002 and 2003 for the truancy of their respective children emphasises this.

Employment and education

Employment statistics show that the white population has higher employment rates than black people. According to *Labour Market Trends*, September 2002, 58 per cent of the working-age population of ethnic minority groups were in employment (1.6 million people), compared with 76 per cent of white people. All ethnic groups had lower activity rates for women than for men, most notably the Pakistani and Bangladeshi groups (33 per cent and 21 per cent respectively for women, compared with 74 per cent and 69 per cent for men).

In summer 2002 the highest working-age activity rates were for white women (75 per cent) followed by women from a mixed race group (66 per cent), and then black women (64 per cent). Asian women had the lowest overall activity rate at 52 per cent. However this hides the diversity of experience for women from different Asian backgrounds, with Indian women having the highest activity rate of 69 per cent and Bangladeshi women the lowest of 22 per cent. The highest activity rates for men were for the white group. The lowest activity rates were from men from the 'other ethnic group' (69 per cent) followed by the black men group (77 per cent).[7]

Black minority ethnic (BME) youngsters were much more likely to be in education than the white group (49 per cent, compared with 30 per cent). The Chinese ethnic group had the highest proportion (71 per cent). Young women were slightly more likely to be in full-time education than young men in the white ethnic group (32 per cent compared with 29 per cent). The reverse was true among ethnic minority groups as a whole, where 50 per cent of men were in full-time education, compared with 48 per cent of women.

Black people still face racism in employment. A case reported in *The Times* (31 July 2002), of a black postal worker shows how racism at work can also affect well-being. A 26-year-old man, Jermaine Lee was subjected to bullying and racism by his supervisors. He was found hanged at his home in Hall Green, Birmingham, in November 1998 after ending a shift at Aston sorting office. The Royal Mail admitted that some of its senior staff had treated him in an 'utterly shameful' manner and this had contributed to his decision to commit suicide. The following have been summarised from everyday news reports:

In July 1998, four young Asian women won nearly £50,000 compensation for what the CRE described as 'one of the most serious' cases of race discrimination in the

---

[7] See *Labour Market Trends*, December 2002, p. 661.

workplace. Shabnum Sharif, 18, Naheed Akhtar, 19 and 21 year old twins Saima and Asma Nazir were banned from observing religious holidays, told not to speak in their native language and taunted with racial abuse by their employer.

In June 2001, The Football League apologised to an Asian referee after it prevented him from being promoted to Premier League matches. Gurnam Singh had been allocated less prominent games because he was Asian. The league was also found to have unfairly dismissed Singh, aged 47, even though he performed consistently well on the pitch.

In April 2002, managers at Ford were found guilty of victimising and abusing an Asian worker, Shinda Nagra at an engine plant in Dagenham. Mr Nagra, 44, told how some employees walked out because they did not want to work with him because of his race.

A number of research studies suggest that black graduates have to apply for more jobs before being offered interviews and attend more interviews before being offered a job. In 2001, 13 per cent of black graduates were found to be still unemployed six months after graduating compared with just six per cent of white graduates (cited in *The Guarding Rise,* 28 September 2002[8]). Although discrimination partly explains the discrepancy between employment rates for black and white graduates, this 'is not the whole story' according to Beverly Bernard, deputy chair of the Commission for Racial Equality (CRE). She points out that 'It is very difficult for black graduates because in many cases white graduates have contacts through their parents. Some will know people who work in the city or media. Black graduates do not always have these contacts'. Although some white graduates may not have contacts or know influential people, race still plays a big part in obtaining employment.

Racism in education and employment may compound lack of access to legitimate opportunities. The difficulties faced by some black people in the British education system, the labour market and housing create a higher proportion of black people among those at high risk of offending. It is therefore possible that although the direct cause of offending (cited by black and Asian offenders) may be the desire to accumulate money (Lawrence, 1995; Barker *et al,* 1993), this desire may be less possible to achieve legitimately among black people because of the difficulties they have faced in employment and education.

Mental health

The London borough of Brent, where half of the population are from an ethnic minority background, has the highest number of deaths of black people between the ages of 14-24 (Brent Council, 2001). Suicide rates are the highest among black men in this age group. The pressures of high employment and discrimination can in part contribute to this. According to McKenzie (2001), 40 per cent of the users of London's psychiatric services are from minority ethnic groups, though they make up only 25 per cent of the population of London. Depression is more common among black people than amongst white people in the UK. McKenzie states that African-Caribbean women are twice as likely as white British women

---

[8] See 'Is the Future Bright for Black or White? Minorities Face Additional Hurdles When Job-hunting', *The Guarding Rise,* 28 September 2002.

to suffer from depression, and African-Caribbean men are more likely than white British men to suffer from depressive ideas and worry. These differences derive mainly from information about non-manual workers, the prototypical black middle-class.

According to Mackenzie (2001), the highest rates of depression in black women are mainly amongst non-manual workers, predominantly in the African-Caribbean middle-classes. In the UK these women have a much higher risk of depression than do manual workers of Caribbean origin. There is also a high suicide rate in the African-Caribbean population, rising to epidemic proportions. The only other country with a higher rate of mental illness amongst the African-Caribbean community is The Netherlands.

Why is it that when black women find themselves in managerial posts, they become more prone to depression? What is needed is the tackling of institutional racism, which would enable black women to function free from race concerns. Problems in this area might arise from white colleagues (male and female) and other people in an organization who might have problems with a black woman manager. Black women in management might also encounter gender problems from both white and black males.

McKenzie also argues that since suicide rates are increasing among black people, the possibility of self-harm should be more important to psychiatrists than the perceived danger to others from people suffering illnesses such as schizophrenia. He questions the 'one-size-fits-all' concept of psychiatry that has come under pressure since discussion of institutional racism has come to the fore. He states that the real causes of mental illness are social. The biggest risk factor to developing schizophrenia is living in a city. If someone has his or her aspirations thwarted, for example through being excluded from school, or not getting the job they want or the promotion they desire, this multiplies their chances of developing depression (*ibid*).

Being under financial strain increases by 50-60 per cent the chances of a person developing depression. Eighty-five per cent of the Caribbean population in the UK have less than £1,000 saved. McKenzie points out:

> This means when times get hard there is nothing to fall back on. This means things are stressful for black people, things that other populations might be able to cope with become a crisis.

Racism, he states, is

> . . . hugely linked to your likelihood of developing a mental illness. It has been observed that if you have been a victim of a racist incident, you have two-and-a-half times the risk of developing depression and four-and-a-half times the risk of developing schizophrenia. So racism and racist incidents have a link to one's chance of developing mental illness later in life. There are more social causes: a bad work environment, moving down the social scale, such as many of the parents had done when they moved to the UK, are bad for mental health. Losing a parent, either through migration or being part of a single family or being put into care, again is bad for mental health.

> Life events such as imprisonment or somebody in your family being imprisoned are all bad for mental health, as are uncertainty and worry about the future. As well as

individual risk factors, there are risk factors in the community. The community can make you ill … Communities that can get together in order to change their [members'] lives are good for mental health. Communities that are disorganized, where there are lots of different people coming in and out whom you don't know or you don't trust increase your amount of worry and anxiety and also increase your chance of developing mental illness.

Moral panic and black crime

There sometimes appears to be a moral panic and hysteria over crimes such as robbery. On 21 February 2003, for example, the *Mirror* devoted eight pages to 'revealing the true face of lawless, violent Britain', concluding that we are 'drowning in a tidal wave of violent crime'. The *Sun* newspaper told its readers in March that the UK was in a state of 'anarchy' and that crime needed to be 'smashed with an iron fist'. And it was not just the tabloids. The *Daily Telegraph* carried an article that seriously argued that British citizens should have the right to bear arms. *The Sunday Times* carried a special 'investigation into Bandit Country UK'. New York-style 'zero tolerance' policing was the *Evening Standard's* preferred option.[9] This is not, however, supported by the *British Crime Survey* which shows violent offences have fallen by 36 per cent since the mid-1990s.

The headlines in the British press—both broadsheet and tabloid—over recent years could suggest that Britain is in the evil grip of a drug that is tearing communities apart. Areas of our inner cities are reported to be under siege from gun-wielding, drug-crazed gangs fighting for turf, and mowing down innocent bystanders who get caught in the crossfire. Recurring themes in such articles include the association between crack and Britain's black community; the association between the use of guns and the crack market; and the level of black-on-black violence that is associated with this 'epidemic'.

The view that crack is associated with black people was expressed in an article posted on No. 10 Downing Street's website: 'Communities urged to step up fight against crack cocaine', which declared that the Government would support and help in this fight, and added: 'speakers at a major national conference on the impact of crack cocaine identified poor urban communities in general, and the black urban community in particular as most at risk of harm'.[10]

Crack is associated with poverty—it has been described as the poor man's cocaine. Many of Britain's black population live in poverty in deprived inner-city areas. The reporting of problems of drug misuse and violence in these areas in a sensationalist way—which associates crack with a particular ethnic community rather than with poverty and deprivation—is not helpful either to the cause of social cohesion in the inner cities or reducing the level of racism in society. But it does, of course, sell newspapers.

What about the level of 'black-on-black' violence? This is being depicted by the media as a new phenomenon, and a consequence of crack cocaine and its

---

[9] See also the example of the article about black people in *The Spectator* given overleaf.
[10] 24 June 2002. This claim was followed by a reference to a finding from the *British Crime Survey* 2000 that two per cent of black respondents, but only one per cent of white respondents, had reported use of crack cocaine, and a statement from the Home Office Drugs Minister to the effect that crack is exceptional in this regard and which concluded: 'Some areas are more at risk of suffering the potentially devastating impact that crack cocaine can have upon individuals, families and whole communities'. For 'some areas' read 'areas mainly inhabited by black people'.

impact on black communities. The fact is that the majority of crime has always been intra-racial, that is to say black people tend to commit crime against other black people, and white people against other white people. This is true in all multi-ethnic societies (*Safer Society*, Autumn 2002, p. 8).

The Metropolitan Police Service, through initiatives such as 'Operation Trident', tackling drugs related shootings amongst London's black community, has been able to make a significant impact on gun crime. A critical part of the Trident approach has been the involvement of community leaders to provide advice and support with witness appeals. The clear-up rate for murders within the Trident remit, traditionally some of the most difficult to solve, has risen from 24 per cent to 70 per cent (*New Nation*, 27 January 2003).

There are those in the black community who are not convinced about labelling an operation as being for tackling black crime in the black community. The investigations by the Operation Trident Unit—which eventually led to long prison sentences for three white men who were found guilty of selling guns and ammunition destined for the inner city streets to undercover policemen—shows that there is really no need for such operations to be designated for black crimes as in white areas you are still going to find criminals who will be white people committing crimes in their own neighbourhoods. In these areas when the locals complain about crime the colour issue is never be raised.

After the shooting of two black girls on New Years Eve, 2002, David Blunkett MP, Home Secretary in January launched a misguided attack on rap music and claimed that there was a direct link between gun violence, Class A drugs and such music. Culture Minister Kim Howells MP likewise claimed that rappers fuelled gun violence. He also lashed out at garage bands such as So Solid Crew— who have had three of their members proceeded against for incidents involving guns in the past 18 months.[11]

All but two of the 20 London boroughs with the highest incidence of gun crime feature on the Government's list of the country's most deprived areas. And Birmingham and Manchester, the cities with the highest number of shootings outside London, are first and second respectively in the poverty league table. But should we really be blaming these statistics on urban music or the disenfranchised, ghetto-styled inner cities that these youngsters all grow up in?

STEREOTYPING AND SIMILAR INFLUENCES

In some quarters, black culture is seen as being to blame for crime among black people. In January 2003, *The Spectator* published an article entitled 'Thoughts and Thuggery' written by Taki Theodoracopulos, in which he described black Britons as 'the causes of crime', 'thugs, the sons of black thugs', as well as 'multiplying like flies' ('New Nation', 27 January 2003). It began, 'Oh boy, was Enoch,[12] God rest his soul, ever right! Now there's a man who was tough on the causes of crime long before crime had been Blaired'. Commenting on the New Year's Eve 2003 shootings of two black girls in Birmingham, he went on to say that, 'Only a

---

[11]   One member was convicted in an earlier case; two are currently on trial facing such allegations.

[12]   Enoch Powell MP a long time campaigner against post-war (and later) immigration (see, generally, the *Appendix*). At the time of this book going to press, Scotland Yard's Diversity Directorate, which includes the Racial and Violent Crime Taskforce was conducting an investigation.

moron would not surmise that what politically correct newspapers refer to as disaffected young people 'are black thugs, sons of black thugs and grandsons of black thugs'. The article went on to say, 'West Indians were allowed to immigrate after the war, multiply like flies, and then the great apparatus took over the care of their multiplications. The Rivers of Blood speech by Enoch was prophetic as well as true . . . '.

At a less biased level, it is perhaps, then, small wonder that interest in black women among researchers has been concerned mostly with aspects of family life, employment and education. This may be rooted in the notion of the 'enslaved black matriarch' who learnt to bring up her children in the absence of a husband and who is deserving of study as her behaviour is different from that of 'normal' women. As argued in later chapters, it may be because the stereotype of the black woman is of someone qualitatively different to her white counterpart that black women have tended to receive different treatment from the criminal justice agencies and to be viewed as 'capable of committing crime'.

Just how misleading stereotypes are can be seen from my own earlier research into the education of African-Caribbean girls[13] which shows that modern-day black fathers play a significant part in the education of their children, are proud of their achievements and do their best to help and encourage them to obtain better qualifications. As some of the girls said:

My father encouraged me to go for 'A' levels. He equated education with success. He says that being black you won't get anything without education.

My father has always been very ambitious for us. He wants us to work hard at college so that we can get a job.

Closely related to stereotyping, black women may also suffer from 'secondary punishment' or what I will call 'guilt by association'. By being the mothers or sisters of black youths (themselves stereotyped as 'criminal') they may find themselves in trouble with the police—who may, e.g. come to their homes to arrest or search for their menfolk (see further in *Chapter 3*). It can be argued that secondary punishment affects all black families in terms of harassment and in some cases brutality by the police and it can lead to questionable treatment, poor procedures, false accusations or malicious prosecutions—as a number of high profile cases have shown in recent times.

'Deviant' cultures and 'deviant' women

Just as the police may regard black women as suspects because of the assumptions they make about their lifestyle (*Chapter 3*), the way they are portrayed by the media and others is also relevant. Overall, they are labelled 'deviant' because they do not conform to what British society conceives to be 'correct behaviour', and they are powerless to protest in individual cases because of their class, economic status or lack of social position. The following press report is indicative:

---

[13] 'Not Victims Not Superwomen: The Education of Afro-Caribbean Girls', Chigwada R, *Spare Rib*, No. 183, 1987.

Young black men commit a disproportionately high number of violent crimes in London because most black mothers, when they are young girls, have children out of wedlock and are not supported by the fathers. There appears to be less stigma attached to single parenthood in the black community. The only hope is that somehow the West Indian marriage can be encouraged and supported.[14]

The implications are that black women, as single parents, deviate from the norm and in so doing are to blame for the criminality of their young men. As far back as 1973, it was reported that the Broadwater Farm Estate in North London was occupied by:

Problem families and the sight of unmarried West Indian mothers walking about the estate aggravated racial tensions.[15]

There is a well-known saying in Africa: 'It takes the whole village to raise a child'. It is acceptable in the black community for a child to be allowed to be raised, e.g. by an aunt or uncle if they are in a better position financially and have good moral values. This is expected to help the siblings and parents. The practice may be gradually diminishing, but it still practised widely. The tradgedy of the Victoria Climbié case (of a young child abused and murdered by the aunt and uncle with whom she had been sent to live in England) was that the aunt and uncle turned out to be wicked and heartless people and Victoria's parents had no way of telling how the substitute parents were going to turn out.[16] But as a result of this case, black culture and ways of raising children came under attack. According to *The Observer*, 'The question few have dared ask Victoria's grieving parents, Francis and Berthe Climbié, is how they could send a child thousands of miles away with someone they barely knew'. Another newspaper described 'a back street trade in babies' and claimed that this trade caused Victoria's death (*The Voice*, 3 February 2003).

Race and class may often mix with 'deviance'. In 2001 the *Daily Mail* dealing with Jamaican 'mules' reported:

Pearl [was] 39 and lived in St Catherine's, a rural area to the west of Kingston. Illiterate and uneducated, she made a bare living buying and selling vegetables and knick-knacks at small markets. But her profits were not enough to feed her children— seven of them ... Between them, the seven children had five different fathers. (29 December 2001: 20)

The article went on to give the reasons why Jamaican women have children by different fathers:

---

[14] *London Evening Standard,* 12 December 1987.

[15] *Hornsey Journal,* 11 May 1973.

[16] Victoria Climbié came to the UK from the Ivory Coast and was entrusted into the care of her aunt who promised to provide her with education and a new life. The Inquiry Report by Lord Laming into the circumstances surrounding the tragic death of this eight year old found that there was a gross failure of the system, which was inexcusable. It blamed all the agencies who could have saved the child's life: Victoria was known to three housing authorities, four social services department, two child protection teams, the Metropolitan Police and a specialist centre managed by the NSPCC. She had been in two different hospitals due to suspected deliberate harm.

Many Jamaican women see having children by more than one father as the equivalent of spreading investments. If one man deserts you, perhaps the other will stay. If one loses his job, or refuses to support his child—well, maybe one of the others will help ... Pearl was very unlucky with the fathers of her children. She picked five losers—none of them stayed with the family or gave financial help.

This negative stereotyping of black women can only contribute to their being seen as irresponsible, promiscuous and deserving of the punishment they get from British 'justice'.

Visher has suggested that lenient or harsh treatment by law-enforcement agencies at any stage of the process depends on the degree to which a woman's behaviour is in accordance or at variance with the female role. This research concluded that chivalrous treatment at the arrest stage depended upon a larger set of gender expectations that exist between men and women in their encounters with police officers and that '... those female suspects who violate typical middle-class standards of traditional female characteristics and behaviour (i.e. white, older and submissive) are not afforded any chivalrous treatment in arrest decisions'.[17] Other researchers have made similar points, arguing that '... the processual consequences of stereotypes not only shape public attitudes and behaviour towards deviants, but guide the very choice of individuals who are to be so defined and processed'.[18]

Because black women are seen as capable of committing crimes and are blamed for their crimes, not seen as victims, they do not benefit from the mitigating factors such as responsibility for a child that help to keep 'normal' or middle-class white women out of prison. Studies of sentencing patterns suggest that childcare is a factor that makes judges reluctant to impose a prison sentence. For black women race and class are also factors. Female prisons are full of working-class white and black women.

Penal outcomes depend on constructions of culpability—on how much offenders are held to blame for their crimes. There are no hard and fast distinctions between being a victim and being an offender, but, rather, there is a continuum of blameworthiness that has important criminal justice implications. Black men and women are at one end of the continuum so constructed, wholly to blame for their crimes. They fit the stereotype of a 'suitable enemy' rather than 'ideal victim' (Christie, 1986a; 1986b). White women are at the other end of the continuum with white men in between. This means that for white women, the line between being a victim and being an offender is somewhat blurred, and can be crossed (Dally, 1994). Women can benefit from leniency through being seen as little to blame for their offences if they are conscientious mothers. For such women there is a good chance that they will be seen as needing help rather than punishment, and their identity as victims will mitigate their culpability as offenders.

Black women—who are seen as independent and unconventional and sometimes also as defiant, and with a succession of partners and children in care—will be held more blameworthy than white women for comparable offences. Circumstances such as having children, needing money, being addicted

---

[17] 'Gender, Police Arrest Decisions and Notions of Chivalry', Visher C, *Criminology*, 21:5-27, 1983
[18] *Deviance and Social Control* (1977), Swigert V L and Farrel R A, University of Illinois Press: Glenview, USA.

will be construed differently by judges, magistrates, probation officers and others with the power to make decisions, and will appear as mitigating or as aggravating factors according to the woman's race, sexual status, appearance, demeanour and lifestyle. For example, in one study on probation reports (Hudson, 1988) it was found that when officers asked white women who were mothers about the fathers of their children, the point of the question was to ascertain whether the fathers were supportive: economically and in other ways. When black mothers were asked the same question the point was to find out if the children were by different fathers, or whether the woman had a record of promiscuity and unstable relationships. Thus, in other words, with white women the point at issue was the adequacy of the father's performance of his role; with black women the concern was the mother's sexual lifestyle. These stereotype-led differences in dealing with white and black women meant that, for a white woman, parental responsibility was likely to be a mitigating factor, whereas for a black woman it was seen to be proof of her fecklessness and became an aggravating factor.

Similar attitudes apply to foreign nationals, who are accounting for an increasing proportion of the female prison population: the fact that they may have committed crimes out of extreme poverty as the only way of providing for their families is unlikely to be seen as reducing culpability. They are likely to be judged not as women driven to great lengths to support their families, but as women who have left their families, who have neglected their responsibilities to their children and other dependants.

For women, being seen as less culpable is conditional on being seen as unempowered, whereas in the case of white women, economic, social or personal difficulties are represented not as situations they face and are trying to deal with as best they can, but as constituting the persons they are.

Feminists penologists have rightly been critical of the construction of equality that is inscribed in law and criminal justice, but this does not mean they are opposed to an ideal of equality. The thrust of feminist critique in and beyond criminal justice is that to treat people equally has been taken to mean to treat them the same (Carlen 1990; Eaton 1986; Hudson, 1996). In law, as in other institutions of liberal societies, this means treating women in the same way as men and black women in the same way as white women.

CHAPTER 2

Voices Unheard

Increased attempts to tackle racial discrimination in the criminal justice system (CJS) have not changed the face of British justice which still looks 'very white'. Ethnic minorities are significantly under-represented within the judiciary and the prison and police services, while black people are disproportionately to be found among the prison population. Although the concept of institutional racism has been recognised by the criminal justice agencies, it remains the case that ethnic minorities are being badly served. To an extent this can be explained by the social exclusion that so many people from black and minority ethnic backgrounds face. They are over-represented in school exclusion, deprived areas, the care system, unemployment and health services. However, social exclusion (see *Chapter 1*) alone cannot wholly explain the over-representation of black people in prison and the under-representation of ethnic minorities in key positions.

In *Reducing Re-offending by Ex-prisoners* (*Chapter 1*) the government's Social Exclusion Unit (SEU) highlighted the discrimination that minority ethnic groups can encounter. Black people are five times more likely than white people to be stopped and searched. Once arrested, they are more likely to be remanded in custody than other offenders charged with similar offences. Results from five pilot areas suggest that black and Asian defendants may be less likely to be found not guilty than white defendants. Research also suggests that black prisoners are likely to receive longer sentences than either white or Asian prisoners. HM Inspectorate of Probation has also found that the quality of pre-sentence reports (PSRs) was significantly poorer for black offenders than for white or Asian offenders, something which could lead to courts being more likely to hand down prison sentences. Once in prison, black people are more likely to be found guilty of disciplinary offences and less likely to have access to purposeful activity. These factors contribute to the fact that black people are disproportionately to be found among the prison population and to unequal treatment in prison (for further details see *Chapter 7*).[1]

If black Britain were a nation, it would have the highest imprisonment rate in the world. And if white people were imprisoned at the rate of black people, England and Wales would have almost half a million people in prison. The contrast in staffing levels within prisons could hardly be greater, although the Home Office has been taking the issue of ethnic minority recruitment and retention increasingly seriously. HM Prison Service (HMPS) now has a Race Relations Adviser and a racial equality key performance indicator (KPI). In 2001-2002, the KPI target was for at least 4.1 per cent minority ethnic staff. This was exceeded, with 4.9 per cent of HMPS staff coming from minority ethnic groups, although disproportionately low numbers of minority ethnic people actually worked in operational duties with prisoners. It is not until 2007 that HMPS aims to have a workforce that represents the ethnic composition of society. This compares unfavourably with the National Probation Service (NPS), where

---

[1] See also the *Introduction* and for latest data when going to press the *Postscript* to this work at p.140.

minority ethnic probation officer grades have increased from 3.4 per cent in 1997 to 10.1 per cent in 2001, already exceeding the target for 2009. Encouragingly, though, of those recruited to HMPS in 2001-2002, 7.9 per cent were from minority ethnic groups, as were 6.3 per cent of staff promoted during the year.

The prisons with the highest levels of minority ethnic staff are in London. This is not surprising given that one in three Londoners is from a minority ethnic group. The highest proportion of minority ethnic staff can be found at Holloway, with 29 per cent, followed by Pentonville with 28 per cent and Brixton and Wormwood Scrubs, both with 22 per cent. However, it is a very different picture nationally. Three prisons—Hewell Grange, Kirkham and North Sea Camp—had no minority ethnic staff at all. At Cookham Wood, e.g. 55 per cent of prisoners were from a minority ethnic group, but only two members of staff. Similarly at Send, another women's prison, 60 per cent of prisoners were from a minority ethnic group, but only three staff members.

The situation is particularly noticeable in women's prisons that house large numbers of foreign national prisoners (see further in *Chapter 7*) and are often in white, rural areas, thus making it difficult to recruit BME staff. Although not inevitable, there is a danger that prisons with no or few such staff will not have a great enough awareness of or sensitivity to the needs of the prisoners they hold. Many prisons, e.g. do not have any staff from minority ethnic groups on their race relations committees.

The under-representation of minority ethnic groups among criminal justice staff is particularly marked at a senior level. Just one prison governor, one chief probation officer and no police chief constables are from an ethnic minority. This is despite the fact that ethnic minorities—who number over 3.5 million people in England and Wales—make up seven per cent of the general labour force. Just one of the 160 or so senior judges—Law Lords, Lords Justice of Appeal and High Court judges—is from a minority ethnic group. Nor are any of the 98 Lord Lieutenants in the UK, who are appointed by the Queen and who recommend people for appointment as justices of the peace. Yet these are the people responsible for administering justice or overseeing public affairs in our name and who underpin policy and make key decisions.

If the criminal justice system is to become fair and just, it is essential that it embraces diversity. It should be a cause for concern that black people are eight times as likely as whites to be in prison, just as it should be a cause for deep embarrassment that only a handful of key figures within criminal justice are from a minority ethnic group. Unless the Government demonstrates that it is able to turn this situation around and dismantle the discrimination that scars so many key institutions, it is likely that minority ethnic groups will become even more alienated—including from criminal justice and law and order.

A black woman's experience of the criminal justice process will be very different to that of a white woman. Lack of acknowledgement of this in theoretical studies has resulted in decision-makers such as police, judges or magistrates relying on stereotypical assumptions about appropriate behaviour. This chapter therefore considers some issues concerning black women that need to be taken into account if they are to have an effective voice in the arena of criminology.

TRADITIONAL APPROACHES

There is a need to hear the voice of black women when considering the causes of crime and when dispensing criminal justice. Feminist criminology has largely left out of account black women's specific experiences. As already noted in *Chapter 1*, it has tended to focus on white women (but with more general works on black men). I would challenge the premise that such studies can be used properly to inform discussions about black women.

Although behaviours, reactions and expectations are affected by structural locations, in British society certain reactions and behaviours seem to be more highly valued than others. Typically, critical criminologists have argued that those with economic power also have access to political power, and thus to the ability to influence the scope and shape of the law (Quinney, 1980; Reiman, 1979). This means that the values found in the law will generally be most consistent with the interests of the upper-class. As noted in the *Introduction*, race, gender and class have a strong impact on economic power, and from this flows the idea that people of the dominant race, class and gender will be more likely than other groups to control the political and legal processes. Crime, which is a political phenomenon, will reflect gender, race and class power. The less powerful a person is in terms of race, class and gender, the more likely he or she is to be subjected to the controlling power of the law (and vice-versa). In addition, the less powerful the class, gender and race to which a person belongs, the more likely behaviours common to that group will be treated as criminal (and, again, vice-versa).

According to Gelsthorpe and Morris the lowest common denominator of feminist perspectives means:

> . . . accepting the view that women experience subordination on the basis of their sex and working towards the elimination of that subordination.[2]

One of the purposes of *feminist criminology*[3] is to consider and advance woman's position so far as understanding crime and criminal justice is concerned. It has not yet fully come to terms with issues concerning *black women*—possibly due to the strength of white women in the feminist movement. The agenda may not include those items that are most pressing for black women.

Certain studies have sought to distil how women, and women and crime in particular, have historically been perceived (but have not specifically included black women's experiences). In Lucia Zedner's case[4] this was—given the place and period under research—only to be expected. Zedner studied women's prisons in Victorian England and identified links between society's response to crime, prevailing social values and concerns, and its views about women. She focused on the role of gender in relation to social attitudes and responses to criminality and concluded that it was not possible to understand the history of crime or its control in isolation. Thus:

---

[2] *Feminist Perspectives in Criminology* (1990), Gelsthorpe L and Morris A, Open University Press.
[3] Some people assert that feminist criminology cannot exist, as neither *feminism* nor *criminology* are unified sets of principles or practice.
[4] *Women Crime and Custody in Victorian England* (1991), Zedner L, Clarendon Press.

Changing views of womanhood and women's role in society informed the ways in which criminal women were perceived and treated at every juncture.

Zedner used the example of 'feeble-mindedness', to illustrate how, at the end of the nineteenth century, women were judged as much for moral behaviour as criminal activity. Under the Mental Deficiency Act 1913 those in receipt of poor relief when pregnant or at the time of giving birth could be, and often were, classified as feeble-minded and placed in asylums. Single parent mothers continue to be criticised, yet for many black women single parenthood may be a quite natural state of affairs.

The weakness or frailty—some accounts say evil—of women still prevails in certain accounts of female criminality, thus influencing general perceptions of the female offender and, more significantly, the offender's perception of herself.

Traditionally, women were either seen as more primitive than men owing to innate biological factors, and therefore less culpable or criminal, or more secretive, dangerous, deceitful or maladjusted. Early observations about female criminality sometimes claimed that women's crimes resulted from their inability to adapt to a natural feminine role. Heidensohn[5], and Morris[6] in their reviews of the literature on female crime identified the following problems:

- women's and girls' crime and deviance were explained more often by biological factors than social or economic forces;
- representations of their motives, or of the circumstances leading to their crimes, were often wrong or distorted; and
- sexual deviance—ranging from a broken hymen to 'immorality' or prostitution—merged with criminal deviance.

Such critiques stemmed from sexist assumptions of predominantly (but not exclusively) male criminologists who tried to explain women's crime, without any real understanding of a woman's perspective.

In recent decades theories have emerged which try to explain the increase in the number of women arrested by reference to claims that female offenders are becoming increasingly more aggressive and violent. Proponents of this kind of view include Freda Adler[7] and Simon[8] who analysed women's arrest trends in the 1960s and early 1970s and put forward ideas about women's criminality (somewhat troubling to feminists) which were largely an extension of the assumption that the emancipation of women depended on achieving legal and social equality with men in public spheres.

Both Adler's and Simon's analyses assumed that female criminality had been kept under control by women's limited aspirations and opportunities. They argued that social circumstances, not biology, explained gender differences in crime. For Adler, the lifting of restrictions on women's behaviour gave them the opportunity to act like men—that is to be as violent, greedy and crime prone as their male counterparts. Simon took a more qualified stance based on her interpretation of the statistical evidence. Having found no changes in women's

5   *Women and Crime* (1985), Heindesohn F, Macmillan.
6   *Women, Crime and Criminal Justice* (1987), Morris A, Basil Blackwell.
7   *Sisters In Crime* (1975), Adler F, McGraw-Hill, New York.
8   *Women and Crime* (1975), Simon R J, Lexington, Massachusetts.

share of arrest for violent crimes, she reasoned that their increasing share of arrest for property crime (especially larceny, fraud and embezzlement) might be explained by their increasing opportunities in the public sphere to commit crime. Adler has been criticised for claiming a link between the goal of emancipation for women and an increase in female crime and Simon for assuming that such increases were due to new workplace opportunities for some women rather than increasing economic pressures. On a broader front, both have been challenged concerning whether the trends they described were actually occurring.

Roberts,[9] in her study of women and rape, found that until the last two decades little was known about women's experiences, except what filtered through from indirect sources. Where information *had* been collected, for example in wartime, she considered that this was not through concern for women but because it was part of the 'Chronicle of Male Action'. Similarly, Leonard[10] believed that:

Theoretical criminology is sexist because it unwittingly focuses on the activities, interests and values of men, while ignoring a comparable analysis of women.

TAKING ACCOUNT OF BLACK WOMEN'S EXPERIENCES

The traditional approach described above does not take account of the situation of black women who, e.g. have always had to work and function outside conventional roles. In understanding the forces affecting women as a whole it is necessary to acknowledge and incorporate into the debate the complex interconnections between racial, sexual and economic disadvantage and oppression in the lives of black women. Andrea Canaan, in her essay 'Brownness' describes her experience:

The fact is I am brown and female, and my growth and development are tied to the entire community. I must nurture and develop brown self, woman, man and child. I must address the issues of my own oppressions and survival. When I separate them, I isolate them, and ignore them, I separate, isolate and ignore myself. I am a unit! A part of brownness.[11]

Just as in trying to speak for all people the law itself ends up silencing those without power, traditional feminist criminology is in danger of silencing certain groups—those who have been kept from speaking, or who have been ignored when they spoke, including black women.

It also has to be recognised that even within minority ethnic communities there are often different responses because experiences of racism, though similar in many ways, have not been identical. Official policies have sometimes had a different impact within or across such communities. African-Caribbeans have mobilised far more around their collective experience of the criminal justice process, particularly of the police and courts, whereas Asian groups have been

---

[9]   *Women and Rape* (1989), Roberts C, Harvester Wheatsheaf.
[10]   *Women Crime and Society* (1982), Leonard E, Longman.
[11]   Cited in Marlee Kline (1990), *Stafford Law Review*.

more actively involved in defending communities against violent attacks, racial harassment, racist immigration laws, and violence against women.[12]

In countries such as Great Britain, the storyteller is usually white, and so 'woman' turns out to be a white woman. In feminist criminology, as in the dominant culture, woman is mostly white and socio-economically privileged. Spelman comments:

> The real problem has been that feminist theory has confused the condition of one group of women with the condition of all ... A measure of the depth of white middle-class privilege is that apparently straightforward and logical points and actions at the heart of much of feminist theory guarantee the direction of its attention to the concerns of white middle-class women.[13]

BLACK MOTHERS

The way women deal with cases of sexual abuse in the family is influenced by race. Bernard points out that feminist literature reveals a paucity of work addressing the specificity of black mothers' experiences. A criticism that could be levelled against much feminist work is that it has typically focused on the experiences of white mothers, from which generalisations are made to all mothers. Black mothers' exclusion and marginalisation from debates means the particular problems they face have not been fully explored. There may be strong parallels and similarities between all mothers, but the very different conditions of women's lives operate to shape their experiences. Significantly, race will not only influence attitudes towards black mothers, but will also profoundly frame how black mothers perceive their choices and help-seeking actions in the aftermath of the abuse of their children.

One of the major problems associated with reporting sexual abuse in black families (below) is that there can be a great deal to fear and mistrust of statutory agencies, which are perceived as powerful and white dominated institutions (Mtezuka, 1996). Moreover, sexual abuse is not discussed openly for fear of exposing the black community to coercive intervention by statutory agencies (Wilson, 1993; Jackson, 1996). The threatening nature of a topic like child sexual abuse may make some people hesitant in seeking outside help. For example, telling about the abuse may not be safe for children. From a very early age black children experience racism and cushioning of the effects of racism are usually undertaken with the family network. Here black children are particularly dependent for support on networks of family and this may make disclosure especially difficult. If a black child is abused with their family, it becomes especially traumatic and can be almost impossible for the child to disclose to outsiders what is happening. In addition, he or she may feel they are betraying their families (*ibid.*). As Hooks (1989, p.2) has so cogently argued: 'so many black people have been raised to believe that there is just so much that you should not talk about, not in private and not in public'. The reporting of sexual abuse in black communities generates fear of reprisals and could incur marginalization or even exclusion from families and communities (Bernard, 1997). Furthermore,

---

[12] e.g. Southall Black Sisters represent Asian women's points of view.
[13] *Inessential Woman* (1988), Spelman E, Beacon Press, Boston, USA.

black people may feel alienated from law enforcement (Mama, 1993; Mtezuka, 1996). It is accepted by large numbers in the black community that there will be little justice in the CJS and as a result black people are not confident that their concerns will be taken at all seriously when they are victims of crimes (Mama, 1993).

Also black men's involvement in sexual abuse towards their own children may open up painful and difficult issues for black women. For many, an area of concern is that negative and distorted messages about black men are conveyed through the media and other social institutions (Mercer and Julien, 1988). Dominant representations of black men portray them as feckless, absent fathers. Additionally, black male sexuality is represented as wanton and bestial.[14]

'The family' is, e.g. a main cause of contradictory experiences for black women in ways unknown to most white women. Although both black and white women may experience the family as an institution of violence and oppression, for black women it often functions as a source of support against harassment and racism. It provides a cultural and political retreat from white supremacy. Many black women consider their race a more primary factor than gender in their dealings with the criminal justice agencies, such as when the police come to their homes to arrest their children as described in *Chapter 3*.

These different experiences of family life for white women and black women need to be recognised and taken into account. The failure of feminist criminologists to do so and to concentrate on gender oppression is but one illustration of Bell Hooks' observations that:

> Certainly it has been easier for women who do not experience race or class oppression to focus exclusively on gender.[15]

The various intersections between race, gender and class oppression—and other differentiating characteristics—affect how and when *all* women experience sexism. They are able to ignore the experience of their race because it does not in any way correlate with an experience of oppression and contradiction. For example, Fry[16] (a white woman) states that white women tend not to think of themselves as white, but merely as women. Thus, it must be recognised that the interests and concerns shared by black women and white women are cut across in a variety of ways by interests of class, sexuality, race and ethnicity.

Child sexual abuse in black families

To some degree, the negative stereotypes of black men act to shape the way they are responded to, and may reinforce general racism as directed against them in their dealings with welfare agencies (Bryan *et al*, 1985; Arshad, 1996). Moreover, it is suggested that as the state plays a significant role in the demonisation of black men, for black women to raise the issue of their violence and abusive behaviour in public is to invite a racist backlash (Wilson, 1993; Mama, 1995; Mtzeula, 1996). To name the reality means confronting difficult questions that evoke strong feelings within black communities, and moreover bring the possibility of a racist interpretation (Wilson, 1993). Given this set of

---

[14] See 'Women, Violence and Strategies for Action', *Feminist Research Policy And Practice*, pp. 105-6.

[15] *Feminist Theory From Margin to Centre* (1984), Hooks B, South End Press, Boston, USA.

[16] 1983, USA.

circumstances, perhaps not surprisingly there is reluctance to engage publicly with the issue of childhood sexual abuse in black communities and general resistance to change.

The complex way race intersects with gender have been addressed most interestingly by black feminists to consider how black women occupy a range of multiple and contradictory positions that have implications for their relationship to welfare agencies (Carby, 1982; Mama, 1996). Black feminists interrogate race from a standpoint that examines the intersection of gender, race and class to highlight the multifarious roles of women as mothers and as members of their families and communities. Most significantly, analyses from black feminist thinkers have illuminated the need to examine the gendered experiences of black mothers within the private sphere of their families as well as their relationships to the public sphere to consider how these will profoundly influence their help-seeking behaviour.

An analysis of the intersecting effects of gender and race in black women's lives shows that gender and power relations are embodied in black families in complex ways, and identify the contradictions that are posed for black women and children in giving a voice to their experiences of violence and maltreatment (Mama, 1989). Black feminists' analyses usefully direct us towards an understanding of how the family is both a source of black women's affirmation and a source of their oppression (Carby, 1982).

This contradictory position makes it a site of resistance in struggles against state and police racism and deaths in custody, for example. Yet it is also a site of oppression, and poses dilemmas and challenges for black women in the aftermath of child sexual abuse and other forms of male violence in the home. Exploration of gender relations in black families and communities emphasises some of the contradictions for black women in their families, which have implications for subsequent events such as whether they seek help.[17]

Paradoxically, there is a pressure on black mothers to present themselves as strong and ever-coping. Villarosa (1994) discusses the way black women internalise notions of the 'strong' black woman. She notes that this internalisation can be a hindrance to acknowledging pain and vulnerabilities that may significantly constrain women in seeking help to deal with emotional hurts, particularly on issues that are shameful to reveal. Foremost in the minds of many mothers is that they may experience a negative result as a consequence of accessing formal help. What is also at stake here for mothers is the consequence of involving agencies such as the police, which could result in marginalization or exclusion from their communities (Bernard 1997).[18]

Black professionals
Although black practitioners may be more likely to adopt an anti-racist approach in work with mothers, there may be barriers for them to translate this commitment into practice because of their occupational situatedness (Lewis, 1996); that is, they may not have decision-making powers due to their subordinate status in their organization. Moreover, some may centre exclusively on race and ignore the impact of gendered power in mediating black mothers'

---

[17] 'Women, Violence and Strategies for Action', *Feminist Research, Policy and Practice,* pp.106-7.
[18] *Ibid*, pp.109-111.

experience in their families, resulting in an oppressive practice towards black mothers. Therefore, the differing issues involved for black and white practitioners need to be explored for developing anti-oppressive practice with black mothers (see above).[19]

Sexism

Lewis[20] accounted for the different crime rates for black and white women, focusing on racism and sexism within the criminal justice process. Sexism had previously been thought to explain the 'chivalry' or leniency shown to women, but Lewis noted that this only included those women who adhere to dominant societal gender role expectations. As black women are less often married than white women, more often charged with violent offences, and less 'feminine' in demeanour, they will therefore less often meet such expectations. In addition, Lewis suggests that different personal characteristics may contribute to differences in the nature and extent of crime between black and white women. Black women live in greater relative poverty and both black women and black men are socialised to be independent and assertive. But such characteristics should be viewed with caution, because of the risk of stereotyping black women and ignoring the variations in black communities. They are only useful if they result in a greater understanding of the different roles and expectations of women's behaviour in different cultures. As Kennedy states:

> Until there is a clear appreciation of racism and the social factors which bring black people before the courts, and an understanding of the subtle dynamics which work in the courts to discriminate against them, they will continue to be amongst the sections of the community least well served by the law.[21]

Feminist criminology thus needs to analyse factors such as the disproportionate impact of criminal justice processes on black women, the full effect of race-gender-class on their lives and the perceptions and experiences of black women of the kind described in this book.

It must be acknowledged that society's views about different groups of women may come into play in sentencing. Since race affects dominant perceptions of women's 'badness' or 'goodness' it would help to have some information about how black women are viewed (for example by judges and police officers) to determine whether there might be discrimination on the basis of societal perception. It also has to be recognised that behaviour that may be attributed to a 'good' woman in one culture may have the reverse meaning in another.

An African woman who arranges with some members of her extended family to care for her children while she spends many hours at the market or finding ways of supporting her children may not be seen in English courts as a 'good' mother who cares for them. It may be that black mothers are considered inadequate by the courts more often than white mothers because they fail to measure up to the dominant (white) ideology of motherhood. Government and

---

[19] 'Women, Violence and Strategies for Action', *Feminist Research, Policy and Practice*, pp.112, 114, 116.

[20] 'Black Women Offenders and Criminal Justice: Some Theoretical Considerations', Lewis D, in *Comparing Female and Male Offenders* (1981), Warren M (ed.), Sage, pp.89-105.

[21] *Eve Was Framed* (1992), Kennedy H, Chatto and Windus.

media criticism in the 1990s concerning children from single parent families who may become delinquent is one example of how dominant values can affect people from minority cultures.

Thus, whilst the ideology of motherhood has dictated that white women stay at home, black women have been regarded as particularly suited for work outside the home, often in someone else's home. For example, African-Caribbean women were encouraged to emigrate to Britain specifically to take positions such as domestics, office cleaners and nurses.[22] At the same time, however, the role of black women as mothers to their own children goes unrecognised and is sometimes actively ignored and discouraged.

Claudia Bernard[23] describes how stereotyping of black mothers as bad parents has strongly influenced these women not to involve the child protection agencies in cases of childhood sexual abuse. Mothers in the study felt vulnerable to implied criticism of their parenting and their capacity to protect their children from abuse. There is over-representation of black (in particular, African-Caribbean) children in the public care system. Also many black women do manual jobs with little pay, and as a result find themselves working even more hours to make ends meet. This can mean spending many hours a day away from their children.

Compared with white women, black women may be affected in more complex and contradictory ways by ideological expectations concerning work and motherhood. This is not to deny that some working class white women find themselves working long hours to make ends meet. Women have to conform to an ideology of motherhood that dictates mothers should not work outside their homes, especially when children are still young. Black mothers may then be seen as *failed* mothers, precisely because they are single parents, or because their husband or partner has a low wage or is unemployed. The *Census of Population* reports that black women work longer hours compared to white women, and that a greater proportion work full-time.

As Kennedy[24] points out, black mothers often feel their bond with their children is perceived as less significant and that their views on the child's welfare are less valuable. Kennedy cites one mother who was sentenced to two months in prison for refusing access to her daughter's father (a civil matter). She felt that she was viewed as bloody-minded and obstructive when in fact she was trying to express deep concern for her child's well being. Her ex-boyfriend was a drug user and the little girl returned from visits describing in detail his use of drugs and drug-related involvement with other people. The mother feared that the influence of drugs would affect his ability to care for the child when she was with him, and wanted any access to be supervised. In court her concerns were ignored. She explained:

> The judge thought I was a stubborn determined person who was going out of my way to break a court order. I think had I not had two children by different fathers they would have viewed me as a different type of person. I think the judge was

---

[22]   See, generally, *Appendix I* to this work.

[23]   'Childhood Sexual Abuse: The Implications for Black Mothers', Bernard C, *Rights of Women Bulletin,* Winter, 1995.

[24]   *Eve Was Framed* (1992), Kennedy H, Chatto and Windus.

trying to say, you can't have your children and do what you like with them. I think the colour factor comes into it, but it's something that can never be proved.

Many poor women in prison come from run-down housing estates—a problem faced to a greater extent by black women and defined as areas of 'high risk' by the police.[25] The disadvantages which begin to stem from such a lifestyle seem obvious. Throughout there are issues of race, gender and class. For a black woman it is not always easy to know whether the negative response she receives is due to one element or the other, or whether, say, two or more elements are inter-related. In every black woman's life there are innumerable occasions when she is not only sexually but racially discriminated against.

---

[25] 'Policing of Black Women', Chigwada R, in *Out of Order: Policing of Black People* (1986), Cashmore E and McLaughlin E (eds.), Routledge, Kegan and Paul.

CHAPTER 3

Police and Black Women

In its submission to the Royal Commission on Criminal Justice in 1992 the Runnymede Trust claimed that racially unequal treatment occurred at all stages of the criminal justice process, from first contact with the police through to imprisonment. Studies of police attitudes from the 1960s to the 1990s regularly disclosed that racist attitudes were held by many police officers, a 'canteen culture' carrying over from joking with fellow officers to direct encounters with the public. Much has been achieved since that time, particularly following section 95 Criminal Justice Act 1991 which casts a duty on the Home Secretary to publish:

> . . . such information as he considers expedient for the purposes of . . . facilitating the performance by [people engaged in the administration of criminal justice] of their duty to avoid discriminating against any person on the ground of race, sex or any other improper ground.

But a deal remains to be done to build on the training and monitoring that now take place and on the changed working practices that have been introduced. In particular, discrimination at the start of the criminal justice process may impact at a later stage, when it may be compounded by further unequal treatment. In this context it can be noted that even as late as 2001, HM Prison Service (HMPS) and the Crown Prosecution Service (CPS) were openly admitting to being institutionally racist (as to which in relation to the police see below).[1] Neither is there a focus on black women as such (see the comments in *Chapter 1*).

BACKGROUND

There is no evidence to suggest that people from ethnic minority groups commit proportionately more offences than white people. Self-report studies (considered by many people to be a more accurate measure of crime rates than the number of offenders caught by the police), suggest around one per cent more white people reporting that they have committed a crime than black people, while the number of Asians saying that they have committed a crime is markedly lower. In Neustatter (2002), a 19-year-old white youth serving a sentence at HM Prison Lancaster Farms said:

> Lots of people think of blacks as the worst criminals because they are on the streets so much, and because when people think of crime they think 'muggers' and then they think 'black'. But you know where I come from there's lots of black and Asian kids and they are my friends and I see how they get hassled and picked up when we white kids are overlooked for the same things.

---

[1] For a summary, see *Introduction to the Criminal Justice Process* (2002), Gibson B and Cavadino P, Waterside Press, *Chapter 16*; and for an analysis *Crime, State and Citizen* (2001), Faulkner D, Waterside Press.

Also a black boy in Neustatter's study stated that he could 'be pushed into a situation where I offend. If you're black there's all that stuff with the police on your case the whole time, thinking you've done wrong when you haven't. Sometimes you lose your rag and then they get you for that' (Neustatter, 2002:61). Neustatter argues that the high rate of stopping and arresting of black and Asian youths does not mean that ethnic minorities are more likely to be found guilty of crimes than young whites. Among those accused, ethnic minority defendants are more likely than whites to have their cases terminated early before court proceedings; in magistrates' courts the acquittal rate in contested trials is higher for black and Asian defendants than for white defendants; and ethnic minority defendants are less likely than whites to be convicted. She points out that 'the inequality that ethnic minorities, and especially black young people, experience takes the form of their having a greater chance than young whites of being put through the criminal justice system and of being charged, yet ultimately being less likely to end up with a conviction. However, they are both more likely to be remanded in custody than whites, and to get longer sentences when they are convicted, and hence they are 'over-represented' in prison. (*ibid*)

Police searches of black people's homes in Brixton and Tottenham were thought, in part, to have triggered riots in that area in the 1980s. In each case the suspect's mother was 'at the receiving end' (Chigwada, 1991). The Scarman Inquiry report (Scarman, 1981), published following the Brixton riots in 1981, rejected the notion of an explicit, 'knowing' policy of discrimination—what might be termed 'direct' discrimination. Lord Scarman identified the immediate problems underlying the Brixton riots as an interaction between intense levels of social deprivation and a history of unlawful policing methods, racially prejudiced police conduct and a lack of community consultation. With regard to racial prejudice among the police, he saw this as a problem of individuals (the 'rotten apples' concept), rather than an institutional issue, but with widespread consequences. Thus Scarman admitted that: 'Some police officers ... lapse into unthinking assumptions that all young black people are potential criminals'.

Some 15 years on from those riots, the inquiry into the death of the young black teenager Stephen Lawrence (Macpherson, 1999: 6.34) had broad terms of reference to examine not only the specifics of the murder investigation (and subsequent police enquiries) but also the factors which underlay the evident tensions between police and minority ethnic groups. It considered the evidence that there were a range of different forms of indirect discrimination—including stereotyping Stephen Lawrence and his friend, Duwayne Brookes, at the scene of the murder, patronising behaviour towards the Lawrence family, as well as stop and search powers targeted against young people from ethnic minorities. The inquiry concluded that institutional racism did exist and defined it as:

The collective failure of an organization to provide an appropriate and professional service to people because of their colour, culture, or ethnic origin. It can be seen or detected in processes, attitudes and behaviour which amount to discrimination through unwitting prejudice, ignorance, thoughtlessness and racist stereotyping which disadvantage ethnic minority people.

Thus, formally at least, the problem of institutional racism was recognised by the Association of Chief Police Officers (ACPO) and Home Office. When the Macpherson inquiry report was published, the Home Secretary commented that:

> The enquiry found that, on that definition, institutional racism exists within ... both the Metropolitan Police Service and in other police services and other institutions countrywide ... That is a new definition of institutional racism, which I accept—and so does the Commissioner. The inquiry's assessment is clear and sensible. In my view, any long–established, white-dominated organization is liable to have procedures, practices and a culture that tend to exclude or to disadvantage non-white people. The police service, in that respect, is little different from other parts of the criminal justice system—or from government departments, including the Home Office—and many other institutions.

The then President of ACPO, John Newing, wrote to the Stephen Lawrence inquiry saying:

> I define institutional racism as the racism which is inherent in wider society which shapes our attitudes and behaviour. Those attitudes and behaviour are then reinforced or reshaped by the culture of the organization a person works for. That creates problems in a number of areas, but particularly in the way officers deal with black people. Discrimination and unfairness are the result. I know because as a young police officer I was guilty of such behaviour. (Macpherson, 1999: 6.50, pp.31-2)

STOP AND SEARCH AND OTHER POLICE POWERS

Research continues to show that black people are stopped more often than white people or other minority groups. Home Office figures released in 2002 led to accusations that the police were failing to stamp out racism in the ranks[2] after the figures revealed that black Britons are eight times more likely than white people to be stopped and searched. It would appear that since the 1999 Macpherson inquiry into racism within the police, the situation has worsened for ethnic minorities, with black people five times more likely to be targeted by police using controversial powers. The police carried out approaching a quarter of a million stops in 2001/2, an increase on the previous year of four per cent, according to Home Office figures. But the Metropolitan police saw a huge increase. Officers in London stopped 30 per cent more African-Caribbean people and 40 per cent more Asian people compared to an increase of eight per cent for white people. Nationally, barely one in ten stops led to arrest, meaning that officers' suspicions of more than 70,000 black and 35,000 Asian people, were not borne out. Outside London two per cent fewer whites were stopped, while there was a six per cent increase of African-Caribbeans and a 16 per cent rise for Asians compared with the previous year. Asians were three times more likely than white people to be stopped. *Race and the Criminal Justice System* (Home Office, 2001) also showed that ethnic minorities were over-represented throughout the system, but under-represented as employees.

---

[2]   The problem of racism experienced by black police officers also continues despite initiatives to stamp this out. In January 2002, a black officer in the Metropolitan police was cleared of fiddling £80 worth of expenses, ending an inquiry that had cost the force an estimated £1 million.

When Home Office minister John Denham MP announced a new unit to study the reasons behind the figures this was denounced as a 'waste of money' by Neville Lawrence, father of murdered black teenager Stephen Lawrence who said the statistics revealed that police officers 'had returned to their old ways and were institutionally racist in their approach to crime. We know what the problem is and we don't need another team to sort it out'. Richard Stone, a member of the Macpherson inquiry which found the police to be institutionally racist, said: 'There are still too many police acting in a racist way. Things are getting worse rather than better'. The Macpherson inquiry concluded that police should have to give written reasons for carrying out stops (Recommendation 61).

Amendments to the Police and Criminal Evidence Act 1984 contained in the Criminal Justice Bill (2002) would extend police powers of stop and search to cover items to be used in criminal damage such as spray paints. Previously, the police have been allowed to stop and search if there is a reasonable suspicion that someone is carrying a weapon, drugs or stolen items. This would now be permitted for objects that are not intrinsically 'criminal'—such as paint. As a consequence a far greater use of stop and search is likely to result. This will have a particular impact on black people as the figures noted above show. Success rates for stop and search are fairly low with roughly only one in six searches resulting in an arrest. Liberty's view is that police resources are best targeted at serious crime and that these measures, taken together, are effectively a return to 'zero tolerance', if by another name. Similar issues and problems would arise if controversial proposals made in March 2003 to take fingerprints and DNA samples from suspects, whether or not charged or convicted, given the vaguaries of who might be arrested 'for that purpose'.

Again, there is no research that specifically examines stop and search figures for black women. That by FitzGerald (2002) on policing in London found that young people have a much higher risk of being stopped and that white people overall have a lower risk of being stopped than members of any minority ethnic group, with black people having the highest risk, followed by Pakistanis and Bangladeshis. Nineteen per cent of black car users were stopped as against 17 per cent of Pakistani and Bangladeshi car users, 13 per cent of Indians and 11 per cent of white drivers. FitzGerald found that a man under the age of 30 from a minority ethnic group had an 18 per cent chance of having been stopped in the previous 12-15 months, compared with a two per cent chance for the rest of the sample. London, covered by the Metropolitan Police Service, has a higher proportion of residents from visible minority groups than any other police area. According to the Office for National Statistics (2001) minorities made up 22 per cent of the London population aged 16 or over, compared with four per cent for the rest of the country. Within London, the population classified as Indian formed the largest single group (five per cent), followed by black Caribbeans (four per cent), Black Africans (3.5 per cent), Pakistanis (1.5 per cent) and Bangladeshis (1.5 per cent).

Black professionals also are subjected to police harassment
The following are cases reported in *The Independent*, 8 November 2002, of black professional people who felt they had been unfairly stopped and searched:

Leroy McDowell and his friend Wayne Taylor, who both suffered from the blood disorder sickle cell anaemia, successfully sued the Metropolitan Police for assault and false imprisonment. They were stopped by police in Hackney, east London and their car searched because police said they 'were in a drugs-related area.' Their pleas that they suffered from a serious condition were ignored and they were placed in cells without receiving medical attention. They were charged with public order offences, which were later rejected by a court. The two men were awarded £38,000 by Central London County Court in 1997.

In the past 17 years, Trevor Hall, a senior civil servant, has been stopped and searched by police on 44 occasions, 39 of which were in London. Mr Hall who is in his fifties and who retired earlier this year as a member of the Home Office's Community Relations Unit, acted as a consultant to ministers, advising on community and race relations policies and the prison and probation services.

Garth Crooks the BBC sports broadcaster and former Tottenham Hotspur striker was first stopped and searched at 18, when an officer subjected him to a torrent of racial abuse. The officer was called off by a colleague who recognised him as a rising star at the local club, Stoke City. Mr Crooks has since said: 'Just wearing a baseball cap and driving a Mercedes are not good enough reasons to stop somebody'.

Carl Josephs, 30, a Birmingham caterer, was stopped 34 times in two years.

Being a respectable and a professional black person does not exempt someone from police harassment. Class does not apply to black people in one sense, i.e. that no matter how successful they may be they are still subject to the same suspicion and treatment accorded to the lower classes. Race plays a significant part in how the police choose their suspects for stop and search.

BLACK WOMEN

Without empirical research it is difficult to know whether the racism applied to black men also applies to black women at the same level or for entirely the same reasons. What *is* known is that the police consider black women to be capable of committing crimes in a way that 'normal' or 'good' white women are not.[3] As noted in *Chapter 1*, any such research needs to address issues of race, gender and class and to look at how these inter-relate.

Earlier research shows that black women do receive fewer cautions than white women.[4] They were also seven times more likely to be arrested for prostitution than women of other groups.[5] One explanation for the disproportionate number of such arrests may be that economics and class come into play. Black women prostitutes are often forced to practise their profession 'on the streets' instead of under the protection of a benevolent hotel manager or from a luxury apartment, as many white 'working girls' do. A woman's lifestyle can increase the likelihood of police contact, harassment, vulnerability to arrest

[3]   'Women and Crime in the City', Player E, in *Crime in the City* (1989), Downes D (ed.), MacMillan.
[4]   'Race and Criminal Justice', Nacro, 1989.
[5]   'Hustling for Rights', Haft M G, in *The Female Offender* (1976), Crites L (ed.), Lexington: Massachusetts, 212.

and risk of involvement in other offences as a result of it carrying her into less safe or more crime prone environments:

> As might be expected, the largest proportion of arrests of black prostitutes takes place in the inner cities where living standards are low, the level of desperation high, and police prejudice endemic.[6]

One study disclosed that incarcerated female offenders are more likely than white women to *perceive* the police as excessively brutal, harassing, and unlikely to give them a break through non-arrest.[7] Discretion was exercised more liberally in favour of non-arrest with white women than black women. Moyer and White hypothesise that police officers will apply more severe sanctions to black women than white women, especially if black women are 'loud, boisterous, aggressive, vulgar, and disrespectful'.[8] This was supported by a statement by the Black Women in Prison Scheme, an organization which gives moral and material support and visits black women in prison. It is their view that:

> Black women are often seen as violent and that they have to be dealt with by male officers ... and the officers have been reported to physically rough up these black women in order to prove that they are not like normal white women.

Suspects and other police detainees

A presumption that black people are more likely to commit crime than white people seems to pervade people's thinking in Britain. According to the Penal Affairs Consortium such thinking is misplaced.[9] Black women are the subject of many negative beliefs and attitudes, the victims of racist assumptions which are likely to affect police attitudes towards them. Their sometimes exuberant 'arm-waving' or otherwise excited behaviour may well be misinterpreted.

Common stereotypes afforded to black women include the over-aggressive African woman and the strong, dominant African-Caribbean woman. In contrast, Asian women are viewed as 'passive', 'hysterical', or subject to oppressive practices within the family. Such stereotyping has deterred police from taking action or prosecuting in cases of domestic violence involving black women who are seen as able to look after themselves. Helena Kennedy mentions the trial of a Ugandan woman for grievous bodily harm to her husband by pouring hot cooking-fat over him. It came to light that, although the woman had called the police repeatedly, her violent husband was never arrested. It was suggested to her that she was not telling the truth when making previous complaints. There was no record of the complaints and it was put to her in cross-examination that she was exaggerating her husband's brutality. It was a prosecution witness, a neighbour, who inadvertently came to her aid. He complained in the witness box

---

[6] *ibid.*

[7] 'Incarcerated Male and Female Offenders: Perceptions of Their Experiences in the Criminal Justice System', Kratcoski and Scheuerman, *Journal of Criminal Justice*, 2:73-78, 1974; and see 'The Criminalisation and Imprisonment of Black Women', Chigwada R, *Probation Journal*, pp. 100-105, September 1989.

[8] 'Police Processing of Female Offenders', Moyer L and White G F in *Crime in America* (1981), Bowker L (Ed.), New York: MacMillan.

[9] 'Race and Criminal Justice', Penal Affairs Consortium, September 1996, p.2.

about the number of times he had been awakened—first by her screams and then by police mistakenly ringing his doorbell when they came in answer to her calls.[10]

In March 1996, the *Runnymede Bulletin* reported the case of a man who died after being sprayed with CS gas. The police were called by the man's wife following a domestic disturbance. Some ten police officers arrived and placed him in a police van. When he developed problems with breathing at the police station he was taken to hospital where he died. The police were called to his home between 4 a.m. and 5 a.m. The man died the same morning at 6.23 a.m. Such events are likely to make other black women involved in domestic violence think twice before calling the police, afraid of what might happen to their partners.

Sarah Thomas

Sarah Thomas a 35-year-old black architectural design student died in police custody in Stoke Newington police station on 6 August 1999. She was arrested as she waited for her boyfriend Paul Doyle outside their flat in Finsbury Park. The police maintained that she was acting suspiciously (she was locked out). She was arrested and taken to the police station where the police say she 'appeared to suffer a fit'—then went into a coma. An ambulance was called—but she died two days later. Sarah was healthy and with no police record, or any record of fits. As she was dragged away to the station witnesses reported her screaming 'Help me, help me they're trying to kill me'. Before there had been a full autopsy or inquest the police announced that her coma was drug induced—but there is no real evidence of this.[11]

Joy Gardner

The much-publicised case of Joy Gardner, a black woman of Jamaican origin who died in 1993 in London, lends support to the view that black women can be seen by the authorities as potentially violent. Joy Gardner had overstayed her visa and was visited by the Alien Deportation Group. Her wrists were handcuffed to a leather strap around her waist, bound by a second belt around her thighs, and a third one around her ankles. As she lay on the floor, 13 feet of adhesive tape were wound around her head and face. Mrs Gardner collapsed. She died in hospital a few hours later. Until her tragic death the use of body belts, surgical tape and the existence of a special deportation squad was unknown to the general public. It subsequently came to light that two other African women had been deported in this way.

If Joy Gardner had been an Australian or a New Zealander the police and immigration authorities are most unlikely to have found it necessary to send so many officers to her house, nor would they have used such methods. What underlies those events is the perception of black women as aggressive and troublesome. There would have been horror in white suburbia if a middle-class

---

[10] *Eve Was Framed* (1992), Kennedy H, Chatto and Windus. There have been changes in the policing of domestic violence since that time, including the setting up of national and local Domestic Violence Units—but the point about official responses to black women remains valid.

[11] See http://flag.blackened.net/revolt/arc/sarsh_sept99.html and also Amnesty International, Library, United Kingdom: Deaths in Custody: Lack of Police. pp. 5, 12.

white woman had been treated in the way Joy Gardner was—and it seems almost inconceivable that a white woman would have been 'taped up' in such a fashion.

Three officers were tried for the murder of Mrs Gardner and acquitted. In effect, the trial put the victim in the dock. As if to honour the standard stereotype and myth of the 'big strong black woman', Joy Gardner was described by one of the officers as 'the strongest and most violent woman' he had ever encountered. One of the officers said that the treatment she received was 'reasonable in all the circumstances'. Some politicians used the events to hammer home their anti-black, anti-refugee message. Teresa Gorman, conservative MP for Billericay, said:

> She had been bumming on the Social Services for five years … she had cost the taxpayer an enormous amount … if she had gone quietly none of this would have happened.[12]

This stereotypical notion that black women are inherently more aggressive or troublesome is unfounded. On the contrary, most of black women are subdued at the shock of first-time contact with the criminal justice agencies and, in the case of foreign women, the relative strangeness of British culture.

Kwanele Siziba

On 27 April 1994 Kwanele Siziba, a 27-year-old Zimbabwean woman, with a fractured wrist, fell 12 floors to her death in East London after trying to climb down to the flat below from a balcony. She was afraid immigration officials had called at her sister's flat where she was staying—in fact it had been a bailiff accompanied by two police officers. She had been very frightened after the death of Joy Gardner and wanted to go back to Zimbabwe. She kept saying 'If the police find me I don't want to die'. The bailiff was employed by the Lord Chancellor's Department to collect a debt. He admitted that he had threatened to break the door down if it was not opened. He was questioned at the inquest on the existence of a code of conduct and admitted that he had issued the threat despite having no legal authority to do so. He expressed no regret. He defended his threat to kick the door in despite the fact that he knew there was no other exit from the flat.

The bailiff had clearly acted beyond his powers. He had already retired from his job and there was no possibility of disciplinary action being taken against him. The family was left with no redress. The coroner noted, in summing up, that Ms Siziba's fear of the immigration service caused by the deaths of Joy Gardner and Omasase Lumumba had contributed to the action she had taken and which had led to her death. He expressed regret at her death and delivered a verdict of misadventure.[13]

THREE SCENARIOS

The Newham Monitoring Project (NMP) has documented a number of real-life cases (anonymised for the purposes of this book but all three occurring in the 1990s) which illustrate the type of situation this chapter has sought to convey:

---

[12] *NMP Annual Report* 1995/96.
[13] IRR, 'Black Deaths in Custody', p.6; http://www.irr.org.uk/2002/november/ak000006.html

Mrs A Police officers visited the home of Mrs A, an elderly black woman, to arrest her son. The police mistakenly attempted to arrest Richard in the belief that he was Richard's brother Jason. Both Richard and his mother tried to explain the misunderstanding but the officers forced their way into the house and pulled Richard out, allegedly beating him in the process and pushing his mother heavily in the chest, causing her to collapse with severe chest pains. It is said that if it was not for the swift action of her children Mrs A could have died. Mrs A was admitted to hospital and was there for five days. She and her son sued the police and, in an out of court settlement, obtained £28,000 in lieu of damages for assault, wrongful arrest and false imprisonment. They also won an apology from the police but so far as is known no disciplinary action has been taken against the officers concerned.

Mrs B Mrs B died when police went to her house to arrest her son. She was shot by the police. At the inquest, a verdict of accidental death was returned, thereby absolving the police but, seemingly, vindicating her family's case that the police search contributed directly to the heart attack that actually killed her. Again, no disciplinary action was taken.

Mrs C The case of Mrs C illustrates how police actions can quickly turn a criminal investigation involving a black woman into an immigration issue. Mr and Mrs C lived on an estate. From the day they moved into their first floor maisonette, they were subjected to racial harassment from their white neighbours in a notoriously hostile part of London. One evening, whilst Mrs C was relaxing in her front room, her three young children aged three and two were out playing on the balcony with her three month old baby in his pram. Mrs C said that the children were at no time left unattended, as the front door was open, enabling her to keep a close eye on them. Mr C was at work.

The two-year-old, who had a pedal car, climbed onto it and reached up, thus managing to hang his head over the balcony. Immediately Mrs C saw this, she ran out and shouted at him to get down in her strong Jamaican accent. Her neighbours understood this to mean that she was going to throw the child over the balcony. Within minutes, whilst Mrs C was still outside calming the children down, she saw a police van driving up close to her home. A few seconds later, three male police officers walked straight into her home without invitation, as her front door was still open. Mrs C said she felt intimidated and humiliated by the audacity of the officers, whose form of greeting was to tell her that they had come out in response to her neighbour's report that she was drunk and attempting to throw her son over the balcony. Mrs C, taken aback by what the officers said, became distressed. She could not understand the policemen's view of this information. They did not, she said, even believe that she was the mother of the children. She had to prove this by producing their birth certificates. The officers then asked Mrs C to produce her passport to show what her immigration status was. When she said that her passport was in a suitcase in an upstairs bedroom, she was followed up the stairs by all three officers. Whilst her passport was checked, Mrs C was repeatedly warned that even though she was a *legal* immigrant, she could still be deported and have her children taken away from her. At that point, she broke down in tears, triggering an extraordinary response from the police. They began to ransack Mrs C's drawers and picked up her pants, holding these up to her and asking who she wore them for. Mrs C was not only stripped of her dignity, but as she later told an NMP worker, she was terrified and felt '… like I had been raped'.

Mrs C was told to go downstairs as the officers were taking her and the children to the police station. She was not allowed to clothe or prepare a feed for her three-month-old son before leaving. This was on a cold evening in March. The police officers later said they did that '... to ensure the safety and well-being of the children'. Mrs C was denied the right to make a phone call to her husband, or to hold her baby until she was seated in the police van—where, according to Mrs C, her young son was 'literally hurled' at her.

At the police station, Mrs C and her three young children were put in a cell and left until a duty social worker arrived. The social worker was so alarmed by the way she had been treated that she gave her NMP's emergency telephone. After another three hours Mrs C's husband was finally contacted and told that his family had been removed from their home because there were concerns for the safety of the children.

Mrs C was released without charge and never given a satisfactory explanation. The following morning, Mr and Mrs C contacted NMP for help and NMP contacted the local Social Services Department to find out what, if anything, they knew about the case. The response was that the Social Services department had been contacted by the Child Protection Team, but had expressed serious concerns about the way in which young children were being removed from their homes in the absence of a social worker. The police, however, insisted that this was part of a 'joint' case between themselves and the social services.

In the hope that she would get some recompense, Mrs C put in a formal complaint. The officers concerned denied all her allegations. The Police Complaints Authority (PCA) came up with what now appears to be a standard response. In a letter, Mrs C was told that '... there were no other witnesses to this incident and therefore no means of reconciling the conflicting accounts given. Having carefully studied all the papers contained in the report of the investigation, the Authority have decided that no formal disciplinary action should be taken'. The incident left Mrs C deeply traumatised, so that she had to be put on tranquillisers. As a result, she was not alert for a while, and she could not properly look after her children. During that period, her husband had to take indefinite leave from work to care for his family. Mr C's employers were becoming impatient with him and threatened to sack him.

As a result of the incident it is said that the C family became isolated and the development of the three-year-old's speech more impaired, as he was afraid to go out and play with other children. The experience almost tore the family apart. Fortunately, Mrs C's children were not placed on the local 'at risk' register (another indication that there was no significant problem had the police investigated the matter more thoroughly rather than making assumptions). Instead, Mrs C was assigned the support of a home help during what was a difficult period. Even after a year, she was still feeling insecure and nervous.

Some other cases of mistreatment

After the Brixton riots and the Broadwater Farm riots, black women lived in fear of being separated from their children, either if they, themselves, were arrested (with the likelihood that their young children would be left alone), or if their older children were arrested.[14] Police officers, in many instances armed, visited over 1,000 homes on the Broadwater Farm Estate after the riots and an indication of the fear that such visits caused is provided by the testimony of a black mother:

They (the police) said that he (her son) had been picked up for the murder of the policeman, and it would be better for him if I told them everything I knew about what he was doing on the night of the riot. When I said my son didn't know anything about the murder they called me a 'stupid bitch' and refused to let me see him. I

---

[14]   *The Women of Broadwater Farm* (1989) (local pamphlet).

never had any quarrel with the police, but now I lie awake at night worrying in case the boys have been picked up again.[15]

A *Guardian* article on 17 June 2002, 'White Officers "Beat Up" Black Policeman' does not help in encouraging more black people to join the force. The article stated that 'Scotland Yard is set to investigate allegations from a black police officer that he was beaten up by a group of up to ten white officers . . . Taiwo Oduntan said that his attackers repeatedly smashed his head on a concrete pavement and that he was left bleeding in a police cell for several hours'. In statements seen by *The Guardian*, he said he was kicked and punched while on the ground and handcuffed, and passed out from the attack. Mr Oduntan, 43, claimed he was denied medical treatment after being arrested, in breach of police guidelines, and feared he would die during the attack. Mr Oduntan, a constable with British Transport Police for eleven years, was released without charge after Metropolitan Police officers were called to his home over an alleged assault by him. A doctor who examined him after the incident said injuries he sustained were consistent with his account of the attack. Two of his front teeth were broken and skin was ripped off part of his upper lip, which was also left swollen. He was left with abrasions and grazes on his shoulder, chest, arm, knee and he was limping. He said his foot was stamped on while in custody in a police cell. The alleged incident started when police were called to his home in Northwood, Middlesex over a claim that he had assaulted his partner. The allegation proved baseless. His partner, Suzana Jurcevic, said that the alleged assault on Mr Oduntan by police was vicious. 'The way he was screaming, I thought he was going to die'. She also rubbished suggestions that he had assaulted her.

Mr Oduntan believes he was attacked because of his race. He says he is on anti-depressants and has been diagnosed as suffering from post-traumatic stress disorder. He has been off work ever since. Ravi Chand, president of the National Black Police Association, said the allegations of assault on the officer by white officers were the worst he had come across. Mr Chand called for a full investigation by an outside force and the suspension of the officers involved: 'The officer is clearly traumatised by the incident which has caused a lot of concern amongst black officers across the country and the black community'.

A Metropolitan Police spokeswoman said that during the incident one of the arresting officers had suffered a leg wound, but could not say how that was caused. On arrival at the police station in Uxbridge, Middlesex, a doctor had said that Mr Oduntan was fit to be detained, but not to be interviewed. The spokeswoman added that the alleged victim of the assault, Mr Oduntan's partner, had refused to make a statement. She said Mr Oduntan had become violent and added: 'We can confirm that a complaint was made on April 24 alleging assault by the police. The department of professional standards is dealing with the complaint. No officers have been suspended'.

Again, on 1 February 2003, *The Guardian* reported a case of a black man who was awarded £250,000 damages (one of the biggest awards ever made for police misconduct). Silbert Farquharson who had no criminal record was violently assaulted by police officers and was subjected to racist abuse. Judge Michael Dea, ordered the Metropolitan police to pay damages to 'a respectable, middle-aged

---

[15] 'Return of Broadwater Farm', Platt S, *New Socialist*, April 1986.

family man of good character'. The sum included exemplary damages, which are awarded only against defendants who have acted 'in an oppressive, arbitrary or unconstitutional way as agents of the state'. Mr Farquharson, a delivery driver, had arrived at the scene of an altercation between his cousin and the police in July 1995. He was subsequently 'assaulted by three officers and thrown facedown in the gutter in the presence of members of the public, who were rightly appalled'. He was restrained with two sets of handcuffs and suffered permanent damage to his wrists and left with chronic pain syndrome.

The judge said Mr Farquharson had been 'subjected to explicit racist abuse in the street and a particularly vicious and cowardly form of racist abuse at the police station'. Mr Farquharson and his cousin, Mr Smith were prosecuted, but the case against them was dismissed by the magistrates' court. 'Unhappily, the officers felt obliged to invent an account of events which they knew to be untrue to justify their actions', the judge said. 'This untrue account was persisted in and led to the unsuccessful prosecution. The prosecution had been brought to disguise their unlawful actions'.

He ruled that the police had assaulted, falsely imprisoned and maliciously prosecuted Mr Farquharson and Mr Smith, and assaulted a Mr Washington, who had been taken to Brixton station and strip-searched. No drugs were found. The police settled claims brought by Mr Smith and Mr Washington out-of-court for £80,000, including costs. The judge said he was satisfied that Mr Farquharson's physical and psychological injuries meant that he would never work again and added: 'There is a clear public interest in condemning racist behaviour on the part of persons in authority in order to assure the diverse elements in our community that the police have no warrant to treat any citizen with contempt and oppression' (*The Guardian*, 1 February 2003: 6). The police will also have to pay costs totalling £75,000 for Mr Farquharson's civil claim (*Daily Mail*, February 1, 2003: 23). None of the officers has yet faced disciplinary proceedings, but a number have since been suspended.

BLACK PEOPLE AND IMMIGRATION

Black women's experiences of policing are quite often bound up with Britain's immigration and nationality laws. These have undergone refinement and expansion in the post-war period, but as Paul Gordon has argued, they have not simply been concerned with controlling who has a right of entry to Britain. 'Immigration control has increasingly entailed the growth of controls and surveillance of those (black people) already here. To this end, the police and the immigration services have been given ever-increasing resources, both in terms of personnel and technology.'[16] Such powers and resources have resulted in the police stopping and questioning black people about their nationality as well as conducting controversial passport raids on black communities.[17] Gordon argues that *all* black people are seen as immigrants. Given that some are illegal, it is common to hear comments such as 'The only way to tell an illegal black from a legal one is to suspect the lot'. This has led many black people not to report any crime to the police for fear of it being turned into an immigration enquiry.

---

[16] *Policing Immigration: Britain's Internal Controls* (1985), Gordon P, Pluto.
[17] Institute of Race Relations, 1979: 13-17.

A case reported in *The Guardian* supports this view.[18] A 29-year-old black man of Nigerian parentage but born in the United Kingdom went to a police station in South London in July 1993 to report the theft of his fiancée's car radio. He was arrested and detained for more than three hours after police questioned him about his immigration status. Police took him in handcuffs to his home, where he showed them his passport and birth certificate. He was taken back to the police station, fingerprinted and detained for another one-and-a-half hours. He was not believed when he told the police officers that he was born in England. He sued for false imprisonment, assault and discrimination under the Race Relations Act. He achieved an undisclosed but 'substantial' out-of-court settlement.

The problem of the use and abuse of immigration powers in relation to black women was also highlighted by a case reported in *Campaign Against Racism and Fascism*[19] in which an East African woman who stopped to ask a policewoman for directions was held at the police-station until her passport could be produced. Also, in a 1989 case, a police officer called at the home of a Nigerian woman under the guise of checking her immigration status, which was in fact legal. He threatened her with deportation and demanded sexual favours as insurance against this. Eventually, the woman was awarded £8,000 in damages with the judge stating that the police officer had 'acted behind the shadow of the warrant card and the strength of the law for his own squalid purposes'.[20]

In yet another case, a black woman was taken to the police station by police officers who had come to her flat to look for her partner. After the police had searched the house and found nothing, they took the woman with them to the police station 'to answer questions about a forged passport'. When she pointed out that the picture on the forged passport bore no resemblance to her, the officers said: 'We know you black people, you disguise yourselves'. The police used family responsibilities to force a 'confession' out of her. She was further victimised in that she was not told of her rights and was not seen by a solicitor. On the second day of the hearing, the passport charge was dropped.[21]

Changes concerning domestic violence and people with insecure immigration status are to be welcomed as these will help members of black ethnic minorities to feel they can report such crimes without fear of being deported. On 26 November 2002 the Home Office announced changes to a concession which permits victims of domestic violence who have an insecure immigration status, often linked to their spouse, to remain in the country on showing certain evidence of their plight. Women who suffer abuse by their husbands are often locked in violent relationships because leaving would entail the withdrawal of their residency permit and place them under threat of deportation. The West London campaigning group Southall Black Sisters commented that in the case of the deportation of a victim of domestic violence, the woman often risks abuse on her return due to prevailing attitudes towards female divorcees.

---

[18]   17 March 95.
[19]   Issue No. 7, 1978.
[20]   *The Times,* 1 August 1989.
[21]   'The Criminalisation and Imprisonment of Black Women', Chigwada R, *Probation Journal*, 1989, pp. 100-105.

Margaret Moran, Labour MP and chairwoman of the All-Party Parliamentary Group on Domestic Violence, said that 'women were being forced to leave a terrible situation in this country, only to be subjected to disgrace, humiliation and ostracism by their own families for something that was not their fault'. Moran played a central part in initiating an Internet project in September 1999 to enable survivors of domestic violence to contribute evidence and information about their experiences and thereby gather evidence about their needs and identify key issues in providing effective responses. The project found that:

> Lack of information on the rights of women with uncertain immigration status can make women fearful of approaching agencies for help. They also have difficulty in accessing public funds (such as income support and housing benefit). Local refuge providers find it difficult to offer space to women with uncertain immigration status because refugees rely on rent income from housing benefit to run the safe houses.

Although the government originally introduced the domestic violence concession in immigration cases on 16 June 1999 it did not have the desired impact as the types of evidence to be produced were too restrictive. More recent changes allow a man or woman in a marriage or partnership to remain in the UK if they produce two of the following pieces of evidence (*Statewatch*, Vol. 12, No. 6, Nov-Dec 2002):

- a letter from a GP with the same information as above
- a court order disallowing the spouse contact with the victim
- a police report confirming a visit at the home of the victim
- a letter from social services or a letter of support from a womens' refuge.

MENTAL HEALTH POWERS

A substantial body of research indicates that, for people from black and Asian ethnic minorities, access to and utilisation of treatments prescribed by mental health services differs from that for white people[22]

Section 136 Mental Health Act 1983 covers situations where someone's behaviour is causing a nuisance or offence. Incidents leading to the use of section 136 are usually reported to the police by members of the public and routinely involve minor offences. The provision reads:

> If a constable finds in a public place . . . a person who appears to him to be suffering from mental disorder and to be in immediate need of care or control, the constable may, if he thinks it necessary to do so in the interests of that person or for the protection of other persons, remove that person to a place of safety.

Somebody removed under this provision can be detained at a 'place of safety' for up to 72 hours. The intention is to ensure that 'mentally disordered' people are examined by a registered medical practitioner and interviewed by an approved social worker so as to make arrangements for their care. It is the only provision in the 1983 Act which allows an individual, acting alone (the constable), without medical evidence, to deprive someone of his or her liberty. The appropriateness

---

[22] For a review see Bhui, 1997.

of police involvement in medical issues and the use of police vans instead of ambulances has been questioned by organizations such as the National Association for Mental Health (MIND).

The statutory definition of 'place of safety' includes a police station.[23] As Faulkner has argued:

> Section 136 of the Mental Health Act is essentially a way of dealing with situations that cannot be dealt with by direct recourse to the mental health social services. As such, it is a necessary inclusion in the Act. However, the procedure followed in London (where the section is most frequently used) gives the police greater power with which to detain and refer people, as a result of which both men and women tend to be admitted to hospital for three days following police detention, and are rarely assessed by social workers.[24]

Other studies have shown that young African-Caribbean immigrants are up to 25 times more likely than white people to be committed for detention under Part III of the Mental Health Act 1983,[25] and that African-Caribbean people born in Britain were admitted at four times the rate for whites.[26] Browne examined the extent to which black people are remanded for psychiatric reports when appearing before magistrates' courts, the nature and outcome of psychiatric remands, and the implications for the provision of services to black people who have passed through the psychiatric remand process. He found that 36 (32 per cent) of the people given hospital orders without restrictions were known to be black.[27] Further evidence is provided by studies examining mental illness rates for black people within the community. More generally, the mental hospital admission rate for people born in England and Wales was 494 per 100,000 whilst the rate for the Caribbean-born community was 539 and the number of first admissions for schizophrenia among black people was three times the norm. Dr. S. P. Sashidhartam commented in *The Guardian:*

> The crisis in British psychiatry is not about large numbers of black people breaking down with any given psychiatric diagnosis, but about how such individuals are being inducted into the mental health services and being labelled as having serious mental illness.[28]

The possibility that high rates of police admissions may be partly affected by conscious or unconscious racist attitudes has been a cause of concern among psychiatrists. Writing about clinical experiences in the East End of London, Littlewood and Lipsedge stated that it was 'certainly true' that the police could be behaving in an overtly racist manner as an alternative to arrest, selectively

---

[23]   Given the history of deaths in custody (see earlier in the chapter), the designation of the police station as a 'place of safety' may seem somewhat ironic.

[24]   'Women and Section 136 of the Mental Health Act 1983', Faulkner A, in *The Boys in Blue* (1989), Dunhill C (Ed.), Virago.

[25]   Wards, 1992.

[26]   'The Compulsory Detention of Afro-Caribbeans under the Mental Health Act', Cope R, *New Community*, 1989, April: 343-356.

[27]   'Black People, Mental Health and the Courts' (1990), Browne D, Nacro.

[28]   4 November 1989.

picking out mentally healthy black people and taking them to psychiatric hospitals under section 136.[29]

Dunn and Fahy compared emergency police referrals of black people and white people to an urban psychiatric hospital based in a catchment area with a large African-Caribbean population. They attempted to establish whether rates of referral for black people were different from those for white people, to ascertain the ability of the police to identify mental disorder among different ethnic groups, and to examine the reasons for referral and the outcome of admission among ethnic groups.[30]

There were 268 referrals during the period of their study. Amongst this number 165 (61 per cent) were white and 88 (33 per cent) were black. The majority of the patients had a previous psychiatric history: 73 per cent of white men and 67 per cent of black men had a history of psychiatric admission, in comparison with 87 per cent of white women and 92 per cent of black women. The proportions admitted under section 136 previously were 40 per cent for white women and 32 per cent for black women. Schizophrenia was the commonest diagnosis in all groups, but was made twice as often in blacks as in whites. Personality disorder and alcohol and drug-abuse were more commonly diagnosed in white patients and drug-induced psychosis was more frequently diagnosed in black men.

The study also found that black people were more likely to receive psychotropic medication, especially neuroleptics: 90 per cent of black men as opposed to 63 per cent of white men, and 83 per cent of black women as opposed to 80 per cent of white women. Furthermore, 88 per cent of black men were kept in hospital after the section 136 order had lapsed as opposed to 74 per cent of white men, and 81 per cent of black women as opposed to 73 per cent of white women. Black men (48 per cent) were also more likely to be offered follow-up treatment than white men (25 per cent), as were black women (71 per cent) when compared with white women (58 per cent).

It is also clear from this study that more black women than white women were referred by the police to mental hospitals under section 136. This finding is supported by a Police Monitoring and Research Group study that found many more black women than white women were detained in police stations or taken to mental hospitals under the section.[31] Again, because black women tend to speak loudly and are from a different cultural background their behaviour tends to be misinterpreted and this can result in their being seen as 'crazy' or in need of psychiatric help. MIND found that in a minority of cases the police breached the conditions of section 136 by removing people, mainly women, from their own or other people's homes. Black women could be particularly vulnerable to such breaches. In neighbourhood disputes police tend to take a black woman to the police station or other 'place of safety' if the neighbourhood is white. If the neighbours are both black the police tend to take no action.

There are serious ramifications in being sent to a psychiatric hospital under section 136. The period of detention can be indefinite, the patient is under

---

[29] *Transcultural Psychiatry* (1979), Littlewood R and Lipsedge M, Churchill-Livingstone.
[30] 'Police Admissions to Psychiatric Hospital: Demographic and Clinical Differences Between Ethnic Groups', Dunn J and Fahy T A, *British Journal of Psychiatry*, 1990, 156: 373-378.
[31] 1987, No. 26.

constant observation and 'good behaviour' can mean patients submitting rights to the ward staff. If a patient tries to assert his or her rights, he or she may be labelled as 'disturbed' and this may further prolong their stay. Doctors and nurses have the right to give drugs to a patient against his or her will and the effects of some psychotropic drugs (e.g. Haloperidol and Largactil), which may be given in high doses to black people, have serious side effects. Some people end up walking with difficulty (sometimes called 'the Largactil shuffle') or like a zombie. Once taken to a 'place of safety', psychiatrists tend to diagnose black women and working-class women as suffering from 'psychosis', rather than 'neurosis', which is the preferred diagnosis for white middle-class women. Such labelling in police records may adversely affect a woman's future involvement with the criminal justice process as well as negatively impacting upon other aspects of her life.

MIND found that many black women 'sectioned' due to police action were later diagnosed as 'not mentally ill' at a hospital. More women are detained under section 136 than for criminal charges (often instead of being charged) and their rights are limited. There is no right to see a solicitor and any children may be taken into the care of the local authority. If employed, an individual's job may also be jeopardised. Another problem under this provision is that if a woman is not diagnosed as in need of hospital treatment, but released after the 72 hours allowed by the Act for detention, she has no redress in law, unless she can prove that the police acted 'in bad faith or without reasonable care'.

Studies in London show that Mental Health Act admission rates are higher for African-Caribbeans than for comparable samples of white and other ethnic groups (Bagley, 1971; Bebbington *et al,* 1991; Moodley and Perkins, 1991; Wessely *et al,* 1991; King *et al,* 1994; Callan, 1996; Davies *et al,* 1996). The magnitude of the excess varies in different parts of the city and is likely to depend on both the population and the configuration of the local service (Bebbington *et al,* 1991).[32]

Non-recognition of mental illness by healthcare professionals may reflect a mismatch between the patient's cultural expression of distress and the signs and symptoms sought by the clinician as manifestations of particular diagnostic syndromes. Conversely, culturally sanctioned and seemingly acceptable distress experiences may attract pathological explanations. First-rank symptoms may not have the same diagnostic significance across cultures (Chandrasena, 1987). What psychiatrists call 'paranoid beliefs' have culturally sanctioned value among African and West Indian groups, and assigning pathological significance to them may therefore be flawed (Ndetei and Vadher, 1984).

African and Caribbean people are heavily over-represented among admissions to psychiatric wards on compulsory orders. Statistical surveys vary, but one thing is clear, that mental distress is common in these communities.

Roger Sylvester's Case
Roger Sylvester, a 30-year-old black man was confirmed dead at the Whittington Hospital, north London, after having been restrained seven days earlier. He was a healthy black man who lived in Tottenham. He came from a large and loving

---

32 See also *Mental Illness in Black and Asian Ethnic Minorities: Pathways to Care and Outcomes* (2002), Kamaldeep Bhui and Dinesh Bhugra, pp. 26-29.

family, and had numerous friends. He worked as an administration officer at the Lambo Centre, one of Islington's drop-in mental health centres, and was well-loved by colleagues and service users alike. He was a Unison member. On the night of January 11, Roger was restrained by eight Metropolitan Police officers outside his home. He was detained under section 136 Mental Health Act and the police told the family that this was 'for his own safety'. They also said that he had not been violent towards the police or anybody else. Within 45 minutes he had sustained numerous injuries and remained in coma, effectively dead until his life support machine was switched off seven days later.

From the outset the Metropolitan Police issued partial, inaccurate and seemingly prejudicial information. Scotland Yard issued a press release on January 14 describing Roger was banging on a neighbour's door in an 'aggressive and vociferous manner'. It was quickly established that he had in fact been banging on his own door and that there is no evidence for the assertion that he was acting aggressively. Witnesses only stated that he was acting strangely, a fact reiterated in the transcript of the 999 call made. Despite a complaint to the assistant chief commissioner about this the Metropolitan Police have not only refused to apologise but have suggested that they have information to substantiate this deeply inaccurate press release.

At the opening of the inquest into his death a pathologist described Roger as a crack cocaine addict in an off-the-cuff briefing to journalists outside the coroners court—an allegation subsequently reproduced in newspapers. Following a complaint by the family he was removed and another pathologist appointed. No apology has been received. The family has received no evidence from anybody that Roger's death had anything to do with crack cocaine.

The Times claimed that police officers believed his death was due to his heart being 'swollen by crack cocaine' and that he had been 'flinging himself to the ground' when police called for reinforcements.[33] According to *The Guardian*, 24 July 2001, p. 20, a policeman destroyed notes relating to this restraint death.

Medical support

Cole *et al* (1985) demonstrated that for first episode psychosis in the London borough of Haringey, compulsory admission, admission under section 136 of the Mental Health Act 1983, first contact with services other than health, and no GP involvement were each associated with being single rather than with ethnic group. Also, compulsory admission, admission under section 136 and police rather than GP involvement were associated with not having a supportive friend or relative. Compulsory admission was also associated with having a family of origin living outside of London.

Harrison *et al* (1988) records that 40 per cent of African-Caribbeans made contact with some helping agency in the week preceding admission compared with two per cent of the general population. Burnett *et al* (1999) reported that African-Caribbean people with schizophrenia were less likely than white people to have had a GP referral to mental health services.

Davies *et al* (1996) found that Mental Health Act detention for assessment and treatment was more common among black and Asian ethnic minorities. This applied to all diagnoses and prevalent cases of psychosis. However, ethnic origin

---

[33] 'Unison Remembers Roger Sylvester', *Unison*, p. 3.

is not the only factor. For example, black women in Hammersmith and Fulham (west London) are reported to have lower compulsory admission rates than white women, whereas in Southwark (south-east London), black women have higher rates (Bebbington *et al*, (1991).

Mental health and African and Caribbean communities

According Kamaldeep Bhui and Dinesh Bhugra in *Mental Illness in Black and Asian Ethnic Minorities: Pathways to Care and Outcomes* (2002, pp. 30 and 33) African and Caribbean people:

- are more likely to be admitted to psychiatric hospital following contact with the police and social services, and less likely to be referred by their doctor. They are also more likely to be detained by police in a place of safety under the Mental Health Act
- are less likely to receive diagnosis and treatment at an early stage
- are more likely to be diagnosed as violent and to be detained in locked wards, secure units and special hospitals
- are less likely to receive non-physical treatment such as psychotherapy, counselling and alternatives to institutionalised care, and are more likely to receive physical treatments and strong medication
- are more likely to be detained and face severe difficulties in moving back into the community
- are more likely to have a relapse and be readmitted to hospital secure units.

A draft Mental Health Bill published in 2001 proposed removing the treatability test, which would mean people would have their liberty taken from them not because of what they have done or because they can receive treatment but because of fear of what they may do in future.

Government plans to lock up people with severe personality disorders who have committed no crimes have been widely criticised. For example, at one Mental Health Alliance conference, Carolyn Kirby, president of the Law Society, said proposals in the draft Bill were 'unworkable' and incompatible with the Human Rights Act 1998. Mike Shooter, president of the Royal College of Psychiatrists, said the planned legislation would be 'one of the most racially discriminatory laws ever seen in the UK' because African-Caribbean men face a disproportionate risk of mistaken diagnosis and imprisonment. Professor Shooter's attack on the Bill, quoted in the newsletter of the British Medical Association, came in an address to the British Pakistani Psychiatrists Association. He said there was an element of institutional racism in psychiatry that would be magnified. 'If the draft bill were passed as it stands, it would be one of the worst cases of racially discriminative legislation I have ever seen'. At a Mental Health Alliance conference he said: 'We are talking about effect rather than intent, but if you are a young black male living in the inner city, you are six times more likely to be sectioned under the current Act'. The Mental Health Alliance, a group of over 50 voluntary organizations which has been working with the government on reform of the Mental Health Act, said the Bill was likely to make services worse[34]

INTERVIEWS

Over two-thirds of the women who were interviewed claimed that they had been 'manhandled' by the police at one time or another. One women, speaking of her experience at the police station, said:

> Police officers look at you and talk to you like you are not a human being. They do not know how to handle people and have a bad attitude ... There are some nice officers but the majority are horrible. (Dawn)

> Police were horrible to me. They refused me to speak to a solicitor. (Aisha)

> Police think all black people are criminals. They see us as suspects and stop you. (Karen)

> Police officers seem to think most black people cannot write or read. I told them I can write myself. (Maxine)

The women thus had a negative view of the police, felt that they had been ill-treated because they were black, and that police attitudes to black women are unhelpful. When considering complaints from black people, black people may be viewed as suffering from some kind of paranoia. The women also felt that the police sometimes exceeded their rights. Marva stated that:

> I got searched in the office. When the police went to my flat they were saying that everything in my flat was proceeds of crime. They turned my house upside down.

Lorraine who was pregnant at the time of arrest said that:

> The police pushed me about and took me to the police station with my brother's girlfriend who was also pregnant. Whilst in the police cell, the police went back to my flat broke the door and searched the flat ... There was no need for that ... they could have asked me for the keys. They found nothing but took my filofax, baby clothes and photographs. It was wrong for them to do that. I should have been present. I did not know about all this until the next day. They would not treat a pregnant white woman like that.

Only one woman, who had a criminal record from the age of 13, had anything favourable to say:

> I have nothing bad to say about the police. I would say it depends on your attitude. They have been professional with me and I am always co-operative and it makes life easier for everyone.

---

[34] *The Guardian*, 11 January 2002, p. 11, 'Detention of Mentally Ill: Unworkable and Racist'.

Police officers have been known to take no action if the person responds well to them and respectfully. The way a woman is dressed seems to matter. Police officers in Elaine Player's research stated that '... they would be more likely to arrest a woman who behaved aggressively or who was verbally abusive or obstructive than a woman who was trying to be helpful or appeared to regret what she had done.'[35] But it can also be pointed out that the way the police treat and speak to black women may contribute to the way black women respond to them. Rhona, who had been in trouble with the police a few times, said:

> I feel that black people are persecuted for no reason at all. They can stop you, interrogate you and if they are not satisfied they will arrest you. They will ask you questions like ... 'Where do you get your money from?'. 'Where do you live?' and they will ask you ... 'Can you read and write?' They assume all black people are illiterates.

The women also felt that some police and customs officers take cases personally so that if charges are not brought this seems to reflect failure on their part. In Beatrice's case (see *Chapter 6*), e.g. the prosecutor took the relatively unusual step of obtaining a voluntary bill of indictment for her trial at the Crown Court after the magistrates' court found that there was insufficient evidence to commit the matter for trial by jury:

> The customs officers in my case are taking the case personally. Its like they want us to be found guilty even though they have no evidence. (Beatrice)[36]

COMMENT

At the very least, this chapter discloses a need for further and continuing training if police officers are to understand other cultures and stop racist and sexist behaviour and attitudes towards black women. This is not to say that black women do not commit crimes, but that wrong conclusions are often drawn from their lifestyles and modes of behaviour in general, and that racism plays a significant part in the extent to which black women are stopped, searched, cautioned, charged, prosecuted, held in custody or taken to mental hospitals. Initiatives by the police (and CPS with whom they work increasingly in joint Criminal Justice Units)[37] are to be welcomed, but all initiatives and training need to take account of the hitherto neglected topic of black *women*.

---

[35] 'Women and Crime in the City', Player E, in *Crime in the City* (1989), Downes D (ed.), Macmillan.

[36] As will be seen from *Chapter 6*, it is also interesting to note that Beatrice was found guilty at her first trial where the jury were all white. At the second trial where the jury was mixed, they could not reach a verdict.

[37] The existence of such units is being increased until they cover the country. There is also a proposal, contained in the White Paper, *Justice for All* (2002) that the CPS should take over the initial prosecution decision in all but straightforward or minor cases, or where there is a need to make a holding charge. The tendency to 'criminalise' various forms of anti-social behaviour (where the test at 'street level' and at the 'front end' of the criminal justice process is largely subjective) which has gone hand-in-hand with other modern developments in this field would seem to expose minority groups to further potential discrimination, so that the police, CPS and their joint CJUs should pay particular attention to the kinds of issues addressed in this chapter.

CHAPTER 4

Community Sentences

The National Probation Service (NPS)[1] plays a key role in providing judges and magistrates with pre-sentence reports (PSRs) on offenders and carrying out community sentences imposed by the courts. Increasingly, this function is part of a wider 'partnership' arrangement with HM Prison Service (HMPS) (see, generally, *Chapter 7*) to provide seamless sentences using accredited programmes and providing a consistent level of services for all offenders. There is now a joint NPS/HMPS Correctional Services Accreditation Board.

Background: The key role of pre-sentence reports and probation officers

PSRs contain critical information such as risk assessments, social and family details and recommendations for sentences in individual cases. Also, where offenders are sentenced to a community sentence—of which there now are eight kinds for adults, primarily the community rehabilitation order (CRO), community punishment order (CPO) and the community punishment and rehabilitation order (CPRO)—probation officers manage, administer and enforce that sentence.[2] A main focus of the PSR is the seriousness of the offence, the risk to the public where the offence is a sexual or violent one, and the risk of re-offending, thereby reflecting the considerations for courts discussed in *Chapter 5*. Courts have a general discretion to dispense with a PSR if they deemed one to be 'unnecessary'—a discretion which needs to be exercised carefully if it is not to marginalise black people and those from other minorities.[3]

Probation officers are also responsible for the supervision in the community of most offenders following their release from prison, including where they are released on 'home detention curfew' (often nowadays coupled with arrangements for electronic monitoring). Youth offending teams (YOTs) also have a probation officer on the team.[4]

---

[1] The NPS was created in 2001 to replace the locally-based probation services. It now functions under a central directorate and via local Probation Boards of which the chief probation officer for the area is a member. Community sentences were renamed at the same time: the probation order became the community rehabilitation order; the community service order became the community punishment order; and the combination order became the community punishment and rehabilitation order. Historical aspects of the text need to be understood in the light of these and associated changes.

[2] For detailed information see *The Sentence of the Court*, Watkins M, Edn.4 (2003), Waterside Press. The remaining community sentences are curfew order (with electronic monitoring), drug treatment and testing order, attendance centre order (up to age 20), drug abstinence order (when available) and exclusion order (when available). Electronic monitoring can now be added to any community sentence once arrangements exist nationwide. Electronic monitoring is contracted to the private sector. For an overview, see *The Magic Bracelet: Technology and Offender Supervision* (2001), Whitfield D, Waterside Press.

[3] Special provisions apply to offenders below 18 years of age to ensure a PSR in most instances.

[4] For a general overview see *Introduction to the Probation Service* (2001), edn. 2, revised reprint (with additional material by Mike Nellis), Whitfield D, Waterside Press.

Historically speaking probation policy ignored ethnic minority offenders until well into the 1970s. One early Home Office circular requested that probation areas with a significant African, Caribbean or Asian population appoint a probation officer to develop services for ethnic minorities. The stated opinion at the time was that specialists could mediate any 'cultural misunderstandings'. This position changed following the urban riots of the 1980s (*Chapter 3*), when probation areas began to acknowledge the need to recognise, institute and actively promote anti-racist practice.

Considerable advances were made in the 1990s in the way that the probation service confronted discrimination and discriminatory practices. The preparation of PSRs is governed—as is much other probation practice—by National Standards. These require that PSRs should be free from discrimination on the grounds of race, gender, age, disability, language, ability, literacy, religion, sexual orientation or other basis. All areas of the NPS have developed clear equal opportunities policies with built-in review and monitoring mechanisms. Similar principals affect the provision by the NPS of community sentences (above) and NPS work with prisons and when supervising offenders under the 'early release' scheme.

PSRs seek to give information about possible community sentence provision in the light of the facts of the offence. The very fact that a PSR is prepared may have an effect, such as increasing the likelihood of a community sentence, but the effect can also be an adverse one in the sense that, in the mind of the court it can give an impression of greater seriousness or concern about the offender. 'Gatekeeping' strategies seek to guard against this and various attempts have been made to agree seriousness scales with courts so that reports are only requested in appropriate cases and probation officers deal with their enquiries in the light of some understanding of the court's likely intentions—including the emergence from about 2000 of the specific sentence report (or 'SSR') which is targeted on the possibility of a given type of community sentence. Before the introduction of the present system, the need for welfare-based intervention was identified as a significant factor in relation to a large number of women given probation orders for minor and first offences.[5] The future appears to lie in a more punishment or 'corrections'-oriented system to 'rebalance' the system in favour of victims and the community and within which probation officers will find themselves 'policing' new forms of community sentences and custodial sentences served partly in the community (as many are, in fact, already).[6]

The professional organizations involved in NPS work, including the Association of Black Probation Officers (ABPO), have all taken steps to promote racial equality in every aspect of the service's work, including the production of policy statements and practice guidance. Similarly, strategies begun by the old area probation services have been taken on board by the NPS, and special responsibility for race relations has been given to staff of chief officer grade. There is regular monitoring of PSRs and other reports to courts and other areas of NPS practice designed to ensure that they are non-discriminatory.

---

[5] HM Inspectorate of Probation Report, 1991.

[6] See *Justice for All: Making Punishments Work* (2002), London: Home Office. Surprisingly, perhaps, this White Paper has little, if anything, to say about issues of the kind dealt with in this book.

There has been a significant rise, from 16 to 30 per cent since 1990 in the proportionate use of custodial sentences for indictable offences. There was a dramatic reduction in the use of fines during the same period and a marginal growth in the use of community penalties. Nevertheless there was a 30 per cent increase in probation caseloads, not least because of the increase in post-custody prison licences. There was a 40 per cent increase in PSRs requested, mostly by the magistrates' courts, for roughly the same number of defendants

Rod Morgan, HM Chief Inspector of Probation argues that the courts have become progressively more punitive and interventionist. Many people who ten years ago would have been given the then equivalent of a CRO or a CPO are now being sent to prison, generally for sentences of less than 12 months and many offenders who ten years ago would have been fined are now getting community sentences. Court reports were being requested in the types of cases where previously they would have been judged unnecessary (see above). Alongside this, NPS caseloads were 'silting up' with low level, low risk offenders many of whom arguably do not warrant NPS ministrations and intervention.

There is, in effect, the equivalent of prison overcrowding (see the *Introduction*) in the NPS. This is all hugely expensive and both the NPS and HMPS are being deflected from concentrating their resources and efforts on that part of the offending population for which attention is most needed.

Aspects of discrimination
Despite the duty to avoid discrimination there is a constant need for vigilance. Acknowledging that improved practices have since been developed, research indicates that black offenders are less likely than their white counterparts to be made the subject of what is now a CRO.[7] Proportionately more PSRs or medical reports are requested on women.[8] The courts are more likely to ask for a report on a first offender when that offender is a woman.[9] But, seemingly, this does not apply in the case of foreign black women, where there are only limited efforts to obtain information from abroad.

Modern probation statistics which include ethnic monitoring data show that of offenders starting probation orders in 1998-1999, 4.5 per cent were black, 1.3 per cent Indian, Pakistani or Bangladeshi and 1.5 per cent from other minority ethnic groups. The NPS dealt with more black and less South Asian people than would be expected from their representation in the general population according to the *Labour Force Survey* 1996-1998. The percentage of offenders from minority ethnic groups was similar for most offence categories. However a significantly larger proportion of those offenders who had been convicted of robbery were from minority ethnic groups, with 15 per cent black and 4.7 per cent from other minority ethnic groups (Home Office, 2000).

---

[7] 'Racism and Criminology: Concepts and Controversies' (1993), Hudson B in *Racism and Criminology*, Cook D and Hudson B (eds.).

[8] 'Female Offenders and the Probation Service', Mair G and Brockington N, *Howard Journal*, 27, No. 2, May 1988, pp. 117-126.

[9] 'Women Offenders in Merseyside', Humphreys B, Merseyside Probation Service, Edmunds, 1993.

Commenting on the state of the then research and a Home Office study 'Sentencing Practice in the Crown Court',[10] the Penal Affairs Consortium noted in September 1996 that:

> There was ... a highly significant and disturbing difference in the extent to which reports ... were prepared on different ethnic groups ... 22 per cent of white defendants had no [report] compared with 37 per cent of black and Asian defendants. Part of the reason for this difference stemmed from differences in relation to plea. Eighteen per cent of whites, 24 per cent of Asians and 20 per cent of black defendants pleaded 'not guilty' and reports were prepared in 51 per cent of contested cases compared with 82 per cent of guilty plea cases. However, substantial differences remained in the extent to which reports were provided for different racial groups after allowing for plea.[11]

The consortium also expressed concern that women convicted of minor offences are more likely to receive a CRO in circumstances where men receive lesser sentences.[12] In appropriate circumstances, community sentences, including CROs, are important in that they allow a woman to serve her sentence hopefully doing something constructive and looking after her family. Any children will not have to be taken from the mother and placed in local authority care or accommodation. They will not suffer 'secondary punishment' for a crime they, the children, did not commit. Also, if a woman is placed on a CRO she will not risk losing her flat (often a council flat) or job, and she will escape the label that attaches to an ex-prisoner (see, generally, *Chapter 8*). People who go to prison tend to come out more knowledgeable about crime and how to commit it.

CROs may be used as an alternative to imprisonment for white defendants, but for black women they may equally be used as an alternative to a discharge, fine or some other, lesser punishment, thereby limiting the scope for community sentences in the future. There is a case for arguing for a greater use of community sentences for women generally, few of whom are in prison for violent crimes or other offences which seriously threaten the community. There is, as explained elsewhere in this book, a misleading myth that black woman are aggressive or inherently violent which can cause courts and other criminal justice practitioners to respond differently towards them.

There are certain themes that are common to NPS work and that of other social agencies that are particularly relevant to women users. Gelsthorpe (1989) indicates that administrative and organizational factors, as opposed to fixed assumptions, were responsible for girls and boys being treated differently by criminal justice agencies. Social work has traditionally defined women primarily in relation to their families and particularly in their capacity as mothers and by holding them responsible for maintaining family harmony. Women may be prevented from making their own choices and are maintained in roles dependent on others.[13] All such matters have a heightened effect in the case of black women

---

[10] 'Sentencing Practice in the Crown Court' (1998), Moxon D, Home Office Research Study No 103, Home Office.

[11] 'Race and Criminal Justice', Penal Affairs Consortium, September 1996.

[12] *ibid*.

[13] *Sexism and the Female Offender: An Organisational Analysis* (1989), Gelsthorpe L, Cambridge Studies in Criminology, Gower.

who may deviate from normal expectations as has already been outlined in *Chapters 1* and *2*.

As long ago as 1990, the National Association of Probation Officers (NAPO) identified in its practice guidelines the need to challenge traditional attitudes towards women and cautioned against assumptions that women and black clients were 'more difficult' and that they present more problems than white male clients. Studies of a qualitative nature have looked at references in PSRs and analysed the frames of reference within which they occur. Whitehouse's 1982 study showed how racism may surface. He looked at racial bias in PSRs.[14] The research started from the premise that the cause of black people being unequally represented in various categories of supervision is the cumulative effect of racial disadvantage and the lack of available sentencing options for black people. Disadvantage thus begins, Whitehouse argues, at the referral stage for reports. It continues via the proportion of recommendations for (what are now) CROs and in the concurrence between recommendations and the sentence of the court. Whitehouse noted that social work practice is dominated by the values of the dominant culture (see also the general comments in *Chapter 1* of this work).[15] Attempts to describe other cultures, which may have no bearing on the facts of the case, can seriously affect the outcome.

In the context of the dominant culture, black women may be seen as over-protective of children, over-religious or over-punitive towards their children. This may lead to a black woman being regarded as not a 'good' mother or one who is 'good enough'. Expressions of emotion like anger or affection may be misinterpreted. Value judgements made about sexual or family relationships, work status and parental responsibility, based on a Euro-centric view of society may be used to deprive an individual of her liberty. Such observations are in line with a widespread feeling amongst members of the black community that, whatever the initiatives and 'good practice' a significant number of probation officers and social workers were then racist in the assumptions they made about black families. An extract from an PSR quoted by Whitehouse highlights this:

> Admittedly there is about him a mild paranoid attitude associated with his ethnic propensities. As far as I am able to ascertain, his personality is that of a normally developed person considering his background and origins.

One would hope that the modern-day monitoring process and the various checks and balances now in place would prevent such a patently obvious statement in a PSR today. But many black people stand to be convinced that the sentiment behind it has disappeared also.

Merseyside Probation Service (in its pre-NPS days) produced a resource pack for managing and developing anti-racist practice. This maintains that service delivery in a racist society is essentially different for black clients, and that the unequal power dynamics in the relationship between supervisor and offender in terms of colour, gender and class must be recognised.[16] McQuillan emphasises the need to acknowledge the issue of white authority and to ensure the careful

---

[14] Then called 'social enquiry reports', or 'SERs'.

[15] 'Race Bias in Social Enquiry Reports', Whitehouse P, *Probation Journal*, 1983, 30: 43-49.

[16] *Managing and Developing Anti-Racists Practice Within Probation* (1992), Kett J, Collett S *et al*, Merseyside Probation Research and Information Unit, 1992.

construction of proposals in PSRs to be no more intrusive than is justified by the seriousness of the offence.[17] The powerful use of discriminatory language, racist stereotypes and images should be continually monitored and challenged particularly in respect of black women who face the double oppression of race and gender. Thus:

> Race does not simply make the experience of women's subordination greater, it qualitatively changes the nature of that subordination.[18]

Denney demonstrates how conventions used by probation officers in interviews, written reports and records can be discriminatory towards black offenders. The imposition of a white, Anglicised view of the nuclear family leads to inappropriate judgements about black family life: white women offenders tend to be presented under considerable stress, often due to factors beyond their control, whilst black women are frequently described as impoverished, nervous and taciturn. The perceptions of probation officers, as well as those of the courts, contribute to the 'composite picture' of the way black women are perceived and sentenced.[19]

Other studies have looked more closely at the depiction of black and white defendants as offenders. This is important as the emphasis of probation work has shifted from presenting comprehensive accounts of an offender's background, personality and home circumstances to concentrating on offence seriousness, attitude to offending, compliance with previous sentences and the risk of re-offending.[20] Waters classifies reports according to whether the defendant's race was marginal as a theme in explaining the offending; whether the defendant was depicted in terms of culture conflict; or as being 'alien' in the sense of very much 'other' to the report writer.[21] Pinder looked at explanations of offending offered in reports finding explanations focusing on opposition stances in black defendants and inadequacy in white defendants.[22] Hudson's study of reports, already mentioned, found black offenders being viewed as hostile and aggressive, and not being credited with the same attempts to change to non-criminal lifestyles that were put forward in the case of white defendants.

Crolley analysed how women offenders were portrayed in PSRs, this differing according to the gender of the author, finding little evidence by either men or women authors of stereotyping women as good mothers, wives etc., but that women officers were less likely to have their proposals followed than male officers.[23] It was suggested that the content of PSRs on women might be

[17] *Pre-sentence Reports: An Anti-Discriminatory Perspective* (1992), McQuillan T, Association of Black Probation Officers.

[18] *Women, Oppression and Social Work: Issues in Anti-Discriminatory Practice* (1992), Langan M and Day L (eds.), Routledge.

[19] *Racism and Anti-Racism in Probation* (1992), Denney D, Routledge.

[20] In *Racism and Criminology: Concepts and Controversies in Racism and Criminology* (1992), Hudson B (Eds. Hudson B and Cook D), Sage.

[21] 'Race and the Criminal Justice Process', Waters R, *British Journal of Criminology*, 1988, 28:82-94.

[22] 'Probation Work in a Multi-Racial Society' (1984), Pinder R, University of Leeds Applied Anthropology Group.

[23] Cited in 'A Better Service for Women' (1994), Edmunds M F, MA dissertation, unpublished, University of Exeter.

influenced as much by the politics of gender as a description of the offence and the offender, e.g.:

> There is some evidence that men authors tend to describe women offenders as being *depressed* whilst women authors describe women offenders as being *oppressed*.[24]

One reason which may be contributing to some black women not receiving CROs may be the fact that probation officers—like other criminal justice professionals—are less likely to see black offenders in problem or help terms but more in simple crime and punishment terms.[25] When probation officers are suggesting such orders for black offenders, this is couched in 'nothing else has worked so we might as well try this' terms, and in terms of being able to place strictures and constraints on offenders' lives, in contrast to the positive reasons given in relation to white offenders, where the plan before the court is often posed in terms of supporting the individual in his or her own efforts to change. Circumstances such as unemployment and lack of housing were more often attributed to the subject's own shortcomings or personality defects when the defendant was black, rather than being discussed in relation to the difficulties caused by relationships, finances, and so on. Although women tend to be visited at home when reports are being prepared, it would appear that when it comes to black women they tend not to be because of the stereotype view of black people—again as aggressive or violent.

INTERVIEWS

The women I interviewed about their experiences were asked to give their views of their dealings with probation officers, including prison probation officers. Some interviewees felt that the probation service had the potential to help black women, not only to obtain a non-custodial sentence but also with financial assistance. However, some of them considered that certain probation officers had 'stereotype views' of black women, and that even good PSRs written on black women were not believed in court.

Eight of the women appeared to be content with their probation officer, and with the help they had received. The officer's race did not seem to matter. Ten of the women had white probation officers and felt that the officer had done his or her best to help them. Some felt that if 'represented' by a black probation officer *in court* the judge might not take the PSR seriously, especially if it was a very good one, 'written on their behalf' (something which mirrors the views the women had about black lawyers: see *Chapter 5*). Whatever the colour of the probation officer's skin, the women felt the PSR would not override or influence the judge's perception of them:

> My report was good, but I felt that the judge did not take notice of it. The reason why I committed the crime was not given. (Margaret)

[24]　*ibid.*

[25]　'Penal Policy and Racial Justice' (1993), Hudson B, in *Minority Ethnic Groups in the Criminal Justice System*, Gelsthorp L (ed.), Cambridge University Institute of Criminology, Cropwood Conference Series, No. 21.

It is interesting that this particular woman felt that her probation officer was 'good'. A probation order (as it then was) had been suggested in the PSR. Her barrister was said to be 'no good' as he did not mention the reason why she committed the crime—a mitigating factor. Similarly:

> The report written for the court was okay, but I felt that she (the probation officer) should have asked for a long term of probation ... I wouldn't have got prison. She is good ... she always has time to talk to me and listens. (Dawn)

One woman said that the court rejected her PSR because it was over effusive:

> My report was very good and the judge did not believe it. He felt that it was *too* good. [emphasis supplied] (Nora)

This may be because the judge had a stereotype view of the kind of a life a black woman is supposed to live. The probation officer had written about Nora's good character, saying that she was a fine mother who cared for her children well— which goes against the mental picture that many white people have of the black woman.

One of the women, who got on well with her probation officer, felt that she had let him down by committing further offences:

> David (a white man) is my present probation officer. I have had a few probation officers in the past, but find I can speak to David about anything. I have been arrested a few times but have not told him because I feel I have let him down. (Sarah)

It would appear from this comment that the relationship between an offender and a probation officer, if it *is* good, can have an impact on trying to stay 'clean', or can simply make a black woman evasive.

The other 12 women were dissatisfied with the help they got from the probation service. Josephine said that:

> I get the impression that probation officers are not concerned about you. They see you and just keep a record.

Some of them felt that probation officers patronised them and did not try to understand 'where they were coming from'. But nonetheless some of the women had good words to say about their *prison* probation officers (i.e. working inside a prison or alongside HMPS). Probation officers who helped the women to bring their children or babies into prison were praised and described as excellent:

> When I was sent to prison my baby was three months old at the time. I wrote to my probation officer saying can you help me have my child in prison. She wrote back to say that she did not have time to come as it was too far ... It was the probation officer *in prison* who helped me bring my child into prison [emphasis supplied]. (Valerie)

Another woman who had received practical help from a probation officer in prison said:

> He is excellent. He really helped me. (Anna)

Four of the women felt that if the probation officer had shown more interest it would have helped them to get a lighter sentence. They believed that if probation officers had inquired more about their backgrounds they would have written more persuasive PSRs.[26] Many black people plead 'not guilty': see *Chapter 5*.

One woman was dissatisfied with the probation service and felt that 'they should update their reports regularly' (something which should happen in appropriate circumstances under National Standards):

> The probation service has helped me in the past but I find they use old reports. I feel they should update them ... sometimes I don't feel like talking to probation officers ... Its not their business and ... I don't say much to them. (Edith)

Catherine, now 23 years old, had been in trouble with the law from the age of 14 and in prison before, but at the time of the interview she was on a CRO (then a probation order). She talked about her experiences:

> I abused the probation service because I felt they did not care about me ... and they did not show any interest—they did not want to get down to the real problems. So I just used them to get money for cigarettes etc. ... I feel that it helps to have a black probation officer—that is if she is not a coconut ... then there is no difference. I now have a black probation officer. We have a very good rapport and I feel that the fact that she is black has helped ... as she knows where I am coming from.

It appeared that the colour of the probation officer's skin did not matter as long as he or she 'delivered the goods'. It was also clear that if the probation officer was black he or she needed to be able to understand black people and their problems, in other words they needed to remain black—hence the word 'coconut' meaning 'black on the outside but white on the inside'. Great resentment was directed towards black professionals generally who did not 'behave black'. On this question of 'coconuts' another woman said:

> I felt that my probation officer was very white-minded and was asking me questions I would not expect from a black person. (Veronica)

Measures to deal with racism in probation reports have met with criticism from some judges. One circuit judge described the equal opportunities policies of the probation service, whereby reports were vetted for racial and other bias, as sinister. He claimed that:

> In 30 years at the bar and four and a half years on the bench, I have never seen a probation report which contained any remark I could describe as racist, sexist or stereotyping.[27]

---

[26] PSRs are normally only prepared before the case comes to court if the offender intends to plead guilty, and are thus not usually available where a plea of 'not guilty' is entered and a trial takes place, unless and until there is a conviction and the case has afterwards been adjourned for a PSR to be prepared.

[27] *The Times*, 13 September 1990.

Although some of the women felt that their probation officer had not been helpful and could have done more, it was clear from the interviews that the PSR was seen as *able* to help in reducing the sentence and that a 'caring' probation officer who advised and listened to problems and assisted in practical ways was appreciated and deemed to be 'good'. Annette said:

> The probation officer was no good and I feel she helped me get three year prison sentence.

Conversely, according to Jane:

> I did not see my probation officer until the hearing day. She was not sympathetic.

Judith, a foreign woman, who did not have a PSR prepared on her felt that if she had had one it would have made a difference to the sentence she received. She had been living in the United Kingdom for six years at the time of her arrest. She was a single mother with four children and unemployed at the time of her sentence. The children were back home in the West Indies. Judith said:

> My children were suffering back home ... and I had no money ... I couldn't get a job and was not working. My brother-in-law took advantage of my financial situation when I went home to see my children. He said you won't be in trouble and we will give you money enough for your children's fees. He said think about what the money can do to help you and your children ... I took a chance ... Here I am with a seven year sentence and do not know where my children are.

Geraldine, who is 'black British' (i.e. born in Britain) also did not have a PSR. She felt that one would have made a difference to the sentence she received. She was sentenced to six years imprisonment for smuggling six ounces of cocaine:

> I was finding it difficult to get a job here and decided to go abroad and work for a year. I got mixed up with the wrong crowd. I was a tour guide and also did child-minding on the side. I was doing child-minding when I was told to stay with these people at the hotel. They forced me to carry their luggage ... I did not want to because I was suspicious. They beat me up when I refused and threatened my life. A probation report would have helped ... I have been in prison two years now and only saw a probation officer last week.

A LACK OF 'CONTEXT'

Historically speaking, Green (1989) argued that the probation service in practice denies the racist context in which many black offenders live and the extent to which this contributes to their offending behaviour and personal identity. This is largely the result of probation officers being socialised into the service through its institutional ideology, which is white dominated and where the issue of 'race' has been marginalised (Bowling and Philips, 2000: 210). According to Green, the combination of the court's focus on individual offending rather than its social and economic context, probation officers' emphasis on African-Caribbean family pathology contrasted with a white middle-class 'norm', and their feelings of vulnerability and threats to their professional status raised by black offending behaviour, have led to narrow organizational responses such as recommending that magistrates and judges impose custodial sentences.

Denney's (1992) study supported Green's (1989) conclusions and also found that the language used in reports on black offenders was more often derogatory in nature than was true for reports on white offenders. References to the 'physical presence' of black offenders were common, as were comments about their use of violence. Officers were reluctant to accept black offenders' concerns about racism and how it had shaped their offending behaviour. Instead, probation officers perceived black offenders to be anti-authoritarian, angry and irresponsible.

A probation discourse which was more 'correctional' than 'appreciative' was found in many reports concerning black offenders, who were seen as 'threatening', and PSRs tended to emphasise that there was less possibility for change among such offenders. White offenders, by contrast, were presented as victims of individual circumstance. However, Denney notes that there were no differences in the proportion of white and black offenders who were recommended by probation officers for non-custodial sentences. Neither was there any evidence that probation officers provided practical assistance to white offenders more often than to African-Caribbean offenders, or that they offered differential access to group work for offenders of different racial origins. In contrast, a later thematic inspection on racial equality raised concerns about differences in the quality of supervision of black offenders, particularly in terms of levels of contact during the later stages of an order (Her Majesty's Inspectorate of Probation, 2000).

A lack of dedicated groupwork or other provision

Again, the early evidence identified few groupwork programmes being run specifically for black and Asian offenders. The last notable survey of groupwork programmes conducted over ten years ago, which was responded to by more than three-quarters of the then local probation services in England and Wales, found that only three of the 1,463 groups registered in the survey were black or Asian membership-only groups (Caddick, 1993). The rarity of these groups has been noted in other literature: not only are black or Asian-only groups a 'rare phenomenon', but there is no evidence that any groups give central concern to the differential needs of black, Asian and white offenders (Senior, 1993. p.39).

The Black Offenders Initiative, set up by the North Thames Resource Unit, developed a programme aimed at empowerment and the exploration of black and Asian offenders' experiences. This programme, received positive feedback from both the members and the leaders of the three groups who had completed it (Raynor *et al*, 1994). The Moss Side, Manchester, programme—although it was not set up specifically for black offenders—included members predominantly from the local black community. It targeted offenders involved in drug supply and addressed issues such as policing and rights, pressures, racism, alternatives to offending and opportunities. The project involved people from community groups and created a positive atmosphere within the local community. Project participants have been reported to have subsequently attended college, work or have re-established themselves in business (Brown and Poole, 1997; Briggs, 1996; Briggs, 1995).

A handbook by Tuklo Orenda Associates (1999) for the then South West Probation Training Consortium, *Making a Difference: A Positive and Practical Guide to Working with Black Offenders*, gives extensive guidance, informed by practitioners in the south-west area, on the best way to work with black offenders. It addresses the need to understand racism and for acknowledgement of the differences between black and white values, learning styles, language and manner.

Groupwork programmes specifically for black offenders often appear to be built around the premise that offenders' behaviour is the product of racism and that they therefore require rehabilitation which focuses on empowerment and related issues (Lawrence, 1995). In studies where offenders themselves have been asked their reasons for offending, different explanations have been given. Interviews with a sample of 30 black offenders, 15 black and white staff and 15 representatives from local organizations and community groups (in a project commissioned by the Safer Cities programme) found that the different groups of respondents placed differing emphases on particular explanations for offending (Lawrence, 1995).

More recent research of mixed group work programmes in HM Prisons, involved interviews with black prisoners drawn from 14 different prisons. This study found that a significant number of black prisoners felt that they would have had a more positive experience if they had not been the sole black member of the group (Akhtar, unpublished report).

Other literature recording experiences of a mixed offending behaviour group in Wandsworth Prison has also suggested that there should at least be more than one black member in a mixed group to reduce the possible sense of isolation that one black person on his own might experience. There was a concern that if black members in the group were in a minority they might feel less able to discuss issues from their own perspective. However this was only speculation by the authors and was not based on any empirical evidence (Fisher and Watkins, 1993).

A document published by the former Inner London Probation Service (ILPS) as the result of many workshops with ILPS' practice teachers also notes that encouraging a black student to participate in a discussion on race with a predominantly white group of students exposes him or her to the potential for further racism (ILPS, 1993).

There is also some evidence that when women are placed in probation groups with a majority of men, the women's needs are submerged (Mistry, 1993). It may therefore be possible to draw parallels between this and minority ethnic offenders in mixed race groups. However, it has been found that groups that have a significant number of black members, or are all black can be more supportive. Offenders can give support to each other and can develop 'a sense of belonging' especially when the positive experiences of some minority ethnic members (e.g. in jobs) gives encouragement to others who doubt their chances of succeeding within a hostile system (Raynor, 1994; Fisher and Watkins, 1993). Again, drawing a parallel with gender, it has also been found that women in all female groups are able to develop a support system and give each other emotional and practical help (Mistry, 1993). However it should be noted that if the interviews were conducted by white probation officers or researchers, replies may be inaccurate as offenders may have simply not wanted to draw attention to themselves as being different.

Programmes can be separate or mixed, the important thing being for black offenders to be able to choose a mixed or an all black group. Black and Asian staff have been found to feel particularly unsupported (HMIP, 2000). A study by ILPS (1996) reported that black offenders felt it was important to have black staff available to talk to, as they were better able to relate to the offender. Probation officers should draw on the expertise of organizations and individuals within black communities (Tuklo Orenda Associates, 1999; Denney, 1992).

Explanations for offending by black people

When asked by supervisors to indicate what they believed were the reasons for offending, black and Asian offenders identified financial issues or unemployment, while representatives from community groups placed greater emphasis on education, training and discrimination and probation staff emphasised discrimination, frustration or family circumstances. Interviews with 28 minority ethnic offenders, conducted by the then ILPS suggested that offenders did not feel that a black empowerment group was relevant to their needs because they felt that being black had nothing to do with their offending and they did not have a problem with race:

... it ain't got anything' to do with me offending, being black ...
... I don't feel I got any problems with me race it's another waste of time for me ...
(ILPS, 1996, p.19).

A study by Barker *et al* (1993) suggested money and image as reasons for offending by black people. Forty-five street robbery offenders (of which approximately two thirds were of African-Caribbean origin) were interviewed. In these interviews, offenders gave money as the reason for their offending and by their own accounts they spent the money on expensive clothes, luxuries and cannabis.

Two other reasons behind the offending behaviour of black people may be the difficulties in gaining employment and achieving educational qualifications. Studies show that poor school performance, low income and unemployment are risk factors that can result in criminal behaviour (Farrington, 1997; Farrington, 1996). Evidence gathered by the DfEE shows a clear pattern of continuous underachievement for certain ethnic groups which starts in early education, continues through further and higher education, and persists in the labour market (Pathak, 2000). Underachievement at school may be caused by a combination of reasons including regular truancy, social class, low teacher expectations, conflict and tension with teachers and a high relative probability of being permanently excluded (Pathak, 2000). All of these factors may themselves be influenced by racism.

What is not clear is whether African-Caribbean, Asian and white people do offend for the same or different reasons. Some research has suggested that systematic racism and discrimination has led to black people's criminal behaviour (Fisher and Watkins, 1993; Denney, 1992), whereas other literature has argued the reasons for black and Asian people's offending are likely to be the same as the reasons given by white offenders (that is, primarily a need for money) (Lawrence, 1995; Barker *et al*, 1993).

Offending by black people cannot be explained by racism alone and therefore any programmes that are specifically targeted at black and Asian offenders may need to focus on more than simply empowerment issues. For example if the lack of educational qualifications and difficulties in securing employment are leading to offending by black people, then programmes aimed at these groups will need to include elements of education and employment training.

Racist views of PSR writers

It has been observed that a greater numbers of black offenders are being sentenced to CPOs (i.e. when they were community service orders) rather than CROs due to racist views of PSR writers, who were found to be recommending white offenders for CROs as they felt they would be easier to supervise than black offenders:

> There was a problem in getting probation officers to refer black offenders to the programme. I think it actually comes down to the probation officer saying 'Can I work with this person, or do I want them to go off and work somewhere else?' They tended to send them to do community service [CPO] rather than . . . on individual programmes.

One early study reported that fewer recommendations for community supervision were made by probation officers on black offenders, resulting in a disproportionate number being imprisoned (Green, 1989).

Evaluation of projects: some examples

An evaluation of the (pre-NPS) ILPS' Greenwich and Lewisham Black Self-development and Educational Attainment Group has been conducted. This involved unstructured interviews with group work officers and group interviews with offenders. Fifteen of the 22 people who started in one of the three groups completed all the sessions and the percentage of completers increased as the courses ran. The final course achieved a 100 per cent completion rate despite the demands on participant's time being higher than in the majority of groupwork programmes. Feedback from offenders was very positive and for many, being in an all black group was a new experience that they found valuable and safe. Generally the feedback pointed to offenders being able to use the self-development materials to fundamentally question their previous behaviour and develop new ways of coping with pressures (Durrance *et al*, 2000).

Reconviction analyses were conducted on offenders who attended two of the programmes. A two-year reconviction study was conducted on programme completers of the Black Self-development etc. programme and these results were compared with white offenders completing a comparable programme. The study reported considerably lower reconviction figures for black programme completers compared to white offenders. Only 51 per cent (18 out of 35) black offenders were reconvicted within two years of programme completion compared to 75 per cent (38 out of 51) of white offenders. This is despite risk of reconviction scores being higher for black offenders (Durrance *et al*, 2000).

A reconviction study was also conducted on two groups of offenders completing the Black People and Offending Programme in the (pre-NPS) West Midlands Probation Service. When compared with predicted reconviction data, actual reconvictions were found to be lower (25 per cent as opposed to 50 per cent) two years after the end of the programme, amongst those who completed the programme (Dunn, 2000). However, it should be noted that the number of offenders in this study was very small. The whole study was based on a sample of 13 offenders and only eight of these had successfully completed the programme. This does therefore limit the reliability of results.

The Home Office Research and Development Directorate report 'Offending Behaviour Programmes for Black and Asian Offenders within Probation Services' (2002), found that little data existed to examine the offending behaviour of black and Asian offenders. The research was unable to identify any current evidence-based practice that takes account of either unique criminogenic factors or responsivity issues specific to this offender group.

The findings of a survey by the Association of Black Probation Officers, 'Locked Out: Black Prisoners' Experiences of Rehabilitative Programmes' found that the respondents were strongly of the view that separate provision for black and Asian offenders was desirable.

COMMENT

A great many steps have been taken to remove bias in PSRs, but there is still a way to go. Reports go through a process of quality control that is part of a wider 'equal opportunities' policy. The aim is to ensure that they are not discriminatory in their content or suggestions. It means that the NPS has adapted its practice to take account of the presence of black people in society generally and, in particular, in the offender population. Race awareness and anti-racist training courses have been provided to staff in the hope of increasing their sensitivity to black issues. However, despite widespread monitoring, gate-keeping, anti-racist training and the use of various methods to regulate decision-making, the proportion of black prisoners continues to rise (see the *Introduction*) and the rate of participation of black offenders in community programmes does not seem to be increasing significantly.

It could be said that some—but by no means all—black women face racism, sexism and classism in relation to the work of the NPS. They are sometimes considered difficult clients who are not viewed as able to change their behaviour. If black women are to fully benefit from the work of the NPS, more needs to be done to develop stronger anti-racist, anti-sexist and anti-classist policies and practice in order to deliver appropriate and effective services to them.

Assuming that the Criminal Justice Bill (2002) reaches the statute book, the NPS will have to deal with and manage a range of new community sentences against a generic and less compartmentalised community sentence background, one in which the discretion of individual officers will play a quite significant and seemingly greater part. Given the lesson that where discretion falls to be exercised there is a need for caution, it is to be hoped that the NPS will prepare adequate policies and practices to confront racism and other forms of discrimination in this new era.

CHAPTER 5

Experience of Courts and Lawyers

From the beginning of the 1990s the Lord Chancellor's Department (LCD) and Home Office have issued guidance for courts and other criminal justice agencies enabling them to develop practices designed to ensure fair and equal treatment. The Judicial Studies Board (JSB), responsible for overseeing the provision of training for judges and magistrates, also took an early lead by establishing an Ethnic Minorities Advisory Committee. Training on race issues was introduced for Crown Court judges, recorders, assistant recorders, district judges and the 30,000 or so lay magistrates. From 2000, the common law duty to avoid discrimination (already bolstered by information issued pursuant to section 95 Criminal Justice Act 1991: see *Chapter 3*, p. 42) was reinforced by the European Convention On Human Rights which among other things demands a fair trial under Article 6 and, by Article 14, that all European Convention rights are applied without discrimination (and by all public authorities).

Racial offences and racial and religious aggravation: a note
Concern for victims of racist crime led to the creation in the Crime and Disorder Act 1998 of a number of racially aggravated offences with greater maximum sentences than their non-racially aggravated counterparts, i.e. racially aggravated assaults (including common assault, actual bodily harm, grievous bodily harm and wounding); racially aggravated criminal damage (including arson); and racially aggravated harassment.[1] Such an offence is 'racially aggravated' if:

- at the time of committing it, or immediately before or after doing so, the offender demonstrates towards the victim of the offence hostility based on the victim's membership (or presumed membership) of a racial group; or
- it is motivated (wholly or partly) by hostility towards members of a racial group based on their membership of that group.

Also, under the 1998 Act, a court must normally increase sentence for *any* crime if it is shown to be racially motivated. Elizabeth Burney and Gerry Rose conclude:

> The law is now widely accepted in principle, and a great deal of effort is being expended upon it. For it to work effectively it needs to be used both with greater finesse and more firmly. What matters is not the quantity of prosecutions, but their quality, and it is concluded that victims would agree. [2]

In 2000, comparable provisions were introduced with regard to religiously motivated offences.

---

[1] Two of the original suspects in the Stephen Lawrence case (see later in the chapter) were in 2002 convicted of this offence and sent to prison after driving a car at an off-duty black police officer.

[2] *Racist Offences: How is the Law Working?: The Implementation of the Legislation on Racially Aggravated Offences in the Crime and Disorder Act 1998* (2002), Burney E and Rose G, Home Office Research Study No. 24.

BACKGROUND

Historically in Britain, the law has been made or determined largely by white males and even today many of the people in senior positions in judicial institutions are white men. The basis of knowledge of legislators and judges is thus located in whatever institutionalised discrimination (*Chapter 3*) may exist. Such comments cannot be applied to the lay magistracy which, by 1996, had already become reasonably well-balanced in terms of its make-up (15,858 men and 14,516 women with 9.1 per cent of the total from minority ethnic groups).

Apart from setting out criminal offences, the law, in effect, defines acceptable behaviour (and now seeks to prevent or punish 'anti-social behaviour' also), e.g. affecting marriage, sexual relations, domestic violence and the care of children, and sets the parameters of what is 'normal' or 'proper'. This 'man-made' law sets the context within which courts respond to women, and to particular groups such as black women, mothers, victims of domestic violence, prostitutes and lesbians. Judges and magistrates—many of whom are middle-class white men— then administer the law in the light of their own perceptions of black women. Notoriously, the late Lord Denning, in the original version of his book, *What's Next in the Law?* stated:

> There are white and black, coloured and brown ... some of them come from countries where bribery and graft are accepted ... where stealing is a virtue so long as you are not found out.[3]

Although he was questioning the fitness of black people to serve as jurors, this type of sentiment may indicate how some judges and possibly magistrates still think of foreign defendants. The book was withdrawn and amended.

The tendency to categorise women who do not match the expectations of the dominant culture as possessing criminal potential was noted in *Chapter 2*. Despite positive changes including of the kind mentioned at the start of this chapter and greater actual recognition of equal rights, deep-rooted problems of institutional inequality persist and the administration of the law continues to reflect this through the political, social and economic dominance of white people and to a large extent white men. Their beliefs about the role of women in the home and at work reinforce popular attitudes about women. Kennedy maintains that the law mirrors society and continues to reflect the subordination of women.[4] Similarly, the construction of defendants as white and British (or perhaps nowadays European) reinforces and perpetuates racism.

Flaws in appointment system
The system for appointing judges and members of Queen's Counsel (QCs) lacks transparency and does not do enough to promote a more ethnically diverse judiciary. A first annual report by the Commission for Judicial Appointments concluded that there were 'a number of significant respects' in which the system could be improved. The commission—chaired by Sir Colin Campbell—criticised the 'overwhelming' white male social background of the judiciary: 'We have not

---

[3]   *What's Next in the Law?* (1982), Lord Denning, Butterworths.
[4]   *Eve Was Framed* (1992), Kennedy H, Chatto and Windus.

seen sufficient evidence to be satisfied that the procedures for judicial appointments do enough to promote cultural diversity'. One commission member Millie Banerjee was reported in the *Law Society Gazette*[5] as saying that the lack of diversity was an undeniable problem. 'The facts are clear—most of the judiciary is made up of white men from a very narrow social background . . . The problems with the consultation process are also clear to us, but how to solve these problems is more complex'. The report also noted concerns about the role of the Lord Chancellor, a government minister, in deciding which private lawyers should have a 'quality kitemark'. Ms Banerjee said this was not in the commission's remit, but admitted it was an issue being openly discussed and the commission wanted a proper debate. Law Society President, Carolyn Kirby welcomed the report's publication.

More women and people from ethnic minorities are now being appointed as judges and the very first Muslim High Court Judge (Mr. Justice Mota Singh) was appointed in 2003. Appointments of ethnic minority judges rose to 7.8 per cent from 6.9 per cent in 2000-2001. White applicants were slightly more successful than ethnic minority applicants.

Applications from female and ethnic minority candidates rose over the same period. Women made up 32 per cent of applicants (compared to 26 per cent in 2000-2001) and candidates who declared themselves to be of ethnic minority origin made up 8.2 of all applications (7.1 per cent). The LCD is quoted as saying, 'Although the percentage increase for minority ethnic appointments is small, it is hoped that the significance of a continuing increase will encourage more applications from eligible minority ethnic applicants.'

Sentences on black women

There has been no direct focus on black women's experience of sentencing practice. There are, however, certain clues that suggest there is a need for concern. Because *women* appear before the courts less frequently than men they may be seen as out of place, not as 'offenders' in the way that men are. But this general perception does not seem to apply to *black women*, when it may not be considered at all unusual for them to be involved in criminal activity. Women who appear 'unusual' or 'abnormal' because of their behaviour or lifestyle may be sentenced in a different way to those who conform to a more traditional role.[6] Judges and magistrates, whatever their declared intent, may react negatively to women whose dress or hair is unconventional. This also applies to women whose sexuality or racial origins appear to challenge the court,[7] and it seems obvious that a defendant's demeanour can have an effect on whether a court, e.g. believes a claim of future good intentions or remorse, either of which may affect the outcome. Hedderman suggests that women may receive more lenient sentences than men.[8] However, the repercussions for women who do not subscribe to anticipated behaviour can be quite the opposite, and this would include black women. Being married, for example, has been found to mitigate more strongly

---

[5] 99/39/10, October 2002, p.1.

[6] *Women on Trial: A Study of the Female Defendant* (1984), Edwards S, Manchester University Press; *The Effect of Defendants' Demeanour on Sentencing in Magistrates' Courts* (1990), Hedderman C, *Home Office Research Bulletin No. 29.*

[7] *Paying for Crime* (1989), Carlen P and Cook D, Open University Press.

[8] Hedderman C, 1990: see footnote 6.

against detention for black women in the USA.[9] As noted in earlier chapters, stereotyping and cultural assumptions based on the fact that black women may not act 'normally' can be highly misleading as indicators of criminal behaviour.

Jury trial
Government proposals contained in the White Paper *Justice For All* to ensure that juries are more representative are part of a current legislative programme and would help towards reassuring BEM people about the jury system.[10] But proposals to dilute the right to jury trial will further discriminate against ethnic minorities and serve only to entrench rather than dismantle racism in the criminal justice system. The proposals would favour middle-class, white-collar people, clog up courts with appeals and penalise ethnic minorities who opt for a jury trial more often, because they have less confidence in magistrates and the police. The proposal to remove jury trial from serious fraud and other 'complex' or 'problematic' cases, trying these by judge alone is not a solution (whilst there is a need to simplify the law and provide better guidance).

Evidence
The White Paper's proposals regarding the rules of admissibility are a cause for concern. The government is intent on allowing a far wider range of evidence to be adduced and for the jury to decide what weight to give to it. Placing more hearsay evidence before a jury runs the real risk of convictions being based on rumour, gossip or misleading signals. Relaxing the usual bar on the disclosure of a defendant's previous convictions before conviction is also dangerous. Worse still there is even a suggestion to allow previous acquittals to be put before a jury. This represents a serious attack on the presumption of innocence and would have an impact on black defendants. On a practical level, it is also likely to encourage the relevant authorities, including the police, where it is known that previous incidents might be placed before a jury prior to conviction, to simply 'round up the usual suspects'. In the past, black defendants are more likely to have the case against them discontinued, or to be acquitted, suggesting that charges were brought against them on insufficient grounds, but in future information about such acquittals might become evidence for the prosecution. The system does not always get it right as demonstrated by many cases of miscarriage of justice.

Double jeopardy
It is understandable for government to want to ensure justice when an acquittal is in real doubt, but any relaxation of the bar on trying someone twice for the same offence might result in repeated prosecutions of unpopular defendants to achieve a popular result. This is a dangerous approach and BME communities would be most likely to suffer the consequences. There is a parallel with attempts to deal with racially motivated offences, where the relevant provisions (see earlier in the chapter) are now often used against the very people they were designed to protect. Twenty-five per cent of people arrested for racially motivated crime are

---

[9] 'Structures and Practice of Familial-Based Justice in a Criminal Court' (1987), Daly K, *Law and Society Review*, 21:2.

[10] Although an earlier proposal that minorities be represented on juries has been shelved.

from minority ethnic backgrounds (Black London Forum, 'Response to Government Proposals', 2002).

It is difficult to see how a second trial could ever be fair. The defence case is likely to be seriously compromised by the fact that the prosecution will have had notice of it from the first trial. The abolition of the double jeopardy rule would not automatically lead to a satisfactory outcome in High Court cases such as those of Stephen Lawrence and Damilola Taylor. The principal problems in these cases were caused by the inadequate approach of the police at the outset, not by startling new evidence coming to light after a trial.

The extension of magistrates' courts' sentencing powers

The proposed doubling of the sentencing powers of magistrates' court to 12 months will predictably lead to an increase in the prison population. Research has shown that magistrates tend to use their sentencing powers to the maximum. Often when they commit to the Crown Court for sentence, the higher court finds that the magistrates' existing powers were in fact adequate. Black people have no faith in magistrates' courts (which they tend to term 'police courts'), and hence the higher number of black defendants who elect for jury trial in either way cases.

There is thus a sense that any general increase in magistrates' sentencing powers will greatly exacerbate the problem, identified in the Halliday report,[11] of overuse by magistrates of relatively short custodial sentences. As is now widely acknowledged, such sentences are expensive, contribute massively to prison overcrowding and costs, and do little to prevent further offending.

The most telling evidence as to the likely effect of increasing magistrates' sentencing powers lies in the statistics on recent sentencing practice. As *Appendix II* to the Halliday report points out, between 1989 and 1991 the number of defendants given custodial sentences by magistrates increased nearly three-fold from, 18,200 to 53,000 per year (+191 per cent). In the same period there was a much more modest increase in numbers sentenced to custody by the Crown Court, from 42,600 to 44,600 (+5 per cent). This suggests that it was primarily magistrates who were responsible for the massive increase in the use of prison, especially short custodial sentences of less than six months, in this period. Sentences of less than six months more than doubled between 1989 and 1999.

While the incidence of defendant elections for Crown Court has declined sharply, magistrates have continued to send between ten per cent and 12 per cent of either way cases to the Crown Court, either for trial or sentence, throughout the past decade, despite the introduction of reforms such as 'plea before venue'.

Anti-social behaviour

Early in 2003 an Anti-social Behaviour Bill is anticipated that will introduce a raft of measures including a crackdown on begging and littering and extended use of 'on the spot' fines—as well as a proposal for residential classes for the parents of juvenile offenders. All this is likely to result in more poor, disadvantaged and socially excluded people finding themselves with a criminal record or in prison

---

[11] Home Office (2001), *Making Punishments Work: Report of a Review of the Sentencing Framework for England and Wales.* 'The Halliday report' (after John Halliday, the senior official involved).

for failing to pay the resulting fines or to comply with court orders. Much of the targeted behaviour—e.g. vandalism, graffiti and threatening behaviour—is already criminal under existing law making extra provision unnecessary. Young black and ethnic minorities involved in crime will tend to be characterised and dealt with by the police and other criminal justice agencies as part of a general pattern of criminal or 'anti-social' activity prevalent in the black community, while violent assaults on black people are very often treated by the police as isolated, individual incidents, even to the extent of being portrayed as 'youthful pranks'. Taken together these measures amount to 'zero tolerance' policy by another name. In the past zero tolerance has been found disproportionately to affect the homeless and black communities, causing resentment and inconvenience but with little effect. Begging should not be a crime. If someone is aggressive in the way they approach to ask for money it is likely that they will be committing an offence under the Public Order Act 1986.

COURT DECISION-MAKING

In addition to the paucity of information which exists about the sentencing of black women *per se*, until the 1990s it was not possible to isolate the effect of race in sentencing and to separate this from decisions made at other points in the criminal justice process. Similarly, earlier research studies tended in the main to be inconclusive about unequal treatment of white defendants and black defendants.

Home Office research (Vennard and Hedderman, 1998 and see now the *Postscript* to this work at p.140) found that black suspects were more likely to be treated differently at various points. Differences based on ethnicity emerge from the time of arrest up to disposal by a court. The study found the proportion of black people among those arrested was much greater than their presence in local populations. They were also more likely to have been arrested following a stop and search. Black suspects were more likely to have been arrested for robbery, Asians for fraud, forgery or theft from vehicles. An earlier Home Office study (1994) found that black men were serving longer sentences than white men and that after taking into account factors such as offence, type of court, and number of previous convictions, there were 'significant' differences in sentence length for men for wounding, theft, handling stolen etc. property and drug offences—with ethnic minority men receiving longer sentences than white men.

Roger Hood's Study
In 1992 a thorough and academically rigorous research study was published by Roger Hood, Director of the Centre for Criminological Research at Oxford University. This examined sentences passed in 3,317 cases heard at a number of Crown Court centres in the West Midlands during 1989.[12] The study showed that, overall, black males were 17 per cent more likely to receive a custodial sentence than their white counterparts. Even after controlling for 15 key variables relating to the seriousness of the offence and other legally relevant factors, the study

---

[12] *Race and Sentencing: A Study in the Crown Court* (1992), Clarendon Press; see also *A Question of Judgement: Summary of 'Race and Sentencing'* (1993), Commission for Racial Equality (CRE).

disclosed that black people had a greater chance of going to prison, to the extent of between five and eight per cent. In cases of medium gravity—where a judge's discretion was, seemingly, the greatest—this rose to 13 per cent. The study concluded that:

> Eighty per cent of the over-representation of black men in the prison population was due to the disproportionate number of them appearing before the Crown Courts (reflecting of course decisions made at all previous stages of the criminal justice process) and the seriousness of their cases. The remaining 20 per cent ... could only be explained as a result of differential treatment by the courts and other factors influencing the severity of the sentences they received. One third of this 'race effect' was due to the higher proportion pleading not guilty and the longer prison terms they got as a result ... It would not need many courts to behave as the Dudley courts and the courts at Warwick and Stafford appear to have done for it to have a considerable effect on the racial composition of the prison population.

The study also found that significantly higher proportions of black (42 per cent) and Asian (43 per cent) offenders were sentenced without a pre-sentence report (PSR: then known as the 'social enquiry report, or 'SER'). This compared with 28 per cent for white offenders. This was in part due to the fact that more black and Asian defendants pleaded 'not guilty' and the existing practice not to prepare PSRs in advance (i.e. unless a guilty plea is anticipated) but only following conviction and after a subsequent adjournment for that purpose, which a judge is not always prepared to allow. There were also significant racial disparities in the distribution of community sentences. For a general discussion of PSRs and their relationship to community sentences see *Chapter 4*.

After taking account of factors influencing the severity of a sentence, it was found that black adults were given sentences higher up the tariff than white people. Concentrated largely within the 'medium risk of custody' band, black defendants were:

- more likely to receive a custodial sentence;
- less likely to be given community punishment order (CPO) or community rehabilitation order (CRO) (as these orders now are), respectively;
- less likely to be recommended for a CRO; and
- even when recommended for a CRO, less likely to get it.

Among young offenders with offences falling within this band, black offenders were more likely to get a CPO or be sent to an attendance centre and less likely to be placed on a CRO. The study concluded that:

> The evidence supports the contention that black offenders receive sentences which are higher up the 'tariff' of penalties than do whites and, therefore, are put at more risk of getting a prison sentence should they re-appear on fresh charges.

As if to corroborate this, Home Office Statistical Bulletin 21/94 (which among other things examined differences in types of offence, type of court and number of previous convictions) indicates that more black offenders were serving sentences for drugs offences for which sentences are frequently lengthy, more black offenders are sentenced at the Crown Court where sentences tend to be more severe for similar offences—'But significant differences remain in sentence lengths for unlawful wounding, theft, handling stolen property, drugs offences and some others'.[13]

A study of the sentencing of juveniles in Wolverhampton[14] found that African-Caribbean defendants had significantly more high tariff non-custodial sentences (particularly supervision orders with requirements and CPOs) than white or Asian defendants—a distinction which cannot be explained by differences in the seriousness of offences, and which occurred although African-Caribbean defendants had, on average, committed fewer current offences and had shorter existing criminal records.

Roger Hood's study analysed PSRs and showed that these were more likely to propose high tariff sentences on African-Caribbean defendants in circumstances where such proposals would not have been made if the defendant had been white. While, in general, PSRs described African-Caribbean defendants in a positive or balanced way, report writers, for well-intentioned reasons, also included background information on defendants, which was in practice likely to reinforce stereotypical views of black families and lead to more substantial intervention in the form of a high tariff sentence.

In 1993, a paper for the Royal Commission on Criminal Procedure by Marian Fitzgerald, reviewed key findings from existing research concluding that:

> The research available addresses many of the concerns which have been raised by ethnic minorities about their experience of criminal justice. It does not do so definitely, however, and many gaps remain. Yet Hood adds weight to the evidence already accumulated which strongly suggests that, even where differences in social and legal factors are taken into account, there are ethnic differences in outcomes which can only be explained in terms of discrimination.

Bail and remand

Roger Hood's study disclosed that a higher proportion of black people (26 per cent) than white people (20 per cent) had been refused bail. It was estimated by him that there was a 16 per cent greater likelihood of black offenders ending up in custody on remand after taking into account all available relevant factors. Another study by Imogen Brown and Roy Hullin[15] of contested bail applications coming before Leeds magistrates' court during a six months period in 1989 found no difference between the proportion of white and African-Caribbean defendants who were remanded in custody when the prosecution opposed bail. However, there *was* evidence to suggest that the CPS opposed bail in a higher proportion of cases involving black defendants than white defendants. The authors commented:

---

[13] 'Race and Criminal Justice', Penal Affairs Consortium, September 1996, p.5.
[14] *Negative Images* (1996), Kirk, B, Avebury Press.
[15] 'Contested Bail Applications: The Treatment of Ethnic Minority and White Offenders' (1993), *Criminal Law Review*, 107.

... if a larger proportion of ethnic minority defendants make bail applications which are opposed, and are thereafter remanded in custody by magistrates in the same proportion as white defendants, there will be an imbalance in the overall remand picture.

A higher proportion of sentenced black prisoners were refused bail before trial. The data suggests that part of the difference in treatment between ethnic groups may be accounted for by the type and seriousness of the offence (as measured by the sentence length). However, after allowing for this, statistically significant differences still remained for adult males convicted of wounding (where 59 per cent of black prisoners had been refused bail compared with 43 per cent of white prisoners); fraud and forgery (55 per cent compared with 40 per cent); drug offences (74 per cent compared with 56 per cent); and some other offences.

From arrest to sentence

One woman who was unhappy with the way she had been treated by customs officers, the police and the courts asked me to attend the second hearing of her case. Beatrice's case (described in detail in *Chapter 6*) sheds some further light on how black people (including black professionals) can be treated by the courts, illustrating how the criminal justice process can be perceived by black women and possibly how it can go astray. It deals with white perceptions of black women's 'inferior' culture, looking at how race, gender and class are articulated.

In another real life case from Bradford 16 Asian rioters appealed against the lengths of their 'unfair' and 'unjust' sentences imposed in February 2003. They claimed that they were given longer sentences than those handed out to white rioters in comparable cases, including those given to stone-throwing 'yobs' who took part in the Ravenscliffe disturbances immediately after riots in 2001. They argued that sentences ranging from four to six years were 'excessive'. Of 15 cases only four sentences were reduced on appeal. Anti-racist campaigners are of the opinion that many of the sentences were harsh compared to those of white youths, who were mainly given CPOs or lenient sentences. 'One white youth received an 18 months sentence for throwing a petrol bomb and a slab of paving stone at the police, compared to an Asian man who received four years and 9 months for lobbing six stones' (*Eastern Eye*, 7 February 2003). Most adult stone-throwers have received sentences of about three years, with about six years for petrol bombers. The longest sentence so far was eight-and-a-half years. The campaigners want the role of the right wing extremists to be taken into account as they feel their presence in the area helped to trigger the riot. Most of the rioters had no previous convictions (see further *Asian Xpress*, 31 January 2003).

WOMEN AND THE COURTS

Black women's experiences have again lacked specific attention. But, as intimated in *Chapter 1*, there *is* evidence that women in general receive unequal treatment compared with men (at various stages of the criminal justice process). Also, as outlined in *Chapter 4*, foreign women often may not benefit from having a pre-sentence report (PSR) that may serve to mitigate their sentence. Their home or family circumstances are thus not always taken into account. The resulting disproportionate number of black women in prison is discussed in *Chapter 7*.

It has been observed by several commentators that when the defendant is black, offences are more likely to be described to courts in such a way that they come into a more serious category. Crow and Cove found that when black people were charged with assault there were more cases where the 'victim' had suffered no actual injury than when the defendants were white.[16] There must, presumably, have been scope for reduction of the charges' or for non-prosecution. This accords with the evidence from the USA where studies have found that charges against black assailants, especially if the victims are white, are less likely to be downgraded than in the case of white defendants.[17] It has been observed that white victims' sufferings are more likely to be seen as serious, and therefore the assailants deserving of more serious punishment than black victims' assailants.[18] So black on white crime is likely to be sentenced more severely than either white on black or black on black crime, again suggesting that race is a factor in criminal justice decision-making including sentencing.

Legal variables, such as offence type and previous criminal history are not the only ones that affect sentencing. Unemployment and no permanent address, and no family or other community ties, have also been shown to correlate with sentences given by magistrates' courts and Crown Courts. Unemployment in borderline cases may be the critical factor whether someone is sent to prison.

As indicated in *Chapter 4*, there is also room for concern that women convicted of minor offences are more likely to receive CROs in circumstances where men are fined, making it less likely that courts will regard a further such order or other community sentences as appropriate if they reoffend later, and moving them more quickly up the tariff of non-custodial sentences towards custody. There is also evidence indicating that some imprisoned women may have been regarded wrongly as less suitable for community punishment orders or intensive CRO programmes than male offenders in similar circumstances.[19]

It is instructive to consider the profile of women who receive prison sentences. According to the Penal Affairs Consortium:

> Most women prisoners were living in poverty before going to prison, often facing multiple debts. The process of imprisonment frequently results in loss of accommodation and possessions and increased destitution on release, pushing them into a downward spiral of hardship ... Many women prisoners are the mothers of young children who have to be looked after by makeshift arrangements involving relatives or taken into care. Such separations can have a traumatic effect on young children . . . policies supposedly intended to combat crime are increasingly likely to be a cause of crime in future generations ... the trend towards a greater use of imprisonment for women is a mistaken one which will cause more damage to society than it prevents.[20]

---

[16] 'Ethnic Minorities in the Courts' (1984), Crow I and Cove J, *Criminal Law Review*, 413-417.

[17] 'Race and Prosecution Discretion in Homicide Cases' (1985), Radelet M and Pierce G, *Law and Society Review*, 19, 4: 587-621.

[18] 'Making the Punishment Fit the Crime' (1976), Zimring F E, Hastings Centre, Report No. 6.

[19] See 'Women Offenders and Probation Service Provision' (1991), Home Office; 'Provision for Women' (November 1993), Marie Edmonds, Somerset Probation Service.

[20] 'The Imprisonment of Women: Some Facts and Figures' (March 1996), Penal Affairs Consortium.

Women and bail

Before conviction or sentence, black women may be remanded in custody for reasons of perceived offence seriousness linked to race, failure to satisfy what in the case of white people might be bail conditions, or to make themselves available for, or cooperate in the preparation of, PSRs. Groups such as Nacro, the Howard League for Penal Reform and Prison Reform Trust have expressed concern about the disproportionate number of women (compared to men) who are denied bail and who subsequently receive a non-custodial sentence.[21] The Howard League estimated that in 1990 only 23 per cent of women who had spent time in custody on remand were subsequently received into prison under sentence, and that up to 73 per cent of women spending time in custody on remand were there unnecessarily.[22] The difficulties encountered by defendants who are remanded into custody (such as loss of accommodation, separation from relatives and family, lack of contact with a defence lawyer and poor physical and sanitary conditions) are likely to be experienced more acutely by women than men. The limited number of female prison places means that, taking this group as a whole, women are held further away from their home area. Nacro maintains that women in custody on remand effectively serve a prison sentence, often in the most overcrowded parts of the penal system, even if subsequently found not guilty or given a non-custodial sentence. This experience, which may also result in the loss of employment, accommodation, family and other community ties, can increase the risk of offending.

The National Association of Probation Officers (NAPO) considered that women may be remanded in custody because of the limited number of bail hostel places.[23] Many women could, however, be remanded to addresses in their local community. Equally, many women are remanded for medical reports but later receive non-custodial sentences.[24] Schemes to provide access to an adequate number of bail hostel places, bail support programmes for women, and associated bail information provision need to be looked at with a view to their being provided in each court area.

Black women are more frequently refused bail, and this may partly be because of not having what is perceived as a stable family background. There appears to be a general assumption that ethnic minority women will 'disappear into their own subculture' which it will then be difficult for the police to penetrate. In addition poverty within the black community often means that it is difficult to obtain financial sureties or a security (the latter, though relatively rarely used for black people or white people, involves the deposit of a sum of money or other valuables with the court). Such considerations mean that black women who should be on bail may often find it being refused.

This view is supported by Voakes and Fowler who maintain 'that more black people find themselves in prison than whites who have committed the same type

[21] *The Guardian*, 25 March 1994.
[22] 'Discrimination in the Criminal Justice System', Crook F, in *Values, Gender and Offending* (1993), Senior P and Williams B (eds.), Pavic.
[23] 'Women in Custody' (May 1989), NAPO.
[24] 'Sex, Class and Crime: Towards a Non-Sexist Criminology', Gregory J, in *Confronting Crime* (1986), Mathhews , R and Young J (eds.), Sage. pp. 53-71.

of offences, and who are likely to have worse criminal records.'[25] Similarly, Smith[26] urges that 'African-Caribbeans may tend to be remanded in custody rather than bailed because their family circumstances tend not to meet criteria commonly used in making decisions about awarding bail.' Smith concludes that this might affect conviction rates probably because it is more difficult to prepare a defence in custody. It is also a possibility that some people remanded in custody are more likely to receive a custodial sentence, almost as if the very existence of such a remand predicates or justifies this outcome. He suggests that recognition of the African-Caribbean family patterns and traditions as normal could ease the difficulty black people have in obtaining bail and notes the ways in which the laws of England and Wales traditionally 'express national identity' by excluding or marginalising present-day ethnic minorities.

Some black women defendants in criminal cases are at a particular disadvantage because they do not reside in this country and therefore have difficulty getting bail, the authorities fearing that they may fail to surrender at the end of the bail period. Because of the absence of local family ties or local connections, some of them have no one to stand surety (i.e. to vouch for their reappearance at court or at a police station).

The Runnymede Trust in its research report, 'White Justice', found that more black people were denied bail compared to their white counterparts. There are various discretionary reasons why someone can be refused bail pursuant to the Bail Act 1976. The police have to decide whether to release an individual from custody until he or she is due to attend court or whether to keep him or her in police custody until his or her appearance before a magistrates' court. In the case of 'police bail' (i.e. bail granted by the police as opposed to a court) this will be for someone to return to a police station at a later date even though they have not been charged with any criminal offence.

Under the 1976 Act, the main exceptions to the right to bail are that there are substantial grounds for believing that, if granted bail, an accused person will:

- fail to surrender to bail; or
- commit an offence; or
- interfere with witnesses or otherwise obstruct the course of justice.

Bail can also be refused for the accused person's own protection. Reasons must exist and be announced to support a refusal of bail or to support conditions attached to a grant of bail.

The facts relied on when operating the Bail Act may be indirectly discriminatory, the sort of items which may have racially disadvantageous connotations. These include: a home with, say, a spouse or parent; a long-standing tenancy or other residential arrangements; a job, or at least reasonable prospects of employment; community ties to groups or associates that are regarded as 'respectable'. These are the very things black people have greatest difficulty in obtaining or demonstrating, and yet they are the very factors which will often underpin application of the legal criteria for remand decisions.

---

[25] 'Sentencing, Race and Social Enquiry Reports' (1989), Voakes R and Fowler Q, West Yorkshire Probation Service.

[26] 'Race, Crime and Criminal Justice', Smith D, in the *Oxford Handbook of Criminology* (1994), Maguire M and Reiner R (Eds.), Oxford University Press.

LAWYERS

In 1995, four per cent of solicitors and eight per cent of barristers were from ethnic minority groups, compared with 1.3 per cent and four per cent respectively in 1989. Although the proportion of all Crown Prosecution Service staff from minority ethnic groups rose from 5.9 per cent in 1991 to 7.5 per cent in 1995, the proportion in the higher grades fell from 1.9 per cent to 1.6 per cent. [27]

What has been described as 'low pay and overbearing bureaucracy' may force many 'legal aid'[28] solicitors to reduce or even quit publicly funded work in the next five years, reductions that will have a discriminatory effect. Almost two-thirds of solicitor's firms (62 per cent) reported recruitment problems for qualified and support staff (*Gazette*, January 2003, p.1). If this problem is allowed to continue, black people, many of whom are in receipt of low incomes (*Chapter 1*) and who rely on legal aid to defend themselves will be severely affected: it will become that much more difficult for them to find a lawyer. As can be seen from the women's interviews later in this chapter, some black defendants experience conflict in deciding whether it is better to have a white lawyer who they believe is less likely to lose the sympathy of the court or a black lawyer who understands their own culture.

Police stations (see, generally, *Chapter 3*) have a list of 'duty solicitors' who, mostly speaking, provide 24-hour cover on a rota basis. These solicitors can be called upon any time of the day or night. It is possible that, in some situations, police officers contact those duty solicitors who are 'amenable' to their own police practices, and who they can work easily with, as opposed to those they see as 'working against' them. Given the existence of prejudice in the ranks of the police as described in *Chapter 3*, the outcome may be less acceptable in the case of black people than white people. Something intended to assist in a practical way becomes tainted by individual or institutionalised discrimination.

Difficulties may also be experienced by black women wanting to change their lawyers. It is, of course, difficult to know how much of the dissatisfaction disclosed in the interviews which follow was due to the solicitor being unhelpful, how much was due to disappointment with the outcome of a case and how much to the prevailing mistrust between black women and the criminal justice agencies.

Helena Kennedy[29] discusses the case of a black woman who saw her solicitor on only a few brief visits and her barrister, whom she had never met before, who arrived just 15 minutes before the start of the case. Her regular solicitor was away on holiday, so there was no familiar face at court. Defendants in such cases have little power, and at times feel forced to accept second-rate practices from the legal profession.

Kennedy describes another case of a black woman whose English was negligible and she too was dissatisfied with her representation because—

---

[27] 'Race Discrimination and the Criminal Justice System' (1996), NAPO and ABPO.

[28] Now called 'state funded representation' under which representation in magistrates' courts is now free-of-charge regardless of income, but this pre-supposes the existence of a sufficient corps of competent lawyers. Withdrawal from the scheme will have discriminatory effect. A survey (of 270 firms across England and Wales)—backed by the Legal Aid Practitioners Group (LAPG) and the Criminal Law Solicitors Association (CLSA)—indicates that morale plummeted during 2002.

[29] *Eve was Framed* (1992), Kennedy H, Chatto and Windus.

although she had had a conference with a barrister at the prison—someone else turned up at court on the day. She could not believe that it was sufficient for someone to read the papers in the case and to talk with her for as little as half an hour. It is hardly unreasonable for clients to want the opportunity to talk to their lawyers at length if they are facing a significant risk of losing their liberty or a substantial period imprisonment. But there is often a sense of pressure from the court to get a move on, and lawyers tend to fear a judge's wrath. The incidence of such changes can only be reduced if more and more cases are given fixed dates in advance, in short better court listing practices.[30]

Kennedy's description[31] of the experiences of some black women lawyers gives cause for concern—the problem of black advocates not being taken seriously are exacerbated in the case of women and the difficulty of securing authority within the courtroom are even greater. Those who *are* successful, she adds, are constantly told by white colleagues that they do not seem to be black, as though there is some special stamp of blackness that they had shrugged off. Such comments may be intended as compliments but can be deeply offensive. Kennedy mentions a black woman barrister—a rising criminal practitioner— defending a black client—who had a strong feeling that the trial judge, renowned for rudeness, was particularly dismissive of her arguments. At one stage when she sat down, he sent her a note asking whether her accent was English, and if so where she had been to school. She ignored the note, uncertain what it meant, but felt undermined, as though her fluency and education were in question. After this black lawyer's final speech to the jury, the judge summed up to the all-white jury with the words: 'Members of the jury, we are British'.

INTERVIEWS

The women in the sample talked about their experiences of the courts and about magistrates, judges, sentencing, bail and lawyers. They criticised the provision of legal aid as inadequate and believed that for them there appeared to be one justice for the poor and another for the rich.

Judges and magistrates
All the women were convinced that judges and magistrates are racist. Edith said:

> I have no faith in magistrates—I feel you are found guilty the minute they see your colour—I do not think they should go through the procedure of hearing the case when they have made up their minds the minute they saw you.

Magistrates' courts tended to be seen as 'police courts' because, the women said, magistrates are more likely to believe the police. Such views have, seemingly, resulted in a higher proportion of black defendants choosing to be tried at Crown Court whenever they have this option with the greater likelihood of a custodial sentence if convicted.[32] Such moves may also result in longer sentences, as guilty

---

[30] *ibid.*
[31] *ibid.*
[32] 'Sentencing Practice in the Crown Court' (1988), Moxon D, Home Office Research Study No. 103, Home Office.

plea discount is not then applicable. Proportionately more black than white defendants may also be committed for trial at the Crown Court because of representations by the Crown prosecutor rather election for trial with a view to pleading not guilty before a jury.[33] However, this must be viewed in the light of initiatives by the CPS to combat discrimination. The women believed that in some instances, it was arranged that 'tough' judges or magistrates would deal with their cases.

Some of the women talked of certain Crown Court judges being known for being anti-black. Doreen said:

> A black person is guilty before he is even tried. There are judges who don't like blacks. You get to know certain courts you go to ... there are particular judges. The judge in my case was ... anti-blacks. Judges don't sympathise with anyone.

Anthea also said:

> I have been in trouble with the law few times. Where I live every black person knows about this judge in the Crown Court ... He is definitely anti-black and dishes out long sentences to blacks. You just get caught up in the system.

Judge Pickles, during an interview with *The Voice* newspaper, said that:

> A Rastafarian standing in front of you with dreadlocks can look rather intimidating. If we could understand their minds better, we might be able to better understand what they are doing and why they are doing it. There is no deliberate racism but there may be unconscious bias because we don't know enough about the people.[34]

Also in 1990, another judge was reported to have referred to black people as 'nig nogs'. Such a comment illustrates the racism present at influential levels. Seemingly, unless judges are prepared to examine their behaviour and admit that discriminatory practices or racism exists within their ranks, more black people will continue to end up in prison.

Bail

Fifteen of the women complained about not being able to get bail:

> I was refused bail and they said this was because I might commit further offences ... but this was my first offence ... and they had my passport and clothes. (Doreen)

Marva went on to say that:

> I feel I was refused bail because of my colour. Although I am naturalised, I am still treated differently from English people ... My co-defendant is black ... if you are black and born here you stand a better chance compared to a foreign black woman ... Don't get me wrong we are all discriminated against but it's worse if you are foreign.

---

[33] 'A Study of Sentencing in the Leeds Magistrates' Courts' (1992), Brown I and Hullin R, *British Journal of Criminology*, 32,1: 41-53.

[34] *The Voice*, 11 September 1990.

Marva's co-defendant had been charged with the same offence and according to her this was their first time in trouble with the law. Similarly, Susan, a foreign woman, was left wondering why she was refused bail when her co-defendant had been granted it. Four of the other women expressed the same view. They all felt that black women were discriminated against and that if you are a foreign black woman, even though you had lived here for years, you will get 'worse' treatment. She felt this harsher treatment was intended to send a strong message that corruption and criminal activities by foreigners will not be tolerated in Britain. If this is the case, it may be due to unjustified assumptions and racism on the part of the judiciary which sees *foreign* black women as invading their country and coming from corrupt places as if to influence the local good and law-abiding women.

Two of the women felt that the courts asked for a large sum of money which they knew the women did not have, including Josephine:

> They asked for a huge sum of money and my brother's ex-wife put up surety for my brother, my brother's girlfriend and myself. They asked for £2,000. (Josephine)

The relatives would, in effect, have to satisfy the court that they could raise the £2,000 if Josephine absconded (i.e. failed to surrender to custody at the end of her bail period).

Sentence

All the women interviewed felt aggrieved and were dissatisfied with the sentences they were given. They said that after discussing them with other women in prison they realised that white women get shorter sentences compared to black women. The following are the views of some of the women:

> I feel that the judge made up his mind the minute we walked into the court. We were only there for ten minutes. (Karen)

> Before I came to this prison we found out that a white woman who had ten kilos of cannabis was given 18 months and for the same quantity a black woman in the prison was given three years. (Monica)

> I was given two and a half years. I felt it was unfair for a first offence and the barrister agreed with me at the time that the sentence was harsh. One white girl here had two ounces of heroin and was given two years and this is not fair—I had two ounces. (Lorraine)

> I'm not happy with the sentence. I tried to appeal and was turned down. I have found out that white girls here got shorter sentences compared to me—some black girls got even longer sentences than me—especially the foreign ones. (Geraldine)

This was echoed by Dawn who said:

> Courts are not fair. I had one and a half kilos of cocaine and was given ten years and have done four years so far. Since I have been in prison I have found that some white women, although they had more cocaine on them, got lesser sentences. One white woman here had six kilos and was given five years. I feel it's unfair as it is my first offence. (Dawn)

> I was given six years for six ounces of cocaine and have found that some inmates have got lesser sentences even though they had more heroin on them. One white woman had one kilo and got four years. (Cynthia)

It is difficult to say how much of this was due to legitimate considerations (such as the seriousness of the offence, the offender's past criminal record and the exact circumstances of the offence) and how much was due to extra-legal variables (being black, being a woman, belonging to the working-classes). Moreover most of the women interviewed pleaded 'not guilty', thereby forfeiting any discount for entering a guilty plea (usually up to one third: there being a statutory duty to consider this aspect and to give reasons).

Lawyers

An area for concern for the women interviewed was not being able to see a duty solicitor on the first day of their arrest. Twelve of the women had not been allowed to see, or had not been told about seeing, one:

> I was not told about a duty solicitor and did not see one while I was in police custody. (Geraldine)

Sixteen of the women complained about the kind of advice they got from the duty solicitor. Aisha said:

> I felt that the duty solicitor was conspiring with the police. You just couldn't trust him.

This may be partly due to the mistrust that already exists between black people and criminal justice agencies. It may not necessarily be that an individual solicitor is racist, but that, since he or she is part of the system, he or she is not seen as being fair in assessing the position of a black woman suspect or defendant, or in giving advice. Several of the women were convinced that the duty solicitor was not working in their favour but against them:

> The duty solicitor was not helpful and I eventually changed him ... I felt he was helping the police. (Josephine)

> I feel we get solicitors who work for the system—my solicitor—I could not trust him. (Nancy)

Miriam, who wanted to change the duty solicitor but failed, said:

> He was a 'custom' solicitor. I didn't find him helpful. All he said to me was ... tell them the truth and you will be alright. He refused to see me alone. I wanted to change him when I was on remand, but they wouldn't let me.

One woman described how she took over from her solicitor in court and represented herself:

> The solicitor I had was no good. I said I prefer to speak for myself ... and in the end ... I just put on a good show and was given six month's probation [community

rehabilitation (CRO)]. I would have got a prison sentence if I had let the solicitor speak for me. (Doreen)

Another said that because of the experience she had had with solicitors in the past (she had been in trouble with the law since the age of 13) she felt black people should be encouraged to represent themselves:

… There is nothing you can do if you are not happy with a solicitor. You can't really defend yourself. You are not allowed to say anything. Somebody else has to speak for you or defend you … All they do is bring up your bad points especially when you are black. (Cora)

All the women felt that they had been treated unfairly by the courts and ten of them that the 'longer sentences' they received were due partly to the legal advice they were given. Four of the women felt that if you are on legal aid you do not get 'justice'.

I feel that legal aid clients do not get a fair deal. I do not feel that barristers and solicitors take your cases seriously … unless you are paying for yourself. (June)

Some advocates who take on legal aid clients are young, liberal and with a conviction that everybody should get justice regardless of whether they are poor or not. Hence their willingness to take legal aid cases which usually means a long delay in payment and lesser fees than for private client work. It may lead to economies:

My barrister only saw me 15 minutes before the hearing. There is no way he would have known all about me in 15 minutes. (Doreen)

This is supported by the black women prisoner's views as detailed in my own earlier research.[35]

I saw the barrister 20 minutes before the hearing. If he wanted to know more about me and my case he would have seen me earlier or for a longer time like an hour or so before the hearing. (Jackie)

These solicitors and barristers are no good. They forget that the decision is very important to you. (Maxine)

This could be said to be a common complaint by defendants, particularly if not satisfied with the outcome of their case.

Marva felt that the barrister had advised her to plead guilty because he believed she was guilty of both charges despite explaining to him that she was not guilty of either. She felt that the advice she got from her barrister was because '… the barrister believed every black person is guilty' and Marva was also unhappy with the length of her sentence, which she felt was too long.

It is difficult to know what constitutes a good barrister or solicitor (although, two women *were* pleased, or partly so, with their lawyer's performance). To some

---

[35] 'The Criminalisation and Imprisonment of Black Women' (1989), *Probation Journal*, Chigwada R, September, pp. 100-105.

women it did not seem to matter so much whether it was a black or white lawyer, as long as he or she turned out to be 'good'. It would appear that a 'good' advocate is measured by the interest he or she shows in the case, his or her advice, the time he or she spends listening and advising and also partly by the kind of sentence an offender gets. For example Cora said:

> I was convicted of fraud involving £75 at the post office. I was 17 at the time I committed the crime and the final hearing took place four years later. I feel I got a lighter sentence (18 months in prison) because of my good barrister.

Most of the women were aware of the problems which black lawyers face in the system. Four of the women who had been in trouble with the law several times talked about their experiences in court concerning black barristers:

> I've been in trouble with the law a few times so I know how to handle the system ... what I do is to go and see a black solicitor first and then study my case and ask to be represented by a white barrister. I'll study my case and tell the barrister the points I want stressed. (Sarah)

Rhona said:

> I feel black lawyers are looked upon as inferior. I prefer to take my case to a black solicitor's firm because I feel at ease to talk to him about my case ... this is from my experience anyway ... black solicitors understand where black people are coming from. I get a white barrister to represent me in court ... The judges and magistrates have no respect for black lawyers ... I know this is supporting the system ... but that verdict is very important to you ... and sometimes you have to look after number one.

This was echoed by Doreen:

> If I could help it I would not be represented by a black barrister ... they have to be very careful, the judge can belittle them ... or they find themselves apologising more.

Black lawyers are often said to be too close to the client and this is viewed as stopping them from giving professional and independent advice. The judges have been known to belittle black lawyers. This perception is supported by *Beatrice's Case* (*Chapter 6*), where the judge did not seem to have much patience with Beatrice's co-accused's black barrister. (Beatrice herself was represented by a white lawyer for the sort of pragmatic reasons outlined above). The following extracts which led to counsel being called 'incompetent' are instructive:

> **BLACK COUNSEL ...** Your honour, I am under a duty to my client to say what I am about to say. I am very, very concerned about the way your Honour has been interrupting my examination-in-chief. This is a very difficult case both for counsel and for the client, who is obviously not a British citizen. I have to concentrate on a vast number of matters in relation to which your Honour has already used terms such as 'peripheral' and 'see where it will lead us to' in front of the jury ... I must say that with your Honour's constant interruptions I am finding it very difficult to concentrate ... Your Honour is not giving me the opportunity to settle the witness into giving evidence. Your Honour is not giving me the opportunity to concentrate on

matters that I know go centrally to his defence and your Honour is also putting me in the unfortunate position of ... impertinence to the bench, which is not intended ...

JUDGE: Counsel, you will not upset me at all ... I have made it clear to you that you shall have as much time as you want subject to the question of wasted costs. So far, according to my timetable, it is no more than 30 minutes. Let me make it clear that counsel owes a duty to display reasonable competence. These matters in relation to the defendant's business, and the like, are matters on which you have been invited by the Crown to lead. I cannot for one moment see how your failure to accept the invitation can be of any benefit to your client. All it seems to me at the moment is that by conducting a cross-examination which seems to go from point to point, without supplying your client with the documents which the court had, which you have, which the jury have, so that he is quite unable to follow your questions, as indeed I am, does not display that level of competence which I would have expected from counsel ...

BLACK COUNSEL: If your Honour thinks I am incompetent so be it.

JUDGE: Please, I said that in my view it did not display the level of competence which I would have expected of counsel and it causes me regret to have to say it ...

Later in this same exchange, the judge used remarks such as 'It is not for me to teach you how to do your job' and said:

... Your incompetence, and my comment about incompetence was directed to the fact that you were trying to examine a witness on a bundle of documents that he did not have.

As it happened, the witness who was being examined *did* have the documents in question. Nonetheless, the judge, without apologising for his own mistake, continued:

I have told you, and I will repeat, that I expect counsel to show the normal level of competence expected from counsel and I have no doubt that you will do your best to achieve that and if you feel that you can lead, then the invitation as I understand it is there and I shall have to consider the position if you fail to follow the invitation and thereby take up more time than is necessary in your conduct of the case.

The jury heard the beginning of this interchange. It demonstrates the need for the anti-racist training offered to judges to go beyond knowing about other people's cultures and to include courtesy to and respect for black lawyers, whose competence should be acknowledged—as it would be in the case of white counsel—by virtue of their position as qualified, trained and often experienced advocates. They should not be belittled in public or before professional colleagues, and certainly not in front of the jury trying the case.

CHAPTER 6

Beatrice's Case

Of the women in the interview sample, I decided to look in greater detail at the answers given by Beatrice. These help to highlight issues discussed in earlier chapters, including the way in which black women perceive that they are treated by the criminal justice process, equality of treatment, stereotyping, assumptions about black people and other aspects of the race-gender-class analysis. Her story also conveniently demonstrates the hazards faced by black women and their sense of powerlessness when confronted by authority. Apart from Beatrice's personal account (see next section), what follows is based on official court transcripts and my own observations whilst attending the last two of the three Crown Court hearings in which she became involved.

BEATRICE'S ACCOUNT

Beatrice went with her boyfriend to visit one of his friends who was staying at a hotel. When they arrived, both were arrested by customs officers. Unknown to her or her boyfriend, his friend had been arrested at Gatwick airport with packets of heroin in his stomach. The customs officers had visited the hotel where the friend had booked a room to see if anyone was awaiting his arrival.

Beatrice protested her innocence at the time (as her boyfriend did his) and told the officers that she knew nothing whatsoever about the man or any drugs. While in police custody she asked if she could telephone her children (both below eleven years of age) to say where she was. Her request was denied on the ground that contacting home could prejudice the enquiry by alerting other people who might be involved in a smuggling operation.

When Beatrice's home was searched nothing of consequence was found other than a 'prayer letter'—written by her—inside her Bible. This was the only significant evidence in her later trial apart from other circumstantial evidence of her visit to the hotel. This prayer letter is reproduced at the end of the chapter.

ARREST AND CHARGE

Beatrice was arrested and charged with being knowingly concerned in evading the prohibition on the importation of a controlled drug, namely heroin. This offence—which concerns a Class A drug—carries a maximum sentence of life imprisonment. However, the allegation was thrown out at the magistrates' court at the committal for trial stage. Put succinctly, that court concluded that there was *insufficient evidence* for the case to be sent to the Crown Court for trial by jury. When the committal proceedings foundered in this way, the prosecutor obtained a voluntary bill of indictment for Beatrice's arraignment to face trial in the Crown Court (a legitimate but comparatively unusual method of securing trial at the Crown Court, though not a matter from which any ultimate conclusions can be drawn in the context of discrimination or differential treatment). Beatrice was re-arrested the same day.

THE PROCEEDINGS

Beatrice took part in four hearings[1] before she was ultimately convicted. The offence is not a palatable one, nor a natural basis upon which to invite sympathy or attention, but this cannot be allowed to obscure the question whether she was treated in the same way that a white suspect or defendant would have been—or whether her explanations and protestations of innocence were given the same attention or credence as those of someone not tainted by white people's assumptions about black women. There were three Crown Court hearings as follows:

- at the first Beatrice was found guilty by an *all-white* jury (a decision later set aside on appeal when a fresh trial was ordered);
- at the second, where the jury was made up half of *black* people and half of *white* people, it could not reach a verdict; and
- at the third, where the jury was *all-white,* she was found guilty.

Whilst nothing can gainsay the decision of the jury in the third—and technically speaking the only valid—trial, Beatrice was angry and bitter at the way she felt she was treated from arrest to conviction and the persistence with which the case was pursued in the light of what seemed to be flimsy evidence.

THE CROWN COURT TRIALS

At the time of our discussions, Beatrice had served almost two years of a seven year prison sentence and was awaiting being deported. It was her first involvement with the criminal law—both she and her co-defendant were of good character and it was accepted by the prosecutor that they had never been in trouble with the law either in this country or abroad. In her own mind, she had no doubt that racism was rife in the criminal justice process and that she had been treated unfairly: because she was black and foreign (even though living in Britain at the time of the offence).

The jury would need to be satisfied beyond reasonable doubt (the criminal standard of proof) that she realised that a prohibited drug was involved and that she was knowingly concerned in its importation. At all stages she denied *any* involvement with the alleged courier of the drugs or *any* knowledge of the drug or its importation. This she repeated at her trial. Everything turned on the interpretation placed by the jury on the visit to the hotel and the prayer letter. There was no independent or direct evidence against her co-defendant either.

Central to the case, the prosecutor called an expert witness—a white British bishop who had lived in Nigeria for 15 years in colonial times among the Ibo—to give his opinion about the true meaning of the letter.

---

[1] Including one set of abortive committal proceedings. It can be noted that committal proceedings as such would disappear under pending legislation, a further concern for BME people.

A conflict of expert opinion

The white British bishop said that the Ibo were deep believers in written charms. In his experience they would put a charm on someone and, referring to the words in the prayer, 'I'm not afraid', he said he had repeatedly come across this kind of charm and that, overall, the letter was a typical charm or 'juju', a prayer for wealth to be obtained by various means. It was, he concluded, concerned with the importation of heroin—about seeking God's help in smuggling heroin and designed to ensure Beatrice did not get caught.

To counter this, the defence called a minister from the Pentecostal church as an expert witness. He was a black man of Jamaican origin, although he lived in Britain. The black minister said that the letter was *not* a charm *nor* a 'juju', but a prayer letter that was common among Pentecostal members. It was typical of such letters and 'asked for deliverance'.

In his summing up to the jury, the judge emphasised how the bishop had lived in Nigeria for 15 years among the Ibo and that he spoke the Ibo language. He also pointed out that the expert witness for the defence had 'recently qualified' as a minister and that he was employed by London Transport. Another statement by the judge that 'maybe the minister's evidence was what he had been told by the defendant' may have implied that the minister was not capable of thinking for himself. The jury of six black people and six white people failed to reach a verdict and there was consequently a retrial.

The retrial

At the retrial—now a third Crown Court ordeal for Beatrice—similar testimony was relied on. The white bishop continued to refer to the prayer letter as a 'charm' or 'juju', stating:

> ... in my opinion, (the prayer letter) is a typical charm or juju against discovery and to protect the bearer and their immediate associates. The writing is couched in biblical language in order to give it power but the language is changed and gives a particular emphasis. An example of this is the part in the prayer which says 'My God gives me power to be rich. The Lord will give me the treasures of the Kingdom of Darkness and hidden riches of secret places of that Kingdom.

This was, he said:

> ... a typical reference to the manner in which drugs are commonly brought from Nigeria to the United Kingdom. The quotation ... 'For the wealth of the wicked is for me the just that I may know' ... refers in my opinion to the profit that can be gained from smuggling drugs.

He continued that the words

> I am not afraid of them be it customs, immigration officers, police both in London and in Nigeria, devil and his cohorts wicked spirit of any order or class spirit of heroin for the Lord my God is with me.

These were typical of a charm to protect against discovery. In his opinion, the same was true of the sentence beginning 'Nobody searcheth me or my baggage'. His final conclusion was:

It may be difficult for someone living in England to understand the power and depth of belief that a charm such as this would have for someone coming from a Nigerian culture. To any Nigerian the reality of the world of the spirit is quite strong, if not stronger than the world of factual and material things … In any enterprise it is therefore important to the Nigerian to protect themselves against bad or malign spirits or influences which might be adverse to the enterprise.

During cross-examination by defence counsel, substantial parts of the letter were accepted by the white bishop as capable of perfectly innocent or alternative interpretations to those put forward by him and consistent with Beatrice's protestations of innocence and the Pentecostal faith, but he refused to place a virtuous interpretation on these items himself:

Q 'Hidden riches' is capable of being construed as a reference to those souls yet to be saved. They are potential riches for the kingdom of God, but they are not yet actual riches because they have yet to come within that Kingdom?
A All that I can say—as you say, you are pressing me on this—is that is not my interpretation. It is not the way I would read it.
Q The Pentecostal Evangelist faith is a very zealous faith, is it not?
A Yes.
Q Zealous, in particular, in saving souls?
A Yes.
Q Souls not yet saved are regarded as souls held by the Devil are they not, in the very literal interpretation the Pentecostalist commonly places upon it?
A That interpretation can be put on it. Yes, it can.
Q The souls of the unbelievers are regarded as 'ripe', if you will forgive that expression, for being brought into the Kingdom of God? They are potential recruits?
A One can put any interpretation on it. I mean, I can only say what I read the total thing to mean. If one abstracts individual sentences and says, 'Could another interpretation not be put on this'? The answer very often is 'Yes.' But it is not the interpretation, reading it in the whole, that I put on it, I am afraid …

It is also worth noting that at the second of the Crown Court trials, this outcome had occurred, in one instance, with the judge's intervention:

Q … if customs, immigration and the police had previously caused a person difficulty or distress, the belief will be not that those people were themselves evil, but that the Devil was employing them to do his evil work through their offices?
A No; I am sorry, I do not think I can place that interpretation on it.
Q If the person has had a great deal of distress brought into their life as a result of contact, innocent or otherwise, with heroin, it is entirely possible that somebody in his faith would name that devil in order to ask God to cast it out, is it not?
A Yes, it is possible.

Judge (intervening)

Q In the terms in which it is done in this letter? If somebody was trying to cast out heroin, because it has affected some part of their life, would you see it written in the way in which it is written here in the context in which it is here?
A No, your Honour, I would not.

It is fair to say that the judge did point out that, at the end of the day, it was a matter for the jury, not the bishop, to decide the status of the letter and what it meant, but by then a message (albeit possibly misleading) may have registered with some members of the jury that the judge may not have thought much of the answers being elicited in cross-examination, and that he preferred answers which were more telling as against the defendant.

In his evidence for the defence, the black Pentecostal evangelist minister disagreed with the white bishop's interpretations. According to him:

It is the custom of many Pentecostal Christians to write prayer letters as a means of asking God to act and help on their behalf for the goodness of personal deliverances or deliverance for others. One of the fundamental beliefs as a Pentecostal is to take the promises of God literally and spiritually.

He went on to explain that the prayer letter was a typical letter from someone who had experienced problems in the past and that in his opinion it was *not* a prayer to protect from discovery of illegal acts or operations. The fact that Beatrice, in the letter, mentions her pastor as well as her husband, he interpreted as meaning that:

She wants her husband to be with her in her faith and she wants her pastor to be stronger or to continue in the faith. In the Pentecostal faith we pray for brothers and sisters who are in the faith and pastors who are leading to lead with simplicity and honesty ... A pastor would not be included in the letter if its intention was for evil or to avoid discovery.

He said that Beatrice had stated that she was not 'afraid' of people or circumstances because God would help her through her troubles. She was asking for help to see her through a difficult period and to cast out the evils from her life:

Many people who have encountered great problems are afraid and use these phrases (as in the prayer letter) to give them strength to face their fear. It is not a prayer against discovery, it is a prayer to give strength to carry on.

Where the prayer letter refers to 'my people' and 'my brothers', the minister considered that it was praying for the whole world to be engulfed in faith. His conclusion was that:

Asking for riches to spread the word of God, to give or to help to instruct in the word of God ... is common to many churches, not only the Pentecostal—it is not a reference to profit that can be made from importing drugs.

Beatrice's evidence
Whilst under arrest and when she later gave evidence in court after electing to go into the witness box and to explain to the jury on oath the meaning of the prayer. Beatrice described the letter as 'a prayer of deliverance and renewal of my life.' She was 'very religious' and of the Pentecostal faith (she had set up bible classes in prison and letters were read out in court written by people on her behalf about her religious beliefs).

Beatrice explained that her husband had been arrested and charged with possession and supply of heroin about a year before she was arrested and charged with the present offence. He was now serving a prison sentence that had caused problems for their marriage and they were now separated. Beatrice believed that *he* was involved with drugs and that this was a result of being influenced by evil spirits. She said that she wanted him delivered from this problem and had written the prayer letter to exorcise the evil influence of heroin. She had written it partly due to police harassment she was suffering due to her husband's activities. She said that '… after my husband's arrest the police would come to my house at any time to search for things and sometimes take pictures of me and my children without prior warning.'

She said that where the prayer mentions protection from 'customs, immigration and police' it was because she feared the blacking of her name as a result of her husband's conviction. She also said that after her husband had been arrested and imprisoned she had started an export and import business to support her children. A customs officer had been to Nigeria to verify this and found no evidence to link her with drugs or wrongdoing. The officer investigated and 'cleared' the business of her co-defendant. It was established that he was a successful businessman with legitimate profits of £42,000 net per year.

The summing up
The essential features of the judge's summing up to the jury are as follows:

> The Crown called, in order to help you (the jury)—to understand the true meaning of this letter, the bishop—He is a bishop and the defence expert witness happens to be a minister in the Pentecostal Church and also a bus driver. It might be tempting to say that it is a bit unfair, bishop obviously outranks him—The bishop is an Anglican, not a Pentecostal but he does have as he told you, at least 15 years of actual experience of ministry in Nigeria and amongst Ibo people. He (the bishop) says this is a letter from his experience of those people practising their Pentecostal religion designed to protect her in her search not for spiritual riches but material riches through the evil trade in heroin. In general the bishop said that although it may seem paradoxical, it is not uncommon, certainly not unheard of, for these prayer letters, apparently couched in religious terms and indeed no doubt penned by persons who believe in the power of their God, to none the less use them to ask for protection from doing something very unchristian which is really the opposite of what the minister was seeking to say to you.

He continued:

> It is right to say, first of all on the plus side, the minister is himself a Pentecostal, although his background is in the West Indies, in particular in Jamaica, and he has absolutely no experience of Nigeria or the Ibo people. So he was speaking from a Pentecostal point of view, but a Pentecostal point of view from either West Indian or English points of view.

The jury retired at 3.32 p.m. and returned with their verdict at 5.17 p.m.—'guilty' in respect of both defendants. There was no pre-sentence report pursuant to the Criminal Justice Act 1991. The judge stated that the probation officers at the prison had said they could not produce one for Beatrice because of pressure of work. Sentencing went ahead without one.

SOME ISSUES RAISED BY BEATRICE'S CASE

Having followed Beatrice's case closely and discussed it at length with a number of people, I believe that the events throw some light on extra-legal factors which may affect decisions to arrest, charge, convict and sentence black women:

- if the prayer letter at the centre of the case had been found on a white person it is unlikely that it would have been given credence without further substantial evidence. But the popular image persists of black people being involved in 'mumbo jumbo', charms, superstition and 'black magic'.

- the judges in both of the last two Crown Court hearings appear to have sought to discredit or undermine the evidence of the black minister who one of them described as 'working for London Transport' and the other as a 'bus driver'. In the interests of avoiding prejudice, this seemingly gratuitous information might have been better avoided altogether, its only real effect being to undermine the evidence of the minister, the implication being that he was not as well qualified or suited to the task of interpretation as the bishop, or that he lacked authenticity or was not clever or intelligent enough for his understanding of theology to count. There were no counter-balancing comments to the effect that the white bishop did not appear to have a particularly high opinion of the African people he had served for 15 years—in respect of whom he uses what many black people would regard as 'racist' and 'contemptuous' remarks—in somewhat outdated, colonial times! He seems to have remained prejudiced in his personal views about the Ibo. Why did the judge choose to give the bishop a fair wind rather than to point out, for example, that it is unlikely a *white* person would understand and relate to Nigerian culture as well as a *black* minister, albeit Jamaican? He simply assumed that the white bishop is capable of being an expert on black people!

- the fact that the bishop lived in Nigeria during colonial times would say a lot about his stereotyping of black people. In that era, black people had no say and were ill-treated by their white masters who simply assumed white superiority.

- the entire proceedings seem to disclose a view of black people as primitive simply because their culture is different to that of the dominant culture of the white majority in Britain. It is nowhere commented on, for example, by the judge that many black people in Britain are exceedingly religious. (One of the ways some black people respond to racism in this country is by turning to the evangelical type churches).

- it is also worth considering the extent to which Beatrice may have been viewed by white jury members as someone whose behaviour or lifestyle were inappropriate to her role as a woman: see, generally, *Chapter 2*. Arguably, this may also have affected the decision to dispense with a PSR and possibly the length of her sentence. The events seem to be littered with examples of where Beatrice may have been sanctioned for 'inappropriate behaviour'. As argued in *Chapter 2*, black women are seen as having a propensity for criminal behaviour that is not matched in the case of white women.

Beatrice's sentence of seven year's imprisonment and the associated recommendation that she be deported after that presented her with a dilemma. She protested her innocence and wanted to appeal, but withdrew her application when it was pointed out to her that if she did not she would have to remain in prison for the decision of the appeal court.

THE PRAYER LETTER

The prayer letter that was at the centre of Beatrice's case is reproduced below. It was typed out, but corrected by hand and is set out in its original form (including the sometimes unusual punctuation—which, in one instance puts a comma at the beginning of a line—insertions and uncorrected spelling), except that the phrases 'spirit of heroin' and 'my husband Frank' each appeared in a loosely drawn box as opposed to just being underlined:

My God gives me power to be rich.
I that wait upon the Lord shall renew my strenght, I shall
mount up with wings as eagles, I shall run and not be weary
and I shall walk free and not faint. for the <u>tree</u> beareth her fruit
               Jesus
, the fig tree and the vine / do yield their strength, I
rejoice in the Lord for he has given me former rain moderately
and will cause it to come down on me, the former rain and the
Latter rain in the <u>forth</u> month then the abundance of God's
blessing will overflow in my Life for the days are at hand to
the effect of every promise and vision in now for I The Lord
of the abundance rain is here   the kingdom
has spoken/for the Lord will give me the treasure of darkness
of   of that kingdom
and hidden riches in secret places, for the wealth of the
wicked is for me the first that I know that My Lord which
I call by name is My God of Abundance and prosperity. Praise God.
       (page 2)
I am strong and of Good Courage I fear not, <u>I am not afraid</u>
<u>of them, be it Customs, immigration officers, police both in</u>
<u>London and in Nigeria, devil and his cohorts, wicked spirit</u>
of any order of class, <u>spirit of heroin</u>, for the Lord my God
is with me. He will not fail me or forsake me, It's He that
go before me, He is with me He will not fail me neighter
                 No body
forsake me. I fear not neighter will I be dismayed. For he has
searcheth me or my baggage   and about my
made a hedge about \ and about my household and about my people
baggages   me
and about the body of Christ and about my brothers and about
               including my
my pastor and about all that I have on every side. He has blessed
children and <u>my husband Frank</u>
the work of my hands and my substance is increased in the Land.
I have travailed and given birth to this and many more and they
had manifested in Jesus name.   Amen

CHAPTER 7

Black Women in Prison

As noted in the *Introduction*, many prisons have become overcrowded. HM Prison Service (HMPS) has an obligation to accept all prisoners sentenced to imprisonment or detention in a young offender institution or remanded in custody by a court. It has no control over the numbers it receives. At the end of May 2002, over 13,000 prisoners were held in overcrowded accommodation, of whom 11,412 were living two to a cell. At the end of July 2002, 93 out of 138 HMPS establishments were overcrowded and this prompted an announcement that police cells would have to be used to contain prisoners, for the first time since 1995.[1] Overcrowding restricts the extent to which prisons are able to meet HMPS key performance indicators (KPIs), i.e. their efficiency and effectiveness targets (and in 2001-2002 the service failed to meet six of these). The KPI on what is termed 'purposeful activity' for prisoners has been met just once in the past seven years. Only 46 per cent of prisons met this target in 2001-2002.

In 2001, a men's jail with 350 places became the third that year to be converted to a women's prison, and HMPS has commissioned two new prisons for women which will create a further 800 places.[2] Both the Lord Chief Justice and Director General of the Prison Service have urged judges and magistrates to think hard before sending women to prison whilst court rulings have acknowledged that the capacity of HMPS to deal with offending behaviour and reduce crime is undermined by overcrowding.[3]

Increasing reliance on prison sentences is described by Smith and Stewart (1998) as 'the most notable penal development of the mid 1990s' and England is generally seen as following the US lead in this. Higher levels of fear of crime have created a climate in which 'protection', 'incapacitation' and 'risk management' are government priorities (Home Office, 1999b).

Ethnic monitoring

Ethnic monitoring of prisoners began in 1984 to assist monitoring of 'race relations' in prisons. The first outcomes in 1986 (Home Office, 1986) showed that in 1985, eight per cent of the male prison population and 12 per cent of the female prison population were of West Indian, Guyanan or African origin, whereas these groups comprised between just one and two per cent of the population generally. Asians made up 2.5 per cent of the male prison population and two per cent of the female prison population, compared with three per cent of the general population. This pattern of disproportionate representation still continues with increasing numbers of black people in prison—and most markedly in relation to women (Bowling and

---

[1] In an effort to overcome the problems of overcrowding, successive governments have embarked on prison building programmes (even if building new prisons has not proved to be an overall solution). In the last ten years, 19 new prisons have been opened. Of these, 15 are already overcrowded (Prison Reform Trust, *Prison Overcrowding: The Inside Story* (2002)).

[2] *Women and Punishment*, 2002.

[3] See *R v. Mills* (14 January 2002) in the context of the increase in the women's prison population. The more frequently cited case is *R v. Kefford* (5 March 2002) in relation to men's prisons.

Phillips, 2001). In England and Wales currently over 15,000 prisoners—some 22 per cent of the total prison population—are from a minority ethnic group. Black prisoners alone account for 15 per cent of the total number in prison and their imprisonment rate is a staggering 934 per 100,000, over seven times that for either Asians or whites (126 per 100,000 and 114 per 100,000 respectively).

Black women's experiences of imprisonment

In October 2002 there were 3,782 adult women and 613 women young offenders (between 15 and 21 years) in prison, giving a total women's prison population of 4,395. In 2000 there were 3,350 women in prison, so that the population had actually increased by almost one-third in just two years. By comparison, in 1991 it stood at 1,510.

Angela Devlin—in her acclaimed work *Invisible Women*[4]—states that black women are routinely regarded as 'troublemakers', heavily supervised, given the harshest punishments and manhandled:

> Six officers—men and women—came along and shouted. 'We're taking you down the block!' They tried to restrain me by grabbing hold of my head. I'd already got a scar on my head from where they restrained me during my last sentence . . . plus I had a bruise on my arm. So I fought them off and they held me by the head. They told me, 'This is the usual procedure', and when they said that I kicked an officer I got 28 days added on for that and ten extra days for pushing an officer. I was a YO[5] but I still got 38 days added on. They manhandled me through that door.

This passage is one of many describing force used on female prisoners as recounted to Devlin. They provide a shocking insight into the cruelties and harshness of prison life. Even more significant, however, was the fact that these accounts of violence all came from one particular group: British-born black women.

The accounts of violence were so numerous and specific to British-born black women that Devlin felt compelled to find out why: 'I wanted to start with a clean slate,' she said, 'I just went in and listened to what the women and officers had to say. I was very shocked at this use of extreme force which I hadn't heard of with white women or foreign nationals.' She struggled to understand why such force was necessary but as she interviewed increasing numbers of prisoners and prison officers a distinct pattern began to emerge. There was a very definite stereotyping (see, generally, *Chapter 1* of this work) of groups of women within prisons, which had seriously negative implications for British-born black women. This is illustrated by two terms commonly used in women's prisons. As Devlin explains in a chapter called 'Poor Mules and Strong Fighters':

> I found distinct differences in the way black British women and foreign national black women are regarded. The term 'poor mules' exemplifies the patronising but often sympathetic attitudes to foreign—in my sample, black African—women serving long sentences for importing drugs from abroad. The term 'strong fighters' refers to the prevailing view among prison officers that black British women prisoners are physically strong, aggressive and often dangerously violent.

---

[4] *Invisible Women: What's Wrong with Women's Prisons?* (1998), Devlin A, Waterside Press.

[5] Young offender, i.e. the term used for offenders below 21 years of age.

The reasons behind this perception, Devlin discovered, were to be found in age-old stereotyping. British black women prisoners were often described as 'big and strong', 'big black girls', 'violent' and 'difficult to control'. Other descriptions used, especially by male officers, were 'loud', 'mouthy', 'gobby' and 'noisy'. These perceptions came across clearly in an interview Devlin held with a white male race relations liaison officer (RRLO) in a women's prison, who said: 'We have no problems with the Indians and Pakistanis. It's the Afro-Caribbeans who are troublemakers. They are a lot noisier and get more excited'.

Devlin believes this has much to do with false equations. 'People seem to think noise equals trouble,' she says. The point was underlined by a black police officer whom Devlin interviewed for another project. The officer spoke of similar misconceptions among his white colleagues when confronted by groups of young African-Caribbean men on street corners:

They'd say, 'These lads are causing trouble, let's nick 'em!' but I'd say, 'They're doing no harm, just listening to loud music and hanging out. That's what happens back home in the Caribbean'.

Devlin found that many of the black women she spoke to seemed able to explain, at least in part, why this misconception occurs. 'Young, black women,' she writes, 'were anxious to point out that though they may appear assertive, noisy and physically tactile, these characteristics should not be misinterpreted as signs of aggression: "That's just what we're like".' But there are many other nationalities well-known for being noisy and expressive, such as Greeks and Italians. There is little evidence to show that these groups are treated any differently from white British women in prison. A false equation is occurring: noisy plus black people equals trouble. Preconceptions about black women could be explained more simply—as old-fashioned racism.

Another generalisation affecting the way black British women are regarded is related to drugs. Devlin states:

Because the offences for which African-Caribbean women are jailed are so often directly or indirectly drug-related there is, they claim, an automatic assumption by staff that they are likely to be using crack cocaine which will make them aggressive and dangerous.

This assumption, combined with cultural stereotyping, builds a forbidding image that has direct consequences for treatment. Although Devlin admits that both black and white prisoners can behave violently, she nevertheless found that British-born black women are subject to heavier supervision, harsher punishment and a prejudice which singles them out as troublemakers from day one.

DEATHS IN CUSTODY

Since the early 1990s there has been a disturbing pattern of deaths in custody following the failures by police officers or prison officers. There have also been a number of deaths following medical neglect. The disproportionate number of deaths, particularly of Africans and African-Caribbeans, following the use of force has reinforced the idea that many of these deaths are a reflection of racism within the police and HMPS and that black people are amongst those singled out for potentially lethal restraint. The repeated failure of the CPS to prosecute prison officers and police officers involved in such deaths, even when there is an inquest verdict of 'unlawful killing', has done little to reduce levels of mistrust within black communities that racially-motivated conduct is tacitly condoned at every level.

Cheryl Hartman

Cheryl Hartman, a 20-year-old black woman, died in HMP Holloway in June 2000. She had a history of self-harm and psychiatric admissions. In 1999 she had been arrested for assault and affray and bailed. The offences were committed whilst under the influence of alcohol and heavy doses of (prescribed) medication. In February 2000 she was taken to hospital suffering from an overdose. On March 24 she appeared and was convicted at the Crown Court and the case adjourned for sentence. Cheryl was remanded in custody and held on the medical wing at HMP Holloway.

Psychiatric reports showed that Cheryl had a 'borderline personality disorder'. One such report concluded: 'Were she given a custodial sentence I would recommend that she continues to receive psychiatric supervision and treatment within HM Prison Service'. The court officer's report recorded her counsel and probation officer's concerns that Cheryl was at risk of self-harm, but this was not conveyed immediately to the prison. She was placed on the psychiatric wing. In May 2000 she was sentenced to nine months detention in a young offender institution (though still held in Holloway), the judge commenting that he hoped the authorities could 'find appropriate help' for her.

She had daily contact with a psychiatrist at the prison and was kept under 15-minute observation. In June she was moved to a dormitory with two other girls in a normal location on the young offenders wing to prepare her for release. The psychiatrist explained to her that if this did not work out she could come back to C1 wing, and recorded in her Inmate Medical Record (IMR): 'If she is not coping—or should deteriorate—we would be willing to take her back'. Hartman was assaulted by another prisoner and sustained a black eye.

On June 12 it was noted that she was 'depressed and trembling' and that she should have an urgent appointment with a psychiatrist. Evidence at the inquest showed that Cheryl was depressed but not suicidal. Despite the entry in her IMR that she could go back to C1 if necessary, the prison psychiatrist was not contacted but it was decided instead to refer Cheryl to a visiting consultant psychiatrist. It was expected that the visiting psychiatrist would see her within 72 hours. This never happened.

On June 13 Cheryl was seen by an education advisor on C1 who had gone to the young offender's wing to check on another inmate with a long history of self-harm and suicide attempts who had been moved to the same dormitory. The advisor was worried that Hartman looked unwell, and the other inmate told her that they had formed a suicide pact, but this was dismissed as that other inmate had made regular gestures of this kind. A meeting was held between the advisor, education officer and Cheryl Hartman and following this and discussions with other staff it was decided that there was no need to open a self-harm form. According to the log: Hartman 'was very distressed . . . and discussed feeling suicidal. I didn't open an F2052 (the self-harm form) following a discussion with [the health advisor] who felt she was much better since Friday . . . and has seen her IMR. General staff discussion felt she is depressed and they will keep an eye on her.'

On June 16 Cheryl was assaulted by another prisoner and it was decided to move her to a single cell the next day. On the morning of June 18, she asked to see a doctor, apparently in a panicky state. A nurse spoke for some time to her through the cell hatch and was concerned enough to make an appointment as soon as possible. Hartman wanted to return to C1 but only a doctor could authorise this. She was apparently informed that an appointment had been made at about 10.10am. At about 10.30 a.m. the officer found her hanging by her dressing gown belt from the cell curtain rail. Resuscitation attempts failed.[6]

Edita Pommel (and other women prisoners)
Another black woman prisoner Edita Pommell was found dead in her cell on 5 May 2000 at HMP Brockhill. She had complained of racial and sexual harassment from a prison officer. There have been investigations of the death of three other female prisoners in the last five years (*Black and Asian Prisoners Guide Book and the Law*, 2000; IRR website).

Zahid Mubarek
There are some 90 to 100 deaths a year in custody on average and black people continue to be over-represented in these figures. In November 2002, the Commission for Racial Equality (CRE) announced that it would launch an investigation into racism in the prison system. Earlier that month, Paul Boateng MP, the then Prisons Minister, had categorised the system as 'institutionally racist' and sought the CRE's assistance to deal with the problem. However, the timing of the CRE's initiative was in direct response to a leaked internal inquiry report following the racist murder of Asian teenager Zahid Mubarek by his cellmate Robert Stewart at Feltham young offender institution (YOI) and Stewart's conviction for that offence.

On 21 March 2000, Mubarek was clubbed into a coma by Stewart, aged 20, at 3.40 a.m., just five hours before he was due to be released. Stewart had battered the sleeping Zahid eleven times with a table leg that he had dislodged weeks before the crime. When Zahid was sentenced to 90 days in prison for shoplifting razor blades worth £6 and interfering with a motor vehicle, he and his family were shocked at the severity of the penalty. This was his first offence. Zahid was genuinely sorry and wrote five or six letters to his parents indicating his desire to become more constructive and positive about life. In a letter written a month before the assault, dated February 23, Stewart reveals a chilling intention to kill Zahid. 'If I don't get bail on the seventh I'll take extreme measures to get shipped

---

[6] Mrs Hartman, Cheryl's mother, a diabetic, was alone at home when informed by telephone by the prison that her daughter was dead. Other family members heard of Cheryl's death over the radio. The police told them that the prison had refused to pass on the family's details to enable them to inform family members personally of Cheryl's death. The family had real difficulty in finding out where Cheryl's body had been taken to—and prison staff gave conflicting information as to how she died. There was no personal visit or letter of condolence from the prison. The organization Inquest complained to the prison about how family was treated and a letter of apology was received. It is not known whether procedures have been reviewed to ensure that this does not occur again. For further details, see *Inquest Law Issue*, No. 5, Spring 2002.

out. I'll kill me fucking pad mate if I have to—bleach me sheets and pillowcases white and make myself a Ku Klux Klan outfit and walk out of me pad holding a flaming cross'.

Four months before the attack, Stewart was seen by a registered mental health nurse who concluded that he had a 'longstanding, deep-seated personality disorder.'[7] The family was promised a full and comprehensive inquiry. The internal report is divided into two parts. Part II, unpublished at the time of writing, is expected to consider issues relating to racism in Feltham YOI. Part I of the report was leaked shortly after Stewart's conviction. Conducted by a senior Home Office investigator, it is wholly critical of the prison as an institution but fails to hold any individual to account for the glaring mistakes made. The 50 page report blames a mixture of poor management and communication, outdated emergency plans, a failure in the prisoner screening operation, staffing crises and failure of staff to follow operational procedures, for not being alert to the danger that Stewart posed. The report also pinpoints plentiful evidence that Stewart was a dangerous and violent racist but this was not seen or was ignored by staff making crucial decisions on cell allocations.

Alton Manning

In May 2000, the Lord Chief Justice ruled that the decision of the Director of Public Prosecutions (DPP) not to bring criminal proceedings against any of the officers involved in the restraint-related death of black prisoner Alton Manning at HM Prison Blakenhurst in December 1995 was flawed and must be reconsidered. Further, a press release issued in the name of the DPP to announce the refusal to prosecute in February 1999 did not accurately reflect the true basis of the decision, and that the DPP is under an obligation to give an accurate, reasonable and plausible explanation for a decision not to prosecute in such cases:

> The right to life is the most fundamental of all human rights . . . The death of a person in the custody of the state must always arouse concern . . . If the death resulted from violence inflicted by agents of the state that concern must be profound . . . Where an inquest [into a death] . . . culminates in a lawful verdict of unlawful killing implicating [an identifiable individual] the ordinary expectation would naturally be that a prosecution would follow . . . In the absence of compelling grounds for not giving reasons, we would expect the director to give reasons in such a case.

In essence, the Lord Chief Justice accepted that allegations of ill-treatment or a death in custody require an effective official investigation capable of leading to identification of those responsible for unlawful violence and their punishment through a criminal prosecution. In the absence of such an investigation and ensuing prosecution, legal protection of human rights would be ineffective in practice because it would be possible in some cases for agents of the state to abuse the rights of those within their control with virtual impunity. A decision is awaited.

---

[7] *Legal Action*, January 2001, pp.6, 7. For a comparable case (this time involving a white family but equally disturbing), see *No Truth, No Justice* (2002), Edwards A, Waterside Press.

RACE RELATIONS LIAISON OFFICERS (RRLOs)

For several years now there have been race relations officers (RRLOs) in all prisons. But even where trained RRLOs are available the belief among black women that reporting an incident of violence or racism may further stigmatise them as troublemakers, resulting in loss of privileges such as visits from children and other family members. In defence of HMPS, it was stated:

> It is our aim to make reporting an incident as easy as possible. To help that process we have complaint forms in various parts of the prisons so prisoners don't have to ask the governor and can therefore make a complaint more discreetly. The staff who handle complaints receive special training in addition to the race relations training. If allegations [of racism or violence] are made against a member of staff it is a disciplinary matter and we take it very seriously.[8]

Prison Service staffing and initiatives

So far as prison staff are concerned, five members of the HMPS's 1,020 senior management governor grades (0.49 per cent) and 354 out of 19,325 prison officers (2.4 per cent) are from minority ethnic groups.[9] HMPS has developed a comprehensive race relations policy. In individual prisons, RRLOs have been appointed and race relations management teams established to implement the service's policies.[10] A *Race Relations Manual* was introduced in 1991. Governors are required to set targets for the recruitment of prison officers from minority ethnic groups. Training on race issues has been reviewed and updated, as have the Prison Rules under which prisoners can be dealt with for racially motivated disciplinary offences. An offence of 'racially discriminatory behaviour' is also now included in the HMPS staff disciplinary code.

SOME ASPECTS OF WOMEN'S IMPRISONMENT

Aspects of the way in which the police use mental health powers to ensure that black women are taken to a 'place of safety' are mentioned in *Chapter 3*.

Distance from home

Because there are fewer women's prison establishments, women are more likely to be held at a distance from their homes, with all that this entails for family ties, visits by relatives and children, and probation officers or social workers from their home area. Mounting pressure on accommodation has meant that less attention is now paid to social or rehabilitative factors than the immediate task of finding available space.[11]

The Social Exclusion Unit (2002) found that black prisoners, in particular, are less likely to receive visits than white or other ethnic minority prisoners, e.g. 30 per cent of white female prisoners surveyed in 2000 received regular visits from

---

[8]   The prison 'requests and complaints' system has since been revised.
[9]   'Race Discrimination and the Criminal Justice System', NAPO and ABPO, 1996.
[10] 'Race and Criminal Justice', Penal Affairs Consortium, September 1996.
[11] 'The Imprisonment of Women: Some Facts and Figures', Penal Affairs Consortium, March 1996.

spouses and partners compared to 15 per cent of black women; 28 per cent of white women were visited by children compared to 15 per cent of black women. Despite black people being over-represented in the prison population there remains paucity in research on 'what works' for them.[12]

Foreign women

As already indicated, a significant proportion of women prisoners are foreign nationals, often serving sentences for drugs offences, including the importation of illegal drugs into the United Kingdom. In addition to the problems usually associated with imprisonment, such women—who are often young black women—face additional difficulties in coping with an alien culture, language problems, isolation, lack of family contact, and acute anxiety about the welfare of children who are either in care or in poverty-stricken conditions in their home country.

Up to a third of women in prison in England and Wales are drug couriers from other countries who will be deported after serving a prison sentence.[13]

Discrimination in custody in relation to black women and women from other ethnic minorities may also include, particularly for foreign women, a paucity of basic information in their own language and lack of a comprehensive or adequate interpreting service,[14] poor catering for special diets, access to appropriate cosmetic products and a failure to access education classes because foreigners, above all black women, are seen as problematic in this last regard.

The *Prison Statistics* show that there are over 7,000 foreign national prisoners in England and Wales (see also now the *Postscript* at p.140) spread across nearly every prison in the country. London has the highest concentration of foreign national prisoners, comprising at least a quarter of the population in each establishment. In HM Prison Brixton and HM Prison Wandsworth they number 300-350, while in Wormwood Scrubs, which caters for most Heathrow airport arrests, the foreign national population is in excess of 50 per cent.

Black women's special difficulties

All women in prison experience difficulties, but for black women there are additional burdens that they encounter on remand, during sentence or on release. These women experience discrimination in prison in many ways. The prison system, in common with other parts of the criminal justice process, was established and designed by and for men and white people. This is evident at all levels: from life-sentence prisoners[15] and services for mentally disordered offenders[16] to lack of appropriate provision for women during sentence and on release.[17]

---

[12] Further aspects of the effects on families are noted in *Chapter 1*.
[13] For an overview, see *Drugs, Trafficking and Criminal Policy: The Scapegoat Strategy* (1998), Green P, Waterside Press.
[14] *Interpreters and the Legal Process*, Colin J and Morris R, Waterside Press, 1996.
[15] 'Women Lifers: Assessing the Experience' (1988), Player E, Cropwood Series.
[16] 'Review of Health and Social Services for Mentally Disordered Offenders' (1992) (The 'Reed Report'), London: HMSO.
[17] 'Post-Release Experiences of Female Prisoners' (1988), Wilkinson C, Cropwood Series.

Stereotypes

The stereotype of the black woman mentioned in *Chapter 1*—for many prison officers a negative stereotype—affects the way black women are treated. Wilson states that:

> We (black women) are ... mad and we commit crime and we sponge off the system ... etc. Black women are not even allowed the patronising treatment of being seen as 'fragile little creatures' who must be protected. We are supposed to be able to cope in whatever situations arise. In prison, for example, black women are often viewed as so violent that they have to be dealt with by male officers ... [18]

Racism

The *Race Relations Manual* for prison officers mentioned earlier in this chapter indicates that racist behaviour or abuse is a serious disciplinary matter. When the manual was first launched in 1991, Angela Rumbold MP, then the Home Office minister with responsibility for prisons, said:

> We all know that discrimination does still occur in our prisons, against both prisoners and staff. Some is overt, perhaps racial abuse of prisoners or harassment of ethnic minority officers. While some is unintentional, like stereotyping which leads to false assumptions about a person's behaviour ... I ... firmly believe that prisoners ... regardless of colour, race or religion, should be treated with equality, humanity and respect.[19]

She emphasised race and colour without mentioning gender, as if racial discrimination is not sometimes—as argued throughout this book—linked to gender or class discrimination. Although it would appear that she recognised that religion can be connected to race, the Home Office has consistently refused to recognise Rastafarianism as a religion, thereby exposing black women Rastafarians to a form of institutionalised discrimination.

Genders and Player (1989) found that some prison officers held racist views and that the prevailing perception of most prison officers was that Asians are 'clean', 'hard-working' and 'no-trouble' whilst blacks are 'arrogant', 'hostile to authority' and have 'chips on their shoulders'. RRLOs sometimes had a difficult time with their colleagues—one was referred to as 'The Sambo-Samaritan'.[20]

Prison visits and prisoners' families

Lucy Gampell of Action for Prisoners' Families (APF)[21] writing in *Criminal Justice Matters* (No. 50, Winter 2002-3), states that the size of the prison population is having a 'devastating' effect on families. Not only are more children, partners and parents facing the trauma of separation and loss caused by imprisonment itself, but prisoners are being held further from their homes, making the logistics of visiting increasingly difficult. Pressure on telephone lines when booking visits

---

[18] 'Black Female Prisoners and Political Awareness' (1985), Black Women in Prison.
[19] Nacro, 1992.
[20] *Race Relations in Prisons* (1989), Genders E and Player E, Clarendon Press.
[21] Formerly the Federation of Prisoners' Families Support Groups. APF exists to draw attention to the effect of imprisonment on the family, influence policy that impacts on prisoners' families and ensure that support and information is made available to those families who need it through a nationwide network of support services.

means some families give up trying and even if they do get to the prison heightened security and inadequate visitors' facilities mean the experience is often a poor one. Although there have been improvements, many prisons still do not have a properly resourced visitors' centre.

Families can and should play a major part in the resettlement of people coming out of prison. The Social Exclusion Unit (SEU) report, *Reducing Re-offending by Ex-prisoners* (2002) identified family ties as one of nine key factors in reducing re-offending. The report contains a detailed analysis of the problem faced by families and the current failure of the prison system and others to ensure they can realise their potential as a positive resource.

Conservative estimates suggest that over 140,000 children a year face the ·experience of a parent being in prison that can lead to anxiety, depression, anger, grief, absence from school, stigma, isolation and a change in their care environment. The Department of Education and Skills has recently revised its guidance to schools on warranted leave of absence, including about aspects of parental imprisonment.

Research consistently highlights a range of risk factors associated with future criminality as including poor parental supervision, harsh or erratic discipline, parental conflict, and separation from a biological parent (Bright, 1992). Domestic violence and a parent in prison are also well documented as risk factors, as are low income, poor housing, deprived neighbourhoods and socially disorganized communities. [22]

Black prison officers

Racism occurs against black *officers* as well. A black prison officer who suffered racial discrimination and victimisation at Brixton prison was awarded record compensation of more than £28,000 by an industrial tribunal in 2002. Claude Johnson, aged 36, a prison auxiliary, was ostracised after he complained that he had seen five officers beating up a black inmate. He was subjected to sustained hostility for more than three years, according to the tribunal ruling.

The case coincided with a new full-page HMPS recruitment advertisement in the ethnic minority press inviting applications from black men and women. The hard-hitting advertisements included personal case histories from black prison staff that openly acknowledged that there is racism behind the prison gates and recorded how they deal with it.

Nicola Francis, who worked at HM Prison Holloway from 1990, is quoted as saying: 'There is discrimination—it's little things. You get racist jokes and you are expected to laugh along with it but that is the way with British people generally, I think. When I joined, some of the people on my course had never seen a black person before.' Johnson said he only learned that HMPS had a race relations policy when he went to the tribunal. The tribunal added that the award would have been higher if the governor had not acknowledged that changes were needed.

Black women prisoners may not report incidents and keep silent because they believe there is nothing to gain by complaining and they do not want to be viewed by staff as 'troublemakers'. Many in my interviews did not know that there were specialist race relations staff.

---

[22] See further *Criminal Justice Matters*, No. 50, Winter 2002-2003.

A report by the Oxford University Centre for Criminological Research found a wide gap between the low number of racial incidents recorded by HMPS and the large number reported to the Oxford researchers, confirming that black people in prison are at a disadvantage, and subjected to racism because of their skin colour, including: victimisation by prisoners and staff, unfair treatment over access to facilities and education, racial abuse and harassment, unfair discipline, bullying and assault.[23]

Religion in prison

One Nacro survey found the provision of facilities with regard to religion not to be the same in all establishments. It cannot be the same in all prison establishments, but religious beliefs can play a significant part in resettlement, particularly for those receptive to the teachings of their faith. It was observed that recognising the practice of different faiths is beneficial for resettlement, especially when community groups are involved. This supports my earlier findings that where black women prisoners were allowed to attend a nearby Pentecostal church they found that they drew strength from their faith and it helped them to cope with the stress of prison life. This is also supported by certain of the women I interviewed for this book. Nacro found that some Muslim prisoners faced additional discrimination based on religion as well as race.

Education in prison

Improving knowledge and skills can have a profound effect on resettlement. Black women in this research talked about education as being the key to their economic independence when they left prison. This is echoed in the findings from the National Prisoners Survey 1991 and the Nacro Survey on Race and Prisons. A snapshot survey indicated a strong interest in education and training before release among minority prisoners. The main findings were:

- black and Asian prisoners (61 per cent) were more likely to attend education and training classes, where they were offered, than white prisoners (44 per cent)
- among those who did not attend classes, more black and Asian prisoners (62 per cent) than white prisoners (44 per cent) said they would like to do so
- 78 per cent of black prisoners thought the classes would be useful after release, compared to 64 per cent of white prisoners
- 66 per cent of black prisoners said they would find employment training useful as preparation. For release, compared to 54 per cent of white and 46 per cent of Asian prisoners.

In Nacro's (2002) report the interviewees complained that the prison establishment did not provide an atmosphere conducive to learning. Respondents in the study felt that much more could be done with regard to education in prison.

---

[23] 'Reported and Unreported Racial Incidents in Prisons' (1994).

Hassan (2000) found that black prisoners saw education about black history as a way of increasing awareness among prisoners that could eventually lead to behavioural changes.

Applications and petitions

Offences *against* prisoners should be treated as seriously as offences *by* prisoners. The chain of communication for complaints (known as applications) starts with wing officers (i.e. the prison officer in charge of the prison wing or a comparable section of a prison), who are often those against whom the complaints were made, so that not all serious complaints reach the prison governor or the Home Office by way of petition.

Prison discipline[24]

Aspects of discipline in prison have been touched upon already. Padel and Stevenson state that:

> Women prisoners are disciplined more than twice as often as men . . . 3.6 offences were punished per head of the female prison population as against 1.6 per head of the male prison population. A much higher proportion of Prison Rules offences committed by women fall into the 'mutiny or violence' category than those by men, which is surprising given that all the major prison riots have occurred in men's prison.[25]

The Prison Rules now contain a number of disciplinary offences referable to racism.

Prison jobs

The benefits of providing relevant work experience in prison cannot be overstated as this gives an essential grounding for employment beyond prison, which in turn creates a regular income, builds self-confidence and reduces the chances of social exclusion. This is supported by a Nacro report (1991) that found a link between inadequate housing, unemployment and offending: about 70 per cent of people being supervised by the probation service were then unemployed.

Nacro's survey (2002) also found that work was regarded negatively within prisons, with one prisoner commenting that 'work, as with most other things, is used as tools to control inmates. This is true for black prisoners who are made to work either as cleaners or in the service'. Another comment was that are 'the percentage of black people working is less than white prisoners. Prison jobs were given out on the basis of your colour'. This view was reinforced by another inmate who commented that 'black people are less likely to get employed in the prison as well as outside'.

Almost all respondents who completed the Nacro (2002) questionnaire faced problems finding a job and a place to live. BME groups explained that their ethnicity, previous convictions and prison sentence(s) weighed heavily against

---

[24] At the time of writing the prison disciplinary system had experienced a period of disarray following the ruling of the European Court of Human Rights in *Okichukwiw Ezeh and Lawrence Connors v. United Kingdom* (15 July 2002) that the practice of governors adjudicating offends the fair trials provisions of Article 6 of the European Convention on Human Rights.

[25] *Insiders: Women's Experience of Prisons* (1988), Padel U and Stevenson P, Virago, 10.

them in the job market. With insufficient means of financial support, about three-quarters of those questioned remarked that they were forced into crime and found themselves back in prison. Almost all had no job to go to.

The same report also found that discrimination in the workplace was racially directed. One respondent at a job interview was told that he had not been successful but was not told why, or how he could have done better. He said black women face a dual discrimination by being black and a woman.

Seemingly, black people can be systematically discriminated against and allocated the worst jobs—labouring and cleaning, whilst the better jobs are given to white prisoners. The case of *Alexander v. Home Office*[26] also emphasises the problem some black prisoners may face in this regard, and similarly in other areas whenever discretion is exercised in prison. In Wandsworth and Parkhurst prisons, Alexander's assessment report and induction report contained the following remarks:

> He displays the usual traits associated with people of his ethnic background being arrogant, suspicious of staff, anti-authority, devious and possessing a very large, chip on his shoulder which he will find very difficult to remove if he carries on the way he is doing ... He is an arrogant person who is suspicious of staff and totally anti-authority.

> He has been described as a violent man with a very large chip on his shoulder which he will have great difficult in removing. He shows the anti-authoritarian arrogance that seems to be common in most coloured inmates.

The prisoner was awarded damages of £1,000. Some black women prisoners may also get 'shit jobs'. For example, a black woman ex-prisoner complained that 'Most of the jobs they give you (in prison) are to make you into a good housewife: cleaning, scrubbing, knitting and sewing'.[27]

Generally speaking research into work done by women prisoners has tended to focus on that allocated to women in general and therefore has not analysed how racism plays a part. Although most problems identified, including isolation from family and children, affect foreign black men as well, the situation of black women is compounded by the finding that foreign black women keep themselves to themselves more than foreign black men when in prison.[28]

Resettlement

Family support during imprisonment is important as it plays a crucial part in resettlement of ex-prisoners back into the community. Imprisonment can be a testing time for families—of working to strengthen the family bond or simply to server it. There are only 19 women's prisons out of 138 and women are often held far away from relatives and friends. For black women the problem is even greater in that in the places where some of the prisons are located there are hardly any black communities (e.g. HMP Askham Grange) and this also means that there are in some cases no black prison officers or black probation officers. This can result in prisoners feeling vulnerable and further isolated.

---

[26] 1988 WLR 968.
[27] *Channel 4*, 19 September 1991.
[28] 'Drug Couriers', Green P, Howard League, 1991.

Financial, accommodation and other worries

Many women prisoners have money worries while in prison and some suffer depression and other mental illness. Family support is crucial in that it can provide emotional support, and can help on a more practical level by providing a home even if only 'in the background'. There are disparities in the housing market and this has resulted in ex-offenders having difficult in securing accommodation. For black women the problem is compounded by race. In the general housing market, black people and Asians are more likely to be, e.g. segregated, excluded from public sector and private sector housing, allocated poor housing and to be diverted into more financially vulnerable housing associations. This partly explains the difficulties black people have in retaining a home while in prison and finding one upon release. In cases where families are unable to help, the National Probation Service (NPS) or voluntary sector organizations dealing specifically with ex-offenders from BME communities may be able to offer support.

Community contacts

Prisoners in the Nacro survey (2002) (above) claimed that contact with community groups brought them hope, and the idea of support from any kind of social or cultural group was well received. It was suggested that such groups could help in the process of resettlement by offering advice and support in social, cultural and financial matters. One respondent in the study said: 'I would have liked to get more support from relevant agencies who could understand my problems and me, especially when you are sent to an area where you are in a minority'. In Nacro's survey, on BME and resettlement needs, two prisoners said that they 'expected quality time with their probation officers rather than just merely signing in and attending what they considered to be pointless meetings every two weeks'. This was also echoed in my earlier research. The Nacro discussion group is said to have emphasised repeatedly that they needed more support from community and statutory agencies for meaningful resettlement after release. 'If we aren't settled how will our kids ever get settled?' was one question asked.

Black women prisoners' specific resettlement needs

Black women have special resettlement needs. These needs can be affected by their cultural backgrounds, the importance of family duties and responsibilities isolation and social stigma faced if they were drug users and by their colour. Black women have to overcome discrimination as well as class and gender issues.

INTERVIEWS

I talked to the women about their experiences in prison, their relationships with prison officers and prison life in general. Over two-thirds of them were in open prisons, two in closed prisons and two under probation service supervision (but had served prison terms in the past). Despite the obvious disadvantages they would face in the future as black women and now ex-prisoners, many of them, especially the older women, had decided to spend their prison sentence as constructively as they could and 'to do something about their situation'.

Education and prison jobs

Most of the women felt that education was a way to a better life, even if provision was diminishing and, so it appeared to them, geared mainly to white women and English-speakers. Some *were* able to take courses and were planning to use the resulting certificates to get a job on release:

> I have spent my time in prison constructively, and have done a few City and Guilds courses. When I leave here all I want is a job and to start all over again. (Angela)

> I go to college outside prison and am doing a secretarial course—I am sitting for my exams next month. I really want to pass. I find education in prison to be only basic. (Dawn)

> I'm doing a hairdressing course at college outside prison so that when I go out I can have my own business and look after my children. (Geraldine)

In open prison it seems that all the women were encouraged to take up education regardless of the colour of their skin. Half were attending classes and were looking at this as their last opportunity to improve their job prospects on release. It follows that half were *not* attending classes, for whatever reason. A black woman prison teacher I interviewed for another project said that she never had any black women in her class and each time she asked about the black women who had put forward their names to attend she was told there were not enough officers to escort them. Again, it may be that black women do not get places because of preconceived notions that they are problematic.

Some of the women complained about lack of continuity of education provision when transferred to another prison:

> There is no continuity—so if you are moved from one prison to another there is no guarantee that in that prison they do that course. For example, where I was before I came here I was doing painting and decorating there, and here they do not do it. (Karen)

The women said that in the closed prisons where they had been sent before being transferred. It was difficult for them to attend education classes as there were not enough prison officers to escort them:

> I'm doing an information and technology—City and Guilds—course. I'm hoping to pass it. (Dawn)

> I'm starting a course in catering in September. I'm looking forward to it. (Karen)

Those women with children in prison appeared to have practical problems with attending classes regularly:

> I attend home economics classes but sometimes I have to miss the class as we take it in turns to look after the children. (Doreen)

> I cannot attend education classes because I'm having difficulties in studying at night as the lights are turned off at 10 p.m. and the dim light comes on—this is affecting my eyes ... I want to study because I now realise that it is time for me to do something ...

to qualify in something so that when I go out I can get a job. I really want to do a child care course so that I can work with children. (Miriam)

Those who were worrying about their children back at home not having enough to live on tended to work rather than attend education classes as this meant having more money, however little. The job allocation system was considered fair in one open prison, even though most of the jobs were in the kitchen or gardening and the women were pleased to be allowed to attend a nearby Pentecostal church which 'helped to keep their spirits up'. Two were doing what they described as 'fulfilling' community work.

Prison officers

All the women expressed displeasure at the way prison officers treated black women prisoners in the closed prison (where each of them had been at some time or other during their sentence). They were more critical of younger officers, for example.

You can only talk to the older prison officers. The older ones are better—the younger ones abuse their power. (Cora)

Ten of the women felt that prison officers were fair but had to look 'tough' and so behaved differently in front of their colleagues. The women felt isolated or used:

Some of them rarely talk to you. When you are in prison what you need is someone you can talk to, someone who can listen to your problems. (Judith)

Some officers were not interested in your problems, but gossip. They only wanted you to tell them about other inmates. (Lorraine)

In that prison I would say all the prison officers are the same regardless of colour. You just had to do what you were told so you were not put on report. (Margaret)

Twelve of the women felt that foreign black women were subjected to harsher treatment. For example, Karen said:

Foreign black women have it tough in prisons ... some of them can't speak English and the prison officers don't bother to explain the rules to them. Most of these women don't know their rights.

Similarly, Maxine and Miriam, respectively, said:

I felt that they were making their rules as they went along. Black women were treated differently—in most cases it was black women who were put on report.

I had to do everything they said because I was missing my children. I wanted to be out as soon as possible. After all, I was only there for failing to pay a fine.

Josephine, talking about her experience at a closed prison, said:

The prison where I was taken to first time, the prison officers there gave me a hard time. I went to ask for some breakfast for my son and happened to mention about variety of food for children—and the prison officer said what do you know about choices—and went as far as saying black people live in huts. I kept quiet because I did not want to be put on report.

Some of the women I interviewed in open prison who seemed reasonably happy with the treatment they were receiving:

The officers here are good ... you can't complain—we all get on well. (Dawn)

They are easy going here—if you don't bother them they won't bother you. There are one or two odd ones though—I wish we had at least one black prison officer or probation officer. (Jane)

Here prison officers are OK. The food is better than in other prisons. There are no black officers though. (Lorraine)

It would appear that a prison officer who is prepared to listen to women's problems is seen as a good officer:

Prison officers here are good. They have time to sit with you and listen to your problems ... You do get one or two odd ones. (Fumi)

In my earlier study, interviewees felt that women in prison who self-mutilate do so because officers do not have time to listen to women's problems. Others said:

When you are in there a lot of things get you down. Women worry about their children, about losing their homes. The officers should sit down and talk to them. (Miriam)

Thus the women felt that prison officers should have more time to talk and to listen to their problems, and this was seen as a way of reducing tensions and problems, including self-harm.

All the women talked about privileges and how they could be withdrawn for trivial matters. Sixteen of them felt that racism played a part.

I feel if an officer takes a dislike to you or if she is racist ... you have your privileges withdrawn more. The officers abuse their power. (Jackie)

The women also felt that they were treated like children:

... to keep on their right side you have to behave like a child ... and do as you are told kind of thing. (Maureen)

Prison discipline[29]
Another problem which was raised by the women was being put 'on report' for minor infringements. This happened to all women but black women felt it was

---

[29] See footnote 24 above.

happening to them more so. Judith was not happy with the advice she had received from the prison governor whilst in prison. She said:

> I absconded when I was first sent to prison—this was a closed prison. I absconded because I was missing my children. I had four children at that time—I got pregnant whilst out. The governor at that prison said 'I'm giving you motherly advice and you must have an abortion—and she was telling the nurses to make me make my mind up quickly as time was running out. I did not plan it—it happened—it was an accident. I just could not bring myself to kill a human being. At times I was confused and used to cry a lot.

At the time when I interviewed Judith, she was pregnant with her sixth child and expecting the baby the following month. This was her second pregnancy whilst in prison and she was in prison with her existing child. She said that:

> When I went home on leave I got pregnant for the second time … Its my luck. I've been crying ever since I got pregnant. The prison officers here are supportive. My boyfriend is supportive and he comes to visit. (Judith)

Some writers have considered that penal policy continues to be dominated by beliefs about women which were pre-eminent at the turn of the century and which reflect moralistic theories about normality and deviance. Dobash, Dobash and Gutteridge found that women in prison are more closely observed, controlled and punished than men, often for more trivial offences.[30] A report by HM Chief Inspector of Prisons endorses this.[31]

Racism

One woman who was refused temporary release at the closed prison when her mother was ill in hospital because she was a deportee said:

> There is racism in prison … The law says one thing and in prison they have their own law. What I found at that prison was that black women were not given temporary release but foreign non-black deportees were allowed to go outside prison to attend college or work. (Dawn)

And others:

> They are horrible to foreign black women, reminding them all the time about where they come from and saying how lucky they are to have this and that. (Jackie)

> The way they talk to you it's like you are nothing—like you are dirty. (Miriam)

> I was put on report for what they called aggressive behaviour, but I was only talking to my friends. (Katherine)

Fumi complained about the state of the toilet. According to her the prison officer replied:

---

[30] *The Imprisonment of Women* (1986), Dobash R E, Dobash R P and Gutteridge S, Basil Blackwell.
[31] *Report of H M Chief Inspector of Prisons 1988* (1989), London: HMSO.

You are lucky to have one... In your own country you would have to go to the bush.

Black women get put on report for 'kissing their teeth', which is considered rude by white officers. When black women are talking they tend to be loud and expressive and when they see a friend they tend to get excited and use their hands to express themselves. This is often misconstrued as aggressive behaviour and some women were put on report for it—in effect for behaving differently to whites.

Strip searches
Eighteen of the women talked about strip searches which every prisoner is subjected to on her first day in prison and also when transferred from one prison to another. They felt that there should be a private room for this purpose:

> I did not like to be strip searched in front of the officers. It is very embarrassing and humiliating. (Miriam)

Ten of the women believed that black visitors were subjected to strip searches more than other people:

> When it is a black woman they really do a thorough search. I did not have many visitors in prison ... Who would want to come and be strip searched like that? (Jackie)

> When it is a black visitor they really harass them and take their time in strip searching them. (Maureen)

Food and hygiene
All the women expressed concern about prison conditions. They said one prison was very dirty and talked about cockroaches, especially at the closed prison. One woman said:

> I was in a dormitory with eight women. We all used the same sink. It was pathetic. In prison you can catch anything. (Dawn)

Ten of the women complained about the food. They felt that better and healthier food should be provided for themselves (and where appropriate for their children). One woman said:

> I lost two stones whilst in prison. I could not eat the food. My face was so spotty. Nobody could recognise me on release. (Maxine)

Those women with children with them in prison complained about the food the children were getting:

> You have to buy decent food from your child benefit money. The food for the children is not good and there is no variety—children are not given fruits. (Annette)

Medication
The women felt that that what women needed was counselling rather, e.g. than psychotropic drugs. The higher rates of offences against prison discipline and the

extensive prescription of tranquillisers and other drugs to female prisoners supports a claim that women's dependency aggravates their emotional and physical isolation.[32] As Bardsley recorded:

> One woman went in for importing cannabis. She came out addicted to Largactil.[33]

Visits
Several of the women talked about prisons being too far from their homes for relatives to travel. They said their families could not afford the fares, but they would have liked visits. For foreign women, isolation is compounded by not having visitors nor receiving money from outside to buy essentials. Some of the foreign women lacked adequate clothing, as they were arrested at ports of entry with only one set of clothes and unsuitable shoes. Penny Green notes that:

> Women prisoners do not wear prison uniforms. They are therefore immediately disadvantaged if they have no friends or family to provide clothes for them. The vast majority of foreign national couriers arrive in Britain with an expectation of staying only five or so days—they bring enough clothes only for these few days, and if they arrive in summer they have no clothing adequate for the British winters ahead. Those they have with them are then all they have when they find themselves imprisoned for six to ten years. One Nigerian woman interviewed burst into tears and lifted her blouse to show she had no underwear at all, her plastic sandals were totally inadequate for the British climate. [34]

Children
A reason why some of the women from the United Kingdom were in an open prison was because they had their children with them, and therefore needed a mother and baby unit which does not exist in all women's prisons. Others were pre-occupied with worries relating to their children in the world outside, about how they were coping (this being magnified in the case of foreign women with children who were still abroad). They also worried about them not having enough money to live on. Some felt guilty about having friends or relatives looking after their children while they were in prison:

> You see the system is not fair. My friend who is herself unemployed is looking after my children and now the social security deduct money from her benefits because of my children. I feel bad about it. (Pam)

> The area I live in there is only whites there. I'm worried about my son because he is experiencing racism at school. (Alithea)

The women said that they preferred their own families to look after their children but realised the financial constraints when relatives were already 'struggling to make ends meet'. The women there were happy that they were able to go home for overnight leave every fortnight or once a month, as they could be with their children.

---

[32] 'Sex and Sentencing', Morris A, *Criminal Law Review* (1988), 163-171; Campell D, *The Guardian*, 11 January 1993.

[33] *Flowers in Hell* (1987), Bardsley B, Pandora/Routledge, Kegan and Paul, p.75.

[34] *Drugs, Trafficking and Criminal Policy: The Scapegoat Strategy* (1998), Waterside Press.

I'm worried about my children. A friend is looking after them. I go home on leave every fortnight. They used to pay for your travelling expenses if you were doing a long sentence. They have stopped it . . . (Lorraine)

Foreign women find themselves in a situation where they might be unable to see their children for, say, five or more years—and may not be able to get in touch with relatives abroad to find out about them. Often these women do not make child-care provisions in the hope or belief that they will be back within a week or so. They are told by drug barons that if caught they will be put on the next plane home. When they are sent to prison their children are left on their own with provisions for a week or so, or with relatives or friends who are told that the mother 'will be returning shortly'. The relatives or friends find it difficult to help the children financially for three or five years and the children have been known to die from lack of care and starvation.

Foreign nationals in Ireland

Women in prison in Ireland make up two per cent of the total prison population. Twenty per cent of the female prison population is made up of foreign nationals. Twelve per cent of the 20 per cent of foreign nationals are black, mostly South African and imprisoned for drug-related offences.

FOREIGN NATIONALS DAY

I attended 'Foreign Nationals Day' in a closed women's prison as part of my research. The women were to discuss the problems they were facing in prison and make suggestions. There were two groups—one conducted in Spanish and the one I attended which was conducted in English. It was attended by black women, mainly African-Caribbeans. The complaints of the women in this group centred around ill-treatment by prison officers and problems associated with making complaints, e.g.:

- One woman felt that if you were outspoken and knew your rights you would find yourself in people's 'bad books' and that a transfer to an open prison would be refused as a form of 'punishment', which she was experiencing at the time.
- A black British woman talked about how she had found herself in trouble with prison officers by advising foreign black women of their rights. She said that whenever she felt the 'screws' were taking liberties with a foreign black woman she would explain to that woman her rights or speak to the 'screw' on her behalf. As a result, she had been labelled a 'big mouth' and a 'bad influence'. Despite having applied many times for a transfer to an open prison she still had not been granted this request.
- There was agreement from nearly all the women present that some prison officers treat them like children and not like human beings. The prison officer in the group said, 'If you treat us with respect we will treat you the same—otherwise you can't speak to us anyhow, if you ask nicely we'll listen'.

- Some women raised issues about the procedure for complaining to the governor about a prison officer. They said that if they wanted to make a complaint they had to go to a prison officer who would ask them the name of the prison officer they were complaining about, and he or she would then warn that officer. The women also said it was difficult, when asked who they were complaining about, to say 'It's you'. The women also felt that some of their complaints were not taken on board and that the prison governor did not get to hear about them.
- One of the women prison officers who was in the meeting stated that there was a way of complaining where it was necessary to write down the complaint so that no-one would know about it apart from the governor. The women disagreed with her. This was sound in theory but they knew very well that it was not possible to complain about a prison officer without that officer or other officers knowing about the subject of the complaint before the governor received it.
- One Rastafarian woman who had been doing pottery since she was in prison, talked about the need for black women to unite and work together. This was said to refer to some problems they had encountered in organizing the 'Foreign Nationals Day'. She said she was aware that many black women were experiencing problems in prison and that she was also aware how difficult it was to cope with these. She said that, as a Rastafarian woman, she was experiencing more problems than other women, as the whole prison culture was alien to her—'the food and everything is not what I'm used to'.

Mature advice

This last woman went on to advise black women in prison, especially the young ones, to use their prison time constructively and not to spend it dwelling on the negative side of imprisonment. She had a sample of some of the pottery she had made whilst in prison and displayed this. She said she had not done pottery before, but when she arrived in prison she felt that instead of spending her time dwelling on her problems and the 'unfair sentence' she got, she would attend classes and learn something.

She reminded the younger black women of the value of obtaining a certificate whilst in prison and how that certificate could help them to get a job on release. One young woman in the group was complaining about her experiences with prison officers and felt very aggrieved with the way she had been treated. She advised her to see time spent in prison as a time to rebuild her life, and not as wasted, and to join an education class and leave the prison with a certificate. She may have been seen by other women prisoners, especially the young ones, as something of a role model.

COMMENT

So what needs do foreign nationals have that set them apart from the bulk of British prisoners? A modest but growing body of research which has focused primarily on male establishments, has found roughly similar problems recurring in most prisons, and which include language problems—which in turn make other problems worse. Written information about prison regimes can be inaccessible and basic rules may inadvertently be contravened, leading to disciplinary measures and adjudications. Also foreign nationals frequently have difficulty in obtaining timely legal advice and are often unfamiliar with the court system in this country. They also tend not to know about things like the parole and early release processes and basic entitlements, such as telephone cards, visits and access to education. They face isolation compounded by the fact that they are serving long sentences, often for drugs importation. Foreign national women, most of whom have dependent children, suffer especially badly from the stress of being separated from their families. The organization Hibiscus has highlighted numerous cases of women being imprisoned for many years after making only short-term arrangements for their children to be cared for in their home countries.

The problem of foreign nationals having to remain in prison after they have served their sentence was raised in my earlier research (Chigwada, 1987). This problem still exits. As Hindpal Singh Bhui notes:

> It is hard to overstate the despair that can result from the threat of deportation and detention after the end of a court-ordered sentence. Where deportation is being considered, the case is often not acted upon until a very late stage, partly because of staff shortages in the Immigration Service and partly because of inefficient bureaucracies in the UK and abroad.

This means that even the many foreign nationals who are happy to be sent home may be imprisoned for indeterminate extra periods. In theory all such detainees should be sent to specialist centres, but a lack of bed space means that a transfer to these more relaxed and better resourced regimes is rare. Detention in Spartan prison regimes creates considerable distress for isolated prisoners and also results in greater pressure on already overworked prison officers who are expected to manage the resultant frustration and human misery.

Bhui points out that in overcrowded and (especially in London) understaffed institutions, services for foreign nationals are subject to the same constraints as every other provision that extends beyond the minimum requirement of containment. Furthermore, there are currently no audited minimum standards, or even guidelines for work with foreign nationals (although there is guidance on working with the relatively small number of detainees in prison). Taken together, these two factors mean that achieving positive and sustainable change is no easy task. Foreign national work is often over-reliant on the personal commitment of individuals, and can quickly run aground when particular members of staff move on to other jobs.

Yet such work is being developed in many prisons in spite of the limitations. The impetus for change has come from a variety of sources, notably the Macpherson report and successive HM Inspectorate of Prisons reports in the mid-to-late-1990s. The effects of the former have been much debated, including the encouragement of a culture of concern about issues of equality and discrimination. The inspectorate meanwhile, has been critical of the treatment of foreign national prisoners, which has helped to focus attention on their specific problems.

Bhui discusses The Wandsworth model which he describes as successful. He states that, Wandsworth was already in the process of making changes late in 1999. The subsequent report made a number of strong criticisms about the treatment of foreign nationals. Bhui states that these concerns were addressed so effectively that the follow-up inspection in 2001 commended the foreign nationals' strategy as a beacon of good practice. The Wandsworth approach has the following basic elements:

- more than a dozen information and support groups a month, with priority given to those identified as having immigration problems or as being at risk of self-harm or suicide
- an advice worker from the Detention Advice Service (DAS), one of the most established independent immigration advice agencies, attends the larger groups and deals with the more complicated follow-up work
- governors, prison officers and staff from many other departments are regularly invited to the groups to discuss issues and answer questions.
- a range of information for foreign nationals and staff working with foreign nationals, much of it translated. This includes a locally developed manual detailing, e.g. the principles of the Wandsworth approach, basic policies affecting foreign nationals, and the contact details of community support agencies and embassies. One of the most important translated documents is a leaflet in 25 languages which includes information about many important issues, including the groups, other specific help for foreign nationals and basic prison rules.

Over time, another key factor has emerged and has now become one of the most important components of the strategy. That is the creation of a number of foreign national orderly posts for prisoners. The orderlies systematically visit new arrivals, help to identify those in greatest need, distribute important information, keep lists of inmate interpreters, and visit vulnerable prisoners on a daily basis, referring prisoners on to staff as appropriate. They also take referrals from officers who identify people in need of the group's support. These posts have been a considerable success, contributing to a calmer, more co-operative regime, because frustrated foreign national prisoners now have an effective means of voicing concerns and obtaining help on a reasonably immediate basis. As a result, the strategy is more likely to be sustainable, especially as the strong commitment from the prisoners themselves is now matched by the support of the majority of prison staff who can see the tangible benefits of their work.

Another objective has been to have a core foreign nationals team consisting of a seconded probation officer/foreign nationals coordinator, specialist immigration advice worker, foreign national prisoner orderlies and foreign national liaison prison officers. Perennial staff shortages mean that the officers continue to be under-represented, despite considerable personal commitment. Their involvement is obviously crucial but has been off-set to some degree by the other elements. The prison's decision to contract a seconded probation officer specifically to drive forward the foreign national work has given the strategy overall coordination and the decision to fund a detention advice service worker for two days a week provided invaluable support; and the volume of work that the orderlies do has added credibility and visibility.

Bhui adds that the strategy has now assumed a greater importance because it led to a Butler Trust award and the support of HMPS headquarters for a subsequent period of research in a number of other prisons. The aim is to test the viability of the approach developed in Wandsworth for different prison environments. This will be done by means of a series of focus groups with foreign national prisoners and interviews with staff in each establishment. Essentially, the conditions, skills and commitment needed for the provision of an effective, sustainable, strategic approach to work with foreign nationals are present in all the prisons surveyed. The process of change is already well under way in many establishments, and the lessons of the research will contribute to new centrally issued guidelines in 2003.

FUTURE INTENTIONS

During the interviews the women also talked about their intentions on release, thereby giving some insight into their attitudes to their offences and the effect that involvement with the criminal justice process had had on them. Many were preoccupied with worries about their employment prospects and accommodation, and what their communities would think of them—as ex-prisoners—when they returned. This is the subject matter of the final chapter.

CHAPTER 8

Hopes and Ambitions

This final chapter looks at the hazards faced by black women after their sentence is behind them. It examines their hopes, ambitions, attitudes and future plans. On their release black women still face all the problems of race, gender and class, but now exacerbated by the fact that they are also ex-prisoners. The chapter concludes with a number of thoughts about the need for change put forward by the women and my own suggestions.

IMMEDIATE PROBLEMS ON RELEASE

For whatever reason, on release from prison fewer black people appear to seek and obtain help from the welfare services (including the National Probation Service (NPS) which is responsible for post-release supervision when legally appropriate). The evidence is largely anecdotal, but it is hardly surprising because, as a general feature, black people resist any arrangements which they believe are part of a process which is discriminatory or 'not for them'. By way of example, one woman in the interview sample had not attended post-release group sessions because she found that the discussions did not relate to black people and that she in turn could not relate to the group. She said:

> It was all right for jobs and that, but you couldn't really discuss your problems as they would not be able to understand them.

There are other difficulties. In general, if someone is sent to prison this normally results in loss of employment and disruption of other ties to their community, family and associates. Other people 'move on' while someone is in prison so that a black woman, in particular, already at risk of being shunned by her former friends and possibly her family on whom she has 'brought disgrace' or unwanted attention from the authorities, may find it hard to re-establish former associations. The stigma of imprisonment is much stronger for black women than it is for people from other groups, so that they may receive little or no support on the one hand whilst coping with discrimination in relation to employment, accommodation and possible fresh involvement with the criminal justice process on the other.

Aisha Tarzi found the stigma of being in prison daunting for the women involved, in particular those from Asia, Africa and South America where a prison sentence is often seen as bringing dishonour and disgrace upon a family. As a result, family members may lose their jobs, engagements may be broken-off and wedding plans cancelled. Marriages can break up and children may be affected in various ways. In some of those countries the prisoners' family is ostracised and forfeits prestige.[1]

Anne Celnick noted that only 40 per cent of black offenders compared to 88 per cent of white offenders claimed that they were given help from family members.[2] Again, in her findings this is largely because of the disgrace brought upon the black person's family by the ex-prisoner. There may be 'guilt by association' for such family members[3] and the black person's family or associates will not want to be thought of as suspects, or otherwise 'criminalised'. They may worry about finding *themselves* in trouble with the law just because they help a relative who has been to prison.

The same kind of considerations prevent some family members from visiting black relatives in prison, or from being supportive in other ways. Sixteen of the women interviewed expressed their concern about the stigma that attaches to having been in prison, and were worried about how their community might react to them if people found out where they had been (this often having been avoided so far). Only two of the women said they had supportive families.

MAKING PLANS

Universally, the women wanted a job when released from prison.[4] Their plans also included 'looking after the children' and 'getting on with life'. In some ways the problems faced after release from prison are a mirror image of those which brought women into contact with the criminal justice process at the outset.

Employment

Sixteen of the women were unemployed at the time of their arrest. Dawn, explaining why she was without a job said:

> I was unemployed because I do not want a low paid—and dirty—job. Why should I—it is very easy to get a low paid job—why should I take a low paid job with unsociable hours? I feel I have a lot to offer, if only they would give me the chance. The kind of job I want careerwise is what black people do not get—as black people we just get pushed to the back of the line.

Poverty among ethnic minority groups is directly connected to unemployment, low pay, industrial structures and racism. Many black women are unemployed or forced into jobs which attract low pay. Those black people who are employed are concentrated in those sectors with the lowest wages, such as distribution,

---

[1] 'Victims of Freedom', Tarzi, A, in *Minority Ethnic Groups in the Criminal Justice System* (1993), Gelsthorpe L (ed), University of Cambridge Institute of Criminology.

[2] 'Race and Rehabilitation', Celnick A, in *Minority Ethnic Groups in the Criminal Justice System* (1993), Gelsthorpe L (ed.), University of Cambridge Institute of Criminology.

[3] Compare the comments on the policing of young men and the affect on their mothers in *Chapter 3*.

[4] Unemployment rates for all the main racial minorities were higher than for whites. Unemployment among white people in Britain was just under ten per cent but soared to 24 per cent amongst Caribbeans and 38 per amongst Africans (*The Voice*, 15 February 1994).

hotels and catering, clothing and leather goods manufacture, and the lower rungs of the medical and health sectors.[5]

For Aisha, the whole 'system' was discriminatory:

> I think the system is like that—we are treated differently. It starts from the time you go to school; you get belittled you get labelled automatically. This is why half of the children end up not going to school—when you check it up—really we get treated in a particular way.

She went on to talk about equal opportunities policies:

> They go on with all this race harmony and equal rights—that's . . . just to quieten things down—to make things look good. As far as I am concerned when they say equal rights—equal education—that's just a cover up. When you get underneath you find something completely different . . . My friends found that each time they tick a box to say they are black British or black African they do not get an interview. We now know if you don't tick a box you stand a better chance of getting an interview. For example, if you fill in a housing form you get asked what ethnic group you belong to. I just leave that part blank—saying black British would not help—otherwise you get categorised automatically.

Generally speaking, the women were aware of the constraints imposed on them as black women, but at the same time they wanted to change their poverty stricken lives. They would need a rehabilitation programme which would include helping them to get employment.

It seems important to note the historical and cultural background to the problems of black people in Britain[6] and how longstanding and deeply rooted are the difficulties—particularly as this affected the women's perceptions about the course their lives would take. Aisha, aged 23, talked about how her parents had suffered racism when they first came to this country and of her determination to overcome prejudice. She was not prepared to tolerate it as she was British:

> From the 1960s things have changed a bit. My parents came here as students and had a hard time . . . I'm British and am not standing for it . . . I know its going to be very hard to change the system—and its in the system—in some way I feel its going to be always like that . . . But I'm born here and feel I have more rights.

Dawn, who felt that she should be treated like everyone else as she was born here, said:

> As far as I'm concerned I'm British, I was born here—obviously white British do not think so—they often tell me to go back to where I come from—even the police have told me that—I tell them I was born here . . . and I *was* born here.

Dee Cook (1993) points out that black ex-prisoners are in a sense denied restoration to full citizenship as they have never received it in the first place. Full

---

5 'Poverty in Black and White: Deprivation and Ethnic Minorities', Amin and Oppenheim, Child Poverty Action Group with the Runnymede Trust, 1992.

6 See the *Appendix:* Historical Background to Modern-Day Problems of 'Immigrant' Labour in Britain

citizenship implies acceptance by other members of society.[7] More often than not, black people known to have been convicted of an offence continue to be stigmatised—even within their own communities—after they have completed their punishment. Failure to achieve full citizenship may itself be a barrier to their reform. Black *people* are disadvantaged and black *offenders* doubly so.

It seems that being *born* in the United Kingdom does not necessarily convey full citizenship if you are black. Because of the colour of their skin, black people are viewed as illegal immigrants constantly having to prove that they are legitimately in the UK, or born here:

> When I was coming from Jamaica, the customs officers found two ounces of cannabis on me. When they arrested me, they took my British passport and I insisted on showing them my British birth certificate. They said 'Why are you showing us that?' When the duty solicitor came to see me he asked where I was born. I said I was British and that they had my passport. He said that when they called him they told him they had a Jamaican woman in custody. (Marion)

Accommodation

Black women are often caught in a vicious circle on release. When they are sent to prison their children may be placed with relatives or taken into local authority care. African-Caribbean women in Britain tend to live in council housing, often flats. This means that if they are sent to prison they will lose their accommodation. Women who are sent to prison for longer than six months have to re-apply for housing, as they are viewed as having made themselves intentionally homeless (in effect, by committing a crime). It means that, on release, they have no accommodation to go to and therefore they cannot get their children back from the local authority that has taken them into care.

Several of the women in the sample were constantly worrying about this, especially those close to their release date. Eighteen had council accommodation and were living under the threat that the council would take their property back if they were going to be in prison for longer than six months. The Housing Benefit, Council Tax Benefit and Income Support (Amendments) Regulations 1995 ended the practice of using housing benefit to meet the rent payments of convicted prisoners serving up to a year in custody. The change applied in respect of new single prisoners entering prison from April 1995 onwards.

The regulations also limited to a maximum of 13 weeks the time for which housing benefit can be paid in respect of an empty property from which a sentenced prisoner is temporarily absent. (The change did not affect unconvicted and unsentenced prisoners, who continue to be eligible for assistance for up to 52 weeks). Under the previous regulations, prisoners serving sentences of up to two years were eligible for assistance, because account was taken of the fact that those serving sentences of this length receive conditional or supervised release after half of their sentence unless release is delayed as a punishment for a disciplinary offence. Under the present system, assistance is confined to prisoners serving sentences of up to six months, who are normally released unconditionally after 13 weeks in custody.

---

[7]   1993.

Other changes in the housing benefit regulations have increased homelessness among released prisoners.[8] The changes have increased the likelihood that prisoners serving from 13 to 52 weeks will lose their homes and possessions. The report states:

> The removal of housing benefit from prisoners serving more than 13 weeks in custody has increased homelessness among released prisoners. We estimate that up to 5,000 additional prisoners could be released homeless each year as a result of this change, losing stable accommodation and all their furniture and possessions. This measure has had particularly harsh consequences for single mothers, often with devastating results for them and their young children.

Such children are often affected in the case of women prisoners because women are more likely than men to be sole carers. When children have been taken into care during a sentence, the loss of accommodation makes it less likely that they will be returned to their mother. When children have been looked after by relatives or friends and returned to their mother on release, if she has lost her home the family faces the prospect of starting again in 'bed and breakfast' and other unsatisfactory forms of accommodation. 'Homelessness and destitution on release greatly increase the risk of reoffending', says the report. It cites research showing that prisoners who are released homeless are more than twice as likely to reoffend as those with homes, and argues:

> Any money saved by the change is likely to be lost several times over by the costs of further offending, including the cost of police time, court time and further prison sentences. In short, this change is short-sighted, inhumane and counter-productive.

Under the regulations, anyone serving over 13 weeks in prison cannot receive housing benefit at all. Local authorities have no discretion, e.g. to pay for a few weeks to bridge any gap. Also, as some local authorities insist on four weeks' notice to terminate a tenancy, even if the prisoner acts promptly to give notice, four weeks' arrears accrue which the prisoner owes on release and must clear before being considered for rehousing as a homeless person.

The Penal Affairs Consortium illustrated the impact of the changes by citing a series of cases in which prisoners lost their homes and possessions as a result of the regulations.[9] The consortium called on the government to reinstate prisoners' eligibility for housing benefit to enable them to keep their homes during periods of up to 12 months in custody. Mary Honeyball, the then General Secretary of the former Association of Chief Officers of Probation (ACOP),[10] said:

> There seems little logic in a policy that cuts benefits to create 'savings' when those same cuts actually cause greater expense in other departments. There is still less logic in making ex-prisoners homeless when we know it is such a powerful trigger in causing crime. It has been callous, costly and, by contributing to crime, entirely counter-productive as a useful public policy.

---

[8] 'Housing Benefit and Prisoners' (1996), Penal Affairs Consortium.
[9] 'Housing Benefit and Prisoners', Penal Affairs Consortium, 1996, pp 5-7.
[10] Chief probation officers are now members of the Association of Probation Boards.

Paul Cavadino, the then chair of the Penal Affairs Consortium, concluded that:

> When courts pass prison sentences, they sentence offenders to be deprived of their liberty. They do not sentence them to lose their homes, their possessions and their children, yet that has been the effect . . .

One woman prisoner said:

> I am worried about losing my council flat. My outside probation officer is helpful. The council want the flat back and I have two children who are with my sister at the moment. (Judith)

Miriam who was in prison for handling stolen goods wanted a transfer from where she was living. She was constantly worrying about going back to the notorious council estate in north-west London which she felt was not a good place to bring up children:

> I am worrying too much about my children and about where I am going to live when I finish my prison sentence—I would like to leave the estate—or the area altogether. I need a transfer. I have been asking for a transfer for a long time but they still have not transferred me. I know if I go back to that estate I'll be back here again . . . things are so hard. There is a lot of crime on the estate—for example drugs—it is not good for the children—they come up selling some really nice clothes for the children and very cheap price! You just find yourself tempted . . . I don't want that again.

Prisoners who are homeless are more likely to be reconvicted. But up to third of prisoners lose their accommodation during custody and face severe difficulties accessing other housing on release. Some social housing providers have banned ex-offenders, although the Homelessness Act 2002 now makes blanket bans unlawful.

A TIME FOR REFLECTION

Several of the women spoke of the impact that imprisonment had had on them and, in some cases, how this would affect them in the future:

> No way would I find myself in such a situation again. I don't smoke or take drugs . . . I was forced to bring those drugs. I just want to do my sentence and leave. (Dorothy)

> This was my first time in trouble with the law . . . It is my first time in prison. I know what I did was wrong and risky, but at the time I was desperate for money to feed and clothe my children. (Jane)

Monica said that she had 'found God' whilst in prison and spoke of her future as follows:

> I regret that I did mix with the wrong crowd and got myself involved in handling stolen goods. I have now found God . . . and now believe in God . . . I will be living a clean, Christian life when I leave here.

She felt that if she had not been in prison she would not have seen the need to change her life:

> Prison has given me time to think about my life and to have time to study the Bible.

Doreen, who was on a CRO said:

> I have now decided to go to college. It is of my own accord. It's got nothing to do with me having been in prison or on probation. You have to make a decision at some time in your life.

THE CRIMINAL JUSTICE PROCESS

Whatever the theory may be about Britain being a multi-racial society it is clear from my research that this ideal is far from being a reality. Throughout the book, the women in the sample are quoted putting forward ideas, suggestions and criticisms of the criminal justice process. The following random items serve to give some indication of the women's perceptions and thus the scale of the problem which needs to be overcome if black women are to accept that criminal justice can be delivered in what they see as a largely male dominated, white, Euro-centric society:

> There should be a change in police custody. The way they talk to you like you are not a human being—they have to change the way they handle people. They abuse their power and some are racist. (Karen)

> One day I was at the social security and there was some trouble there and police officers came to arrest a man—a whole lot of them, including a police sergeant in the lift. I pressed a lift to go downstairs and the sergeant said to me 'look at your black cunt'. That's what he said to me—the sergeant—and they were all laughing. So I abused him back. You have to know your rights in this country otherwise they will walk all over you. (Alithea)

> There was no black jury in my case. I feel black people would understand you better. (Rhona)

> There should be more black lawyers, probation officers and police officers. This would give us more confidence in dealing with them. Even though my black probation officer was not helpful, I still feel more comfortable talking to black professionals. (Sarah)

> More black judges would make a difference—whites need to see us as human beings. (Lorraine)

> There should be more black prison officers otherwise its like 'them against us'—you see. (Dawn)

> Some black lawyers give you the impression 'I have gone that one step further and I'm better than you.' I still feel we need more black lawyers though. (Aisha)

I live on a very notorious council estate in London. They went and employed five black officers and they were given hell—as sell outs. When they are doing their raids they try to include a black officer. It may help if they employed a black officer from the black community—from the ghetto. (Marva)

There should be more black lawyers because I feel that some white solicitors are still racist—they press you to plead guilty because they are convinced that you did commit the crime. (Rhona)

I don't think having more black lawyers would make a difference—it would come to the same thing—there are some black lawyers who think, or are, more white than whites. (Judith)

The solution is not to have more black police officers or lawyers but to accept black people as they are. Black people have to sacrifice their identity to get on in life. You can't work for the system—remaining black—and getting promoted. When black people are too professional they become white minded—they put on airs and graces—that is the only way they can be accepted and succeed in this system. (Aisha)

SOME CONCLUDING THOUGHTS

The experiences of the women described in this book illustrate that although there are many problems which women as a whole share, there are added problems for black women and that the colour of their skin has a bearing on the way they are dealt with by the criminal justice process. Whatever the laudable and extensive initiatives taken by government departments and criminal justice agencies to combat racism and discrimination, the situation remains one in which the substance of what is actually happening does not match the grand structures which are being built. How else can it be explained in the wake of section 95 Criminal Justice Act 1991, the Human Rights Act 1998, the publication of extensive data and other information by the Home Office and the development of a range of activities to combat discrimination by individual criminal justice agencies that the number of black people and women being drawn into the criminal justice process and ultimately into the prisons of England and Wales is still disproportionate and rising?

Making things happen
There is every difference between acknowledging the existence of a problem, saying that mechanisms have been put in place, and actually changing outcomes. Thus far, a grand agenda has failed to deliver overall improvement in the way that ethnic minorities, women and black women in particular are dealt with. Indeed, there has been a deterioration in terms of equal outcomes. Perhaps the one saving feature is that section 95 itself is still in place when in other parts of Europe and around the world such 'protections' (other than under the European Convention)[11] have tended to recede. It is a question of making *things happen* not just hoping or believing that they will. With this in mind, there are several suggestions which I would like to put forward based on the issues raised in this

---

[11] As noted in *Chapter 5*, the Convention does not confer a free-standing right not to be discriminated against, but provision in article 14 that Convention rights must be applied without discrimination.

book and with particular emphasis on the situation of black women as one of those 'discreet' but 'identifiable' minority groups referred to in *Chapter 1* who until convinced otherwise believe that justice is for other people, 'not for them':

- there should be ready acceptance by people in senior positions within the criminal justice process that racism and discrimination on the grounds of race or gender still exists and that there is a need to re-double efforts if the behaviour of the very many decision-makers for whom they are responsible or accountable is to change
- the training and information made available should concentrate on making decision-makers more aware of the perceptions and cultures of minority groups with a view to avoiding stereotyping and misleading assumptions about black people, about women and black women (*Chapters 1* and *2*)
- there should be recognition of the multiple disadvantages faced by black women and of their general sense that they do not receive justice (*Chapters 1* and *8*)
- there should be better understanding of black women's lives and a recognition that in a multi-cultural society these may not accord with the 'dominant' and entrenched middle-class values of white women (whether of feminists, criminologists or 'ordinary people')—indeed there is no reason why they should. Diversity should not be equated with notions of 'criminal propensity' (see, generally *Chapter 2*).
- the police should display greater sensitivity to matters such as the interviewing, arrest and prosecution of black women and the police and CPS should recognise that failure to do so may be counterproductive in that many black women will be alienated towards crime. In particular, those agencies should recognise that the actions they take have a significant effect on events and responses at later stages in the criminal justice process. Black women should not be treated as if they were 'illegal immigrants' and 'guilt by association' must be avoided (*Chapter 3*).
- caution should attach to the use of mental health powers if intervention relies for its justification on 'abnormal' behaviour (a sentiment that applies at all stages of the criminal justice process, but particularly in relation to 'sectioning': *Chapter 3*)
- the NPS and HMPS should continue their progressive work but with greater emphasis being placed on the special problems of black women in terms of the provision of information to courts with regard to community sentences and facilities and resources for sentences which are *relevant* to black women. It should not be assumed that the existence of strong equal opportunity and anti-discrimination policies and practices will automatically guarantee equality of opportunities in fact, or an absence of discrimination (*Chapters 4* and *7*).
- sustained efforts should be made to recruit black people, including black women, into the higher ranks of the judiciary and legal profession in particular, and progress to higher level posts should not be denigrated or discouraged in day-to-day to day affairs (*Chapter 5*)
- all people concerned with the administration of the courts and with judicial decision-making should obtain a clearer understanding of issues affecting black people and should consider that data which shows how black people

and women have been dealt with up until now. The duty to deal fairly and impartially with *all* people should not be allowed to mask the fact that, on the evidence, that duty has not been fully discharged, something which does not seem to have improved in recent years despite extensive training and the availability of improved information (*Chapter 5*).

- more appropriate and relevant provision should be made for the increasing number of black women (including black foreign women) arriving in prison. There should be major efforts to combat racism and inequalities in prison discipline, as well as to build on the positive aspect that many black women wish to improve their education and future prospects before re-entering their communities. The use of medication, strip searches and psychiatric provision should be carefully monitored to ensure that these do not involve a racist or discriminatory element (*Chapter 7*).

- the fact that black women are faced with multiple hazards of discrimination should be a feature recognised and understood by people across the criminal justice process and should feature prominently on the agenda of all people concerned with equality of treatment.

Apart from obvious and blatant racism, there is a more insidious and subtle racism. Not only is there a need for black people to be properly represented amongst criminal justice professionals across-the-board, but the institutional racism that pervades British criminology also needs to be highlighted and addressed. At present much research into the workings of the system is done by or associated with the state. In an ideal world, the state should not be the main provider, controller or funder of the data by which its own responsibilities ultimately fall to be judged, and there should be greater scope for independent criminologists—including BME criminologists. This might help to avoid accusations such as those made in *The Guardian* (4 July 1994) that ministers were systematically 'shelving' or delaying the publication of research findings that did not support their particular stand on law and order.

Postscript

Throughout this book I have tried to demonstrate how race, gender and class intersect in a way specific and unique to black women, contributing to their over-representation in prison and unequal treatment by the system as a whole. Never perhaps have the problems been highlighted more acutely than by a newspaper report headed 'Prison Boss gets Hate Mail after Attack on Racism'. According to the report, Director General, Martin Narey said that he had become a target of 'extremely offensive' hate mail from prison staff after declaring that HMPS was 'institutionally racist', such that he had passed the unsigned letters, which contained threats towards him, to the police. He said that he had come across 'pockets of malicious racism' within certain prisons and that although most prison governors backed his stand there was still a minority who complained that life was being made too hard for them and that the reform programme was too difficult (*The Guardian*, 14 February 2001).

As indicated in the *Introduction* a feature of criminal justice is that events can change almost by the day. As this book was going to press further figures were released which serve to corroborate or lend weight to many of the points I have made and these are summarised below for readers to reflect upon. The figures are contained principally in *Race and Criminal Justice 2002* (Home Office, 2003).

- the number of black people in prison has increased by 54 per cent since 1997
- there has been a 12 per cent increase in BME (1,470) from the 12,580 held in June 2000
- one in every 100 BME adults in Britain is now in prison and black prisoners now account for 1 in 6 of all inmates
- in June 2001, 14,050 prisoners were known to belong to BME groups
- BME made up 21 per cent of the male prison population and 26 per cent of the female population (where ethnicity was known). This compares with nine per cent of BME in the general population
- black people make up just three per cent of the population of England and Wales but account for 13 per cent of the male prison population and 21 per cent of female prison population
- South Asians and 'Chinese and others' accounted for three per cent and four per cent respectively of the male population and one per cent and four per cent respectively of the female population
- in June 2001, ten per cent of the male prison population were known to be foreign nationals and 19 per cent of the female population
- of female foreign nationals, 50 per cent had West Indian nationalities and 25 per cent were European, while 11 per cent were African nationals and six per cent were Asian
- foreign nationals account for a higher proportion of ethnic minority prisoners than of white prisoners. In 2001, foreign nationals made up four per cent of the white prison population, 31 per cent of black prisoners, 30 per cent of South Asians and 53 per cent of prisoners from Chinese and other ethnic groups. Among black and South Asian female prisoners, the proportions of foreign nationals were 55 per cent and 43 per cent respectively.
- the most frequent type of offence among female sentenced prisoners with foreign nationality was a drug offence (81 per cent). This compares with 30 per cent among British female sentenced prisoners.
- a substantial proportion of female foreign national prisoners have been arrested at ports or other locations and convicted of importing or exporting drugs. These offences carry longer sentences than average, which means that such offenders are disproportionately represented among the prison population
- 72 per cent of female foreign nationals serving sentences for drug offences were black, and 16 per cent were white
- within the sentenced British female prison population, there are considerable differences in offence type between white females and females from BME backgrounds. The proportion of black British females sentenced for drug offences (56 per cent) was more than twice the proportion of white British females sentenced for drug offences (27 per cent). The proportion of black British females sentenced for drug offences was higher than the proportion of black British males sentenced for drug offences (18 per cent). The difference between the proportions of British

white and black females sentenced for drug offences (29 per cent points) is higher than between the proportions of British white and black males sentenced for drug offences (six per cent).

- 65 per cent of adult black prisoners were serving sentences of four years or over. Among other BME groups, the proportions of adult prisoners who were serving sentences of four years and over were 58 per cent of South Asians, 61 per cent of Chinese and others, and 50 per cent of whites.

- among young offenders, BME are also on average serving longer sentences than whites. Seventy-eight per cent of sentenced young South Asians and 83 per cent young black people were serving sentences of 12 months or more, compared to 70 per cent of young whites.

- among adult female sentenced prisoners, 69 per cent of black prisoners were serving sentences of four years and over compared with 34 per cent of white prisoners.

- some of the differences between the sentence lengths being served by the members of different BME groups may be explained by the proportions convicted for offences such as drug offences, which tend to attract longer sentences. (Nevertheless, the *Home Office Statistical Bulletin* 'The Ethnic Origins of Prisoners ' (21/94), concluded that in 1990, black male adult prisoners received, on average, sentences which were 98 days longer than would be expected, taking into account the age of the offender, the type of offence and the type of court sentencing)

- black offenders who were aged below 21 received sentences which were 36 days longer on average than the average of all offenders. Asian offenders (who are not over-represented in the prison population relative to national population) received sentences which were around 45 days longer than the average

- black people are five times more likely to be arrested than white and other ethnic groups

- for violent offences the use of custody was higher for black offenders than white and Asian offenders

- of those dealt with by the Youth Justice Board, black defendants were more likely to be remanded in custody and given conditional, rather than unconditional bail, than white or Asian defendants

- black people tend to serve longer sentences than white and or Asian inmates.

- nine per cent of complaints made against the police came from the black community, six per cent from Asians and two per cent from other BME groups

- BME people are still under-represented at all grades as employees in the prison service

- although the overall number of prison officers fell in 2001 by three per cent there was a growth in the number of Asian officers (10.1 per cent) and overall the proportion of BME officers increased from 2.7 per cent to 3.9 per cent (however, black and Asian people are seen as over-represented in those dismissed or resigning from the police force and prison service. BME represented 5.9 per cent of those leaving the prison service including 6.6 per cent of resignation and 9.6 per cent of dismissals).

APPENDIX

Historical Background to Modern-day Problems of 'Immigrant' Labour in Britain

The first generation to come to Britain in the 1950s and 1960s was actually *invited*. The flow of immigrant labour into post-war Britain was not some 'hostile invasion'. The old British Empire offered the United Kingdom a solution to the problem of acute labour shortages. Thus, for instance, London Transport recruited bus crews in the West Indies and, as Minister of Health (1960-63), Enoch Powell actively encouraged the recruitment of West Indian and Asian nurses by British hospitals. Indeed, for some people, the prospect of losing this cheap source of immigrant labour was worrying:

> In the hot and heavy industries such as foundries—never popular in times of full employment with the home labour force—they [immigrants] frequently constitute the only available pool of labour. In the textile industry, it has been claimed that night shifts would be forced to close down entirely without them. (*The Times*, 4 August 1965)

Such sentiments acknowledge the significant part immigrant labour played in the burgeoning economy of the early 1960s, but at the same time, show the historically vulnerable position of black labour in British society. When an economic boom is followed by a recession, unskilled labourers are often the hardest hit, as the poverty experienced by black people in Britain in the 1990s also shows. Many of the jobs which the first generation had were the dirtiest, often the most hazardous, involving shift work and were frequently in the worst-paid manual occupations. Previous experience and skills were ignored by employers and black workers were increasingly placed in 'new' jobs on the shop floor, opened up by changes in technology—for example, in the iron foundry industry in the West Midlands—where they were shunned by unions and white workers alike, who were concentrated in the older, established artisan and skilled jobs.

The poor conditions and low levels of pay were compounded by racism and discrimination, which were experienced daily, ranging from routine protests by white workers against employing black people to notices saying 'No coloureds' at factory gates.[1]

Also, the first generation experienced housing problems. Widescale research disclosed that black people were living in squalid and overcrowded conditions, mainly in the private rented sector.[2] Often this was in 'lodging houses' in inner cities, along with friends and relatives, but this accommodation was not cheap. Landlords often charged a premium, branded a 'newcomers' tax', or 'foreigner levy'. Before legislation made blatant racism unlawful, landlords discriminated openly against black people by displaying signs bearing slogans like: 'No coloureds. No Irish. No dogs.' The housing levels of black people have not changed significantly. Many immigrants and black people who are British-born live in poor housing conditions in inner cities, and still undertake unskilled or semi-skilled employment.

The older generation remains God fearing and law-abiding; their offspring, often British born, have become criminalised. The second generation is seen to be 'rising up', or 'angry', in refusing low level employment or shiftwork (where there is any to refuse) and generally struggling, or 'hustling', to survive in a variety of ways—legal, semi-legal and illegal.[3]

---

[1] 'Ethnic Minorities and Employment', Block 4, Open University Press, 1982.
[2] Newham Monitoring Project.
[3] 'The Racism of Criminalisation: Police and the Production of the Criminal Other in Minority Ethnic Groups', Jefferson T, 1993.

BIBLIOGRAPHY

ABPO (1995), 'The Association of Black Probation Officers', Leaflet.

Action for Prisoners' Families, *Who Is Guilty?*, Resource Pack, London: Action for Prisoners' Families.

Adler F. (1975), *Sisters in Crime*, McGraw-Hill: New York

Agozino, B. (1997), *Black Women and the Criminal Justice System: Towards the Decolonisation of Victimisation*, Aldershot: Ashgate.

Akhtar, S. (unpublished report), *An Evaluation of the Prison Service Sex Offender Treatment Programme, Enhanced Thinking Skills Programme, Reasoning and Rehabilitation Programme, To See if the Treatment Needs of Black Offenders are Being Met.*

Alexander, C. (2000a), *The Asian Gang: Ethnicity, Identity, Masculinity*, Oxford: Berg.

Alfred, R. (1992), *Black Women Workers in the Prison Service*, London: Prison Reform Trust.

Andrews, D. A. (1995), 'The Psychology of Criminal Conduct and Effective Treatment', in J. McGuire (ed.), *What Works?: Reducing Reoffending*, Chichester: Wiley.

Anthias, F. and Yuval-Davis, N. (1992), *Radicalised Boundaries*, London: Routledge.

Arshad, R. (1996), 'Building Fragile Bridges: Educating for Change', in K. Cavanagh and V. Cree (eds.), *Working With Men: Feminism and Social Work*, London: Routledge.

Aye Maung, N. (1995), *Young People, Victimisation and the Police: British Crime Survey Findings on the Experiences and Attitudes of 12-15 Year Olds*, Research Study 140, London: Home Office.

Aye Maung, N. and Mirrlees-Black, C. (1994), *Racially Motivated Crime: A British Crime Survey Analysis*, Research and Planning Unit Paper 82, London: Home Office.

Bagley, C. (1971), 'The Social Aetiology of Schizophrenia in Inpatient Groups', *International Journal of Psychiatry*, 17, 292-304.

Barclay, G. C. (1995), *The Criminal Justice System in England and Wales, Digest 3*, London: Home Office.

Barclay, G. and Mhlanga, B. (2000), *Ethnic Differences in Decisions on Young Defendants Dealt With by the Crown Prosecution Service*, Section 95, Findings 1. London: Home Office.

Barker, M. *et al.* (1993), *The Prevention of Street Robbery*, Police Research Group Crime Prevention Series Paper No. 44, London: Home Office Police Department.

Bayne-Smith, M. and McBarnette, L. (1996), 'Redefining Health in the Twenty-first Century', in M. Bayne-Smith, *Race, Gender and Health*, Thousand Oaks, CA, London and New Delhi: Sage.

Bebbington, P. E. *et al.* (1991), 'Inner London Collaborative Audit of Admissions in Two Health Districts, 11: Ethnicity and the Use of the Mental Health Act', *British Journal of Psychiatry*, 27.

Bernard C. (1995), 'Childhood Sexual Abuse: The Implications for Black Mothers', *Rights of Women Bulletin*, Winter.

Bernard, C. (1997), 'Black Mothers' Emotional and Behavioural Responses to the Sexual Abuse of their Children', in G. Kaufman *et al.* (eds.), *Out of the Darkness: Contemporary Perspectives of Family Violence*, Thousand Oaks, CA: Sage.

Bernard, C. (2000), 'Shifting the Margins: Black Feminist Perspectives on Discourses of Mothers in Child Sexual Abuse', in J. Radford, *et al.* (eds.), *Women, Violence and Strategies for Action*, Buckingham, Philadelphia: Open University Press.

Bjorgo, T. and Witte, R. (eds.) (1993), *Racist Violence in Europe*, London: Macmillan.

Black Female Prisoners and Political Awareness (1985), London: Black Women in Prison.

Black Police Association (1998), *Submission to Part II of Stephen Lawrence Inquiry*. London: BPA.

Bosworth, M. (1999), *Engendering Resistance: Agency and Power in a Women's Prison*, Aldershot: Dartmouth.

Bottoms, A. E. (1983), 'Neglected Features of Contemporary Penal Systems' in D. Garland and P. Young (eds.), *The Power to Punish: Contemporary Penalty and Social Analysis*, London: Heinemann.

Bottoms, A. (1995), 'The Philosophy of Punishment and Sentencing' in C. M. V. Clarkson and R. Mogan (eds.), *The Politics of Sentencing Reform*, Oxford: Clarendon Press.

Bowling, B. (2002), *Racism, Crime and Justice*, Longman Criminology Series

Bowling, B. (1990), 'Conceptual and Methodological Problems in Measuring Race Differences in Delinquency: A Reply to Marianne Junger', *British Journal of Criminology*, 33, 1, 231-50.

Bowling, B. (1993a), 'Racial Harassment in East London', in M. S. Hamm (ed.), *Hate Crime: International Perspectives on Causes and Control*, Cincinnati, OH: Academy of Criminal Justice Sciences/Anderson Publications.

Bowling, B. (1998), *Violent Racism: Submission to the Stephen Lawrence Inquiry*, Cambridge: Cambridge Institute of Criminology.

Bowling, B. (1999a), 'Arresting the Abuse of Police Power: Review of the Met's Report on Stop and Search, "Diversity on Line"', December 1999.

Bowling, B. (1999b), 'The Rise and Fall of New York Murder: Zero Tolerance or Crack's Decline?', *British Journal of Criminology*.

Bowling, B. (1999c), *Violent Racism: Victimisation, Policing and Social Context* (revised edn), Oxford: Oxford University Press.

Bowling, B. and Phillips, C. (in press), *Racism, Crime and Justice*, London: Longman Criminology Series.

Bowling, B. *et al.* (1994), 'Self-reported Offending Among Young People in England and Wales', in J. Junger-Tas, *et al.*, *Delinquent Behaviour Among Young People in the Western World*, Amsterdam: Kugler.

Bridges, L. (2000), 'The Lawrence Inquiry: Incompetence Corruption and Institutional Racism', *Journal of Law and Society*.

Bridge, D. and McLaughlin, T. H. (eds.) (1994), *Education in the Market Place*, London and Washington, DC: Falmer Press.

Briggs, C. (1995), 'Policing Moss Side: A Probation Response', *Probation Journal*, June 1995, 62-66.

Briggs, C. (1996), 'The Community Strikes Back', *Criminal Justice*, (the magazine of the Howard League), Vol. 14, No. 2, p. 15.

Bright, J. (1992), in *Family, School and Community*, Swindon: Crime Concern.

Broadwater Farm Inquiry (1985), *Report of the Independent Inquiry into the Disturbances of October 1985 at the Broadwater Farm Estate, Tottenham*, Chaired by Lord Gifford QC, London: Karia Press.

Broidy, L. and Agnew, R. (1997), 'Gender and Crime: a General Strain Theory Perspective', *Journal of Research in Crime and Delinquency*, vol. 34, no. 1, pp. 227-306.

Brown, B. (1990), 'Reassessing the Critique of Biologism', in L. Gelsthorpe and A. Morris (eds.), *Feminist Perspectives in Criminology*, Milton Keynes: Open University Press.

Brown, I. and Hullin, R. (1992), 'A Study of Sentencing in the Leeds Magistrates' Court', *British Journal of Criminology, 32,1., pp. 42-53*.

Brown, I. and Hullin, R. (1993), 'Contested Bail Applications: The Treatment of Ethnic Minority and White Offenders', *Criminal Law Review*.

Brown, K. (2001), *No-one's Ever Asked Me: Young People with a Parent or Sibling in Prison*, London: Federation of Prisoners' Families Support Groups (now Action for Prisoners' Families).

Browne, D. (1990), *Black People, Mental Health and the Courts*, Nacro.

Browne, D. (1997), *Black People and Sectioning: the Black Experience of Detention under the Civil Sections of the Mental Health Act*, London: Little Rock.

Browne, D. and Poole, L. (1997), *Evaluation of the New Directions Groupwork Programme*, Manchester: Greater Manchester Probation Service.

Bryan, B. *et al.* (1985), *The Heart of the Race: Black Women's Lives in Britain*, London: Virago.

Bhui, Hindpal Singh (2002), 'Foreign National Prisoners – the Wandsworth Strategy', *Prison Report*, (the magazine of the Prison Reform Trust), October.

Bhui, K. (1997), *Services Provision for London's Ethnic Minorities'* in *London's Mental Health*, London: Kings Fund.

Bhui, K. and Bhugra D. (2002), 'Mental Illness in Black and Asian Ethnic Minorities: Pathways to Care and Outcomes in Advance', *Psychiatry Treatment*, January 1: 8 (1): 26-33.

Bulletin, Runnymede's Quarterly No 329, March 2002.

Bulletin, Runnymede's Quarterly, December 2002.

Burnett, R. *et al.* (1999), 'The First Contact of Patients with Schizophrenia with Psychiatric Services: Social Factors and Pathways to Care in a Multi-Ethnic Population', *Psychology Medicine*, 29, 475-483.

Caddick, B. (1993), 'Using Groups in Working with Offenders: A Survey of Groupwork in the Probation Services of England and Wales', in Brown, A. and Caddick, B. (eds.), *Groupwork with Offenders*, London: Whiting and Birch.

Caddle, D. and Crisp, D. (1997), *Imprisoned Women and Mothers*, Home Office Research Study 162. London: Home Office.

Cain, M. (1973), *Society and the Policeman's Role*, London: Routledge.

Cain, M. (1986), 'Realism, Feminism, Methodology, and the Law', *International Journal of the Sociology of Law*, 14 ,255-67.

Cain, M. and Sadigh, S. (1982), 'Racism, the Police and Community Policing: A Comment on the Scarman Report', *Journal of Law and Society*.

Callan, A. (1996), 'Schizophrenia in Afro-Caribbean Immigrants', *Journal of the Royal Society of Medicine*, 89, 253-256.

Campell D, *The Guardian*, 11 January 1993.

Carby, H. (1982), 'White Women Listen! Black Feminism and the Boundaries of Sisterhood', in The Centre for Contemporary Cultural Studies (eds.), *The Empire Strikes Back*, London: Hutchinson.

Carlen, P. (1983), *Women's Imprisonment*, London: Routledge.

Carlen, P. (1988), *Women, Crime and Poverty*, Milton Keynes: Open University Press

Carlen, P. (1990), *Alternatives to Women Imprisonment*, Milton Keynes: Oxford University Press.

Carlen, P. (1994), 'Why Study Women's Imprisonment? Or Anyone Else's?' in R. King and M. Maguire (eds.), *Prisons In Context*, Oxford: Clarendon Press.

Carlen, P. (2002a), 'Carceral Clawback: The Case of Women's Imprisonment in Canada', *Punishment and Society*, 4(1).

Carlen, P. (2002b), 'Governing the Governors', *Criminal Justice*, 2(1).

Carlen, P. and Tchaikovsky, C. (1996), 'Women's Imprisonment in England at the End of the Twentieth Century: Legitimacy, Realities and Utopias' in R. Matthews and P. Francis (eds.), *Prisons 2000: An International Perspective on the Current State and Future of Imprisonment*, New York: St Martin's Press.

Cashmore, E. (1991), 'Black Cops Inc.' in E. Cashmore and E. Mclaughlin (eds.), *Out of Order?Policing of Black People*, London: Routledge.

Central Council of Probation Committees Steering Group on Inner Cities (1983), *Probation: a Multi-Racial Approach*, London: Central Council of Probation Committees.

Chambliss, W. J. and Nagasawa, R. H. (1969), 'On the Validity of Official Statistics: A Comparison of White, Black and Japanese High School Boys', *Journal of Research in Crime and Delinquency*.

Chandrasena, R. (1987), 'Schneider's First-Rank Symptoms: An International and Interethnic Comparative Study', *Acta Psychiatrica Scandinavia*, 76, 574-578.

Chesney-Lind, M. (ed.), (1997), *The Female Offender: Girls, Women and Crime*, Thousand Oaks, CA: Sage.

Chesney-Lind, M. (2000), Program Assessment of 'Women at Risk Program of Western Carolinians for Criminal Justice', Ashville, North Carolina: Report Prepared for the National Institute of Corrections, Ashville: Women at Risk.

Chigwada R. (1987), 'Not Victims, Not Superwomen: The Education of Afro-Caribbean Girls', *Spare Rib*, No. 183.

Chigwada, R. (1990), 'Black Women and the Law', *Legal Action Bulletin*.

Chigwada R.(1991), 'Policing of Black Women' in *Policing of Black People*, Cashmore E. and McLaughlin E. (eds.), London: Routledge, Kegan and Paul.

Chigwada R. (1996), *Policing of Black Women*, *Policing of Black People*, in Cashmore E. and McLaughlin E. (eds.), London: Routledge, Kegan and Paul.

Chigwada-Bailey, R. (1987), 'Black Women's Experience of Prison Education', *Gender and Education Journal*, Carfax.

Chigwada-Bailey, R. (1989a), Criminalisation and Imprisonment of Black Women, *Probation Journal*, September: 100-105.

Chigwada-Bailey, R. (1989b), 'Black Women's Unequal Experiences of Prison Education', *Gender and Education*.

Chigwada-Bailey, R. (1991), 'Policing of Black Women', in E. McLaouglin and P. Cashmore (eds.), *Out of Order*.

Chigwada-Bailey, R. (1997), 'Problems Facing African Women in British Prisons', *West Africa*, 10 & 17, London.

Chigwada-Bailey, R. (1997), *Black Women's Experiences of Criminal Justice: A Discourse on Disadvantage*, Winchester: Waterside Press.

Chigwada-Bailey, R. (2003) 'Black Women and Criminal Justice', *British Council Gender Network Newsletter*, February.

Cloward, R. A. and Ohlin L. E. (1961), *Delinquency and Opportunity: A Theory of Delinquent Gangs*, London: Routledge and Kegan Paul.

Coid, J. W. *et al.* (2000), 'Ethnic Differences in Admissions to Secure Forensic Psychiatry Services', *British Journal of Psychiatry*, 177, 241-247.

Coid, J. W. *et al.* (2002), 'Ethnic Differences in Prisoners, 1: Criminality and Psychiatric Morbidity', *British Journal of Psychiatry*, 181, 473-480.

Cole, E. *et al.* (1985) 'Pathways to Care for Patients with a First Episode of Psychosis: A Comparison of Ethnic Groups', *British Journal of Psychiatry*, 170-316.

Colin J. and Morris R. (1996), *Interpreters and Legal Process*, Winchester: Waterside Press.

Collett S., Merseyside Probation Research and Information Unit.

Commission for Racial Equality (1989), *Racial Justice in Magistrates' Courts: the Case for Training*, London: CRE.

Commission for Racial Equality (1990), *Sorry, It's Gone: Testing for Racial Discrimination in the Private Rented Housing Sector*, London.

Commission for Racial Equality (1992), *Cautions v. Prosecutions: Ethnic Monitoring of Juveniles by Seven Police Forces*, London.

Commission for Racial Equality (1999), Royal Commission on Criminal Justice, London: CRE (Supplementary Evidence: Racially Mixed Juries), London.

Cook, D. (1989), in Carlen P, *Paying for Crime*, Milton Keynes: Open University Press.

Cook, D. (1993), 'Racism, Citizenship and Exclusion', in D. Cook and B. Hudson, (eds.) *Racism and Criminology*.

Cook, D. (1997), *Poverty, Crime and Punishment*, London: Child Poverty Action Group.

Cook, S. and Davis, S. (1999), *Harsh Punishment: International Experiences of Women's Imprisonment*, Boston: North Eastern University Press.

Cope R. (1989), 'The Compulsory Detention of Afro-Caribbeans under the Mental Health Act', *New Community*.

Correctional Service of Canada (CSC) (1995), Security Management System, Ottawa: Correctional Service of Canada, Federally Sentenced Women's Program.

Criminal Justice Matters, no. 50, Winter (2002), London: Centre for Crime and Justice Studies.

Croall, H. (2001), *Understanding White Collar Crime*, Buckingham: Open University Press .

Crow, I. and Cove, J. (1984), 'Ethnic Minorities in the Courts', *Criminal Law Review* (July).

Crow, I. (2001), *The Treatment and Rehabilitation of Offenders*, London: Sage.

Daly, K. (1994), *Gender, Crime and Punishment*, New Haven: Yale University Press.

Daly, K. (1997), 'Different Ways of Conceptualising, Sex/Gender in Feminist Theory and their Implications for Criminology', *Theoretical Criminology*, 1.

Davies, P. and Jupp, V. (1999), 'Crime and Work Connections: Exploring the Invisibility of Workplace Crime' in Davies, P. *et al.* (eds.), *Invisible Crimes: Their Victims and their Regulation*, Basingstoke: Macmillan.

Davies, S. *et al.* (1996), 'Ethnic Differences in Risk of Compulsory Psychiatric Admission Among Representative Cases of Psychosis in London', *British Medical Journal*, 312, 533-537.

Day, M., *et al.* (1989), 'Black People and the Criminal Justice System': Three Speeches Given at the Howard League Conference on 'Minorities, Crime and Justice', London: Howard League for Penal Reform.

Demuth, C. (1992), *Racism and Anti-Racism in Probation*, London: Routledge.

Denney, D. (1992), *Racism and Anti-Racism in Probation*, London: Routledge.

Denning, Lord (1982), *What's Next in the Law?*, London: Butterworths.

Department for Education and Employment (2001a), *Youth Cohort Study: The Activities and Experiences of 16 year olds: England and Wales, 2000*, London: DfEE.

Department for Education and Employment (2001b), *Youth Cohort Study: The Activities and Experiences of 18 year olds: England and Wales, 2000*, London: DfEE.

Department of the Environment, Transport and the Regions (2000), *1999/00 Survey of English Housing: Preliminary Results*, Housing Statistics Summary No. 7, London: DETR. www.housing.detr.gov.uk/research/seh/

Devlin, A. (1998), *Invisible Women: What's Wrong with Women's Prisons?* Winchester: Waterside Press.

Dkirk, B. M. (1996), *Negative Images: A Simple Matter of Black and White?: An Examination of 'Race' and the Juvenile Justice System*, Aldershot: Avebury.

Dobash R. E. *et al.* (1986), *The Imprisonment of Women*, Oxford: Basil Blackwell.

Dominelli, L. *et al.* (1995), *Anti-Racist Probation Practice*, Aldershot: Arena.

Dowds, L. and Hedderman C. (1997), 'The Sentencing of Men and Women', in C. Hedderman and L. Gelsthorpe (eds.), *Understanding the Sentencing of Women*, pp. 7-22, Home Office Research Study 170, London: Home Office.

Dunn J. and Fahy T. A. (1990), 'Police Admissions to Psychiatric Hospital: Demographic and Clinical Differences Between Ethnic Groups', *British Journal of Psychiatry*.

Dunn, M. (2000), 'Recidivism Report of the Black Offender Group Pilots', West Midlands Probation Service.

Durrance, P. *et al.* (2000), 'The Greenwich and Lewisham Black Self-Development and Educational Attainment Group, Evaluation Report', Inner London Probation Service.

Eaton, M. (1986), *Justice for Women? Family, Court and Social Control*, Milton Keynes: Open University Press.

Eaton, M. (1993), *Women After Prison*, Buckingham: Open University Press.

Edmunds M. F. (1994), cited in 'A Better Service for Women', University of Exeter.

Edwards S. (1984), *A Study of the Female Defendant*, Manchester: University Press.

Elkins, M. *et al.* (2001), 'Prison Population Brief,' Home Office Research and Development Statistics, London: Home Office.

'Ethnic Minorities and Employment' (1982), Block 4, Open University Press.

Farrington, D. P. (1995), 'The Twelfth Jack Tizard Memorial Lecture: The Developing of Offending and Antisocial Behaviour from Childhood: Key Findings from the Cambridge Study in Delinquent Development', *Journal of Child Psychiatry*, 36, 929-964.

Farrington, D. P. (1996), *Understanding and Preventing Youth Crime*, Joseph Rowntree Foundation: York.

Farrington, D.P. (1997), 'Human Development and Criminal Careers' in Maguire, M. *et al.* (eds.), *The Oxford Handbook of Criminology*, Oxford: Clarendon Press.

Farrington, D. P. and Benett, T. (1981), 'Police Cautioning of Juveniles in London', *British Journal of Criminology*.

Faulkner A. (1989), 'Women and Section 136 of the Mental Health Act 1983', in *The Boys in Blue*, Virago.

Fisher, K. and Watkins, L. (1993), 'Inside Groupwork' in Brown, A. and Caddick, B. (eds.), *Groupwork with Offenders*, London: Whiting and Birch.

Fitzgerald, M. (1993a), 'Racial Discrimination in the Criminal Justice System', Research Bulletin No. 34, Home Office Research and Statistics Department, London: Home Office.

FitzGerald, M. (1997), 'Minorities, Crime and Criminal Justice in Britain', in I. H. Marshall (ed.), *Minorities, Migrants and Crime: Diversity and Similarity Across Europe and the United States*, Thousand Oaks, CA: Sage.

FitzGerald, M. (1999), *Searches in London under Section 1 of the Police and Criminal Evidence Act*, London: Metropolitan Police.

FitzGerald, M. and Marshall, P. (1996), 'Ethnic Minorities in British Prisons: Some Research Implications', in R. Matthews and P. Francis (eds.), *Prisons 2000: An International Perspective on the Current State and Future of Imprisonment*, London: Macmillan.

Fitzgerald, M. *et al.* (2002), *Policing for London*, Willan Publishing.

Flood-Page, C. and Mackie A. (1998), *Sentencing Practice: An Examination of Decisions in Magistrates' Courts and in the Crown Court in the mid-1990s*, Research Study 180, London: Home Office.

Frances-Spence, M. (1995), 'Justice: Do They Mean For Us? Black Probation Officers and Black Clients in the Probation Service', in Ward, D. and Lacey M. (eds.), *Probation: Working For Justice*, London: Whiting and Birch.

Gampell, L. (2002), 'Who's Guilty?', *Criminal Justice Matters*, 9, No. 50, Centre for Crime and Justice Studies.

Garland, D. (1990), *Punishment and Modern Society*, Chicago: University of Chicago Press

Garland, D. (2000), 'The Culture of High Crime Societies: Some Preconditions of recent "Law and Order" Policies', *British Journal of Criminology*.

Gelsthorpe, L. (2001), 'Accountability, Difference and Diversity in the Delivery of Community Penalties' in A. Bottoms *et al.*, (eds.), *Community Penalties: Change and Challenges*, Cullompton, Willan.

Gelsthorpe, L. and Loucks N. (1997), 'Magistrates' Explanations of Sentencing Decisions', in C. Hedderman and L. Gelsthorpe (eds.), *Understanding the Sentencing of Women,*. Research Study 170, London: Home Office, pp. 23-53.

Gelsthorpe, L. and Morris, A. (1990), *Feminist Perspectives in Criminology*, Milton Keynes: Open University Press.

Gelsthorpe, L. and Morris A. (1994), 'Juvenile Justice 1945-1992', in M, Maguire, R. Morgan and R. Reiner (eds), *The Oxford Handbook of Criminology*, Oxford: Oxford University Press.

Gelsthorpe, L. and Morris A. (2002), *Women's Imprisonment in England and Wales: A Penal Paradox in Criminal Justice*, London: Sage Publications.

Genders, E. and Player, E. (1989), *Race Relations in Prison*, Oxford: Clarendon Press.

Gilroy, P. (1987a), *There Ain't No Black in the Union Jack*, London: Hutchinson.

Gilroy, P. (1987b), 'The Myth of Black Criminality', in P. Scraton (ed.), *Law, Order and the Authoritarian State*, Milton Keynes: Open University Press.

Gilroy, P. (2000), *Between Camps: Race, Identity and Nationalism at the End of the Colour Line*, London: Allen Lane, Penguin.

Gordon P. (1985), Policing Immigration: British's Internal Controls, London: Pluto.

Graef R. (1989), *Talking Blues*, William Collins and Sons.

Green, P. (ed.) (1991), *Drug Couriers*, London: Howard League for Penal Reform

Green, P. (1996), 'Drug Couriers: The Construction of a Public Enemy' in P. Green (ed.) *Drug Couriers: A New Perspective*, London: Quartet Books.

Green P. (1998), *Drug Trafficking and Criminal Policy: The Scapegoat Strategy*, Winchester: Waterside Press.

Green, R. (1989), 'Probation and the Black Offender', *New Community*, 16(1): 81-91.

Groves, W. B. and Frank, N. (2001), 'Punishment, Privilege and Structured Choice' in J. Halliday *et al.*, *Making Punishments Work: Review of the Sentencing Framework for England and Wales*, London: Home Office.

Haft M. G. (1976), *Hustling for Rights*, Lexington: Massachusetts.

Halliday. J *et al.* (2001), *Making Punishments Work: Review of the Sentencing Framework for England and Wales*, London: Home Office.

Hagan, J. and McCarthy J. (1997), *Mean Streets: Youth Crime and Homelessness*, Cambridge; Cambridge University Press.

Hannah-Moffat, K. and Shaw, M. (eds.) (2000b), *An Ideal Prison? Critical Essays on Women's Imprisonment in Canada*, Halifax: Nova Scotia, Fernwood Publishing Press.

Hannah-Moffat, K. and Shaw, M. (2001), *Taking Risks: Incorporating Gender and Culture into the Classification and Assessment of Federally Sentenced Women in Canada*, Ottawa: Status of Women. www.swc.cfc.gc.ca

Harrison, G. *et al.* (1998), 'A Prospective Study of Severe Mental Disorder in Afro-Caribbean People', *Psychology Medicine*, 18, 643-657.

Hart, S. (2000), 'Daylight Robbery', *The Big Issue.*

Hassan, E. and Thiara R.K. (2000), *Locked Out? Black Prisoners' Experience of Rehabilitative Programmes* , London: Association Of Black Probation Officers.

Hedderman. C. and Gelsthorpe, L. (1997), *Understanding the Sentencing of Women*, Home Office Research Study 170, London: HMSO

Heindesohn F. (1985), *Women and Crime*, Basingstoke: Macmillan.

HM Inspectorate of Prisons (2000), *Thematic Inspection Report: Towards Race Equality*, London: Home Office.

HM Inspectorate of Prisons (2001), *Follow Up to Women in Prison: A Thematic Review*, London: Home Office.

HM Inspectorate of Prisons (2002), *Report on an Unannounced Visit to HMP Ford*, London: HMSO.

HM Inspectorates of Prisons and Probation (2001), *Through the Prison Gate: A Joint Thematic Review by HM Inspectorates of Prisons and Probation*, London: Home Office.

HM Inspectorate of Probation (1991), *Women Offenders and Probation Service Provision*, London: HMSO.

Home Office (1957), *The Wolfenden Committee's Report on Homosexual Offences and Prostitution*, London: HMSO.

Home Office (1989), *The Ethnic Group of those Proceeded Against or Sentenced by the Courts in the Metropolitan District in 1984 and 1985*, Home Office Statistical Bulletin 6/89. London: Home Office.

Home Office (1992a), *Gender and the Criminal Justice System*, London: Home Office.

Home Office (1992b), *The National Prison Survey: Main Findings*, Home Office Research Study 128, London: HMSO.

Home Office (1992c), *Race and the Criminal Justice System*, London: Home Office.

Home Office (1994a), *The Ethnic Origins of Prisoners*, Home Office Statistical Bulletin (21/94), London: Home Office.

Home Office (1994b), *Race and the Criminal Justice System 1994, A Home Office Publication under Section 95 of the Criminal Justice Act 1991*, London: Home Office.

Home Office (1996), *Protecting the Public: The Government's Strategy on Crime in England and Wales*, London: HMSO

Home Office (1997), *Police and Criminal Evidence Act 1984 (s. 66) Code of Practice (A) on Stop and Search*, London: Home Office.

Home Office (1998a), *Entry into the Criminal Justice System: A Survey of Police Arrests and their Outcomes*, Home Office Research Study 185 London: Home Office.

Home Office (1998b), *Statistics on Race and the Criminal Justice System: A Section 95 Publication under the Criminal Justice Act 1991*, London: Home Office.

Home Office, (1999a), *The Government's Crime Reduction Strategy*, London: Home Office.

Home Office, (1999b), *Statistics on Women and the Criminal Justice System: A Section 95 Publication under the Criminal Justice Act 1991*,

London: Home Office, Research, Development and Statistics Directorate.

Home Office (2000a), *Criminal Statistics England and Wales Supplementary Tables 1999*, Vols. 1 and 2, London: HMSO.

Home Office (2000b), *The Government's Strategy for Women Offenders*, London, Home Office.

Home Office (2000c), *Probation Statistics England and Wales 1998*, London: HMSO.

Home Office, (2000d), *Statistics on Women and the Criminal Justice System: A Section 95 Publication under the Criminal Justice Act 1991*, London: Home Office, Research, Development and Statistics Directorate.

Home Office (2001a), *Criminal Statistics for England and Wales 2000-2001*, London: HMSO.

Home Office (2001b), *Prison Statistics, England and Wales 2000*, London: HMSO.

Home Office (2001c), *Probation Statistics England and Wales 1999*, London: HMSO.

Home Office (2001d), *Statistics on Women and the Criminal Justice System*, London: HMSO.

Home Office (2003), *Race and Criminal Justice 2002*, London: Home Office.

Hood, R. (1992), *Race and Sentencing*, Oxford: Clarendon Press.

Hooks B., (1984), *Feminist Theory From Margin to Centre*, Boston: South End Press.

Hooks, B. (1989), *Talking Back: Thinking Feminist: Thinking Black*, London: Sheba.

Hudson, B. (1987), *Justice Through Punishment: A Critique of the 'Justice' Model of Corrections*, Basingstoke: Macmillan.

Hudson, B. (1988), *Content Analysis of Social Enquiry Reports Written in the Borough of Haringey*, unpublished report, Middlesex Area Probation Service.

Hudson, B. (1989), 'Discrimination and Disparity: The Influence of Race on Sentencing', *New Community*.

Hudson, B. (1993), *Penal Policy and Social Justice*, Basingstoke: Macmillan.

Hudson, B. (1996), *Understanding Justice: An Introduction to Ideas, Perspectives and Controversies in Modern Penal Theory*, Buckingham: Open University Press.

Hudson, B. (1998), 'Doing Justice to Difference' in A. Ashworth and M. Wasik, (eds.), *Fundamentals of Sentencing Theory*, Oxford: Clarendon Press.

Hudson, B. (2000), 'Punishing the Poor: Dilemmas of Justice and Difference', in W. C. Hefferman and J. Kleinig (eds.), *From Social Justice to Criminal Justice: Poverty and the Administration of Criminal Law*, New York: Oxford University Press.

Humphreys B. (1993), *Women Offenders in Merseyside*, Merseyside Probation Service.

Immarigeon, R. and Chesney-Lind M. (1992), *Women's Prisons: Overcrowded and Overused*, San Francisco, CA: National Council on Crime and Delinquency.

Inner London Probation Service (1993), *Working with Difference: A Positive and Practical Guide to Anti-Discriminatory Practice Teaching*, London: Inner London Probation Service.

Inner London Probation Service (1996), *Black and Ethnic Minority Offenders' Experience of the Probation Service: June 1995*, London: ILPS.

Jackson, V. (1996), *Racism, Child Protection: The Black Experience of Child Sexual Abuse*, London: Cassell.

Janus, M. (1987), *Adolescent Runaways: Causes and Consequences*, Lexington Books.

Jefferson, T. and Walker, M. A. (1992), 'Ethnic Minorities in the Criminal Justice System', *Criminal Law Review*.

Jefferson T. (1993), 'The Racism of Criminalisation: Police and the Reproduction of the Criminal Other in Minority Ethnic Groups in the Criminal Justice System', Paper presented to 21st Cropwood Round Table Conference 1992, Cambridge: Cambridge Institute of Criminology.

Kalunta-Crumpton, A. (1996), 'The Influence of Race and Unemployment upon Prosecution in Drug Trafficking Trials', *Probation Journal*.

Kalunta-Crumpton, A. (1999), *Race and Drug Trials: The Social Construction of Guilt and Innocence*, Aldershot: Avebury.

Kennedy H. (1992), *Eve was Framed*, London: Chatto and Windus.

Kemshall, H. (1998), *Risk in Probation Practice*, Aldershot: Ashgate.

Kenshall, K. (1998), 'Evaluation of Programmes for Female Offenders', in R. Zaplin (ed.) *Critical Perspectives and Effective Intervention*, Gaithersburg, Maryland: Aspen.

Kett, J. *et al.* (1992), *Managing and Developing Anti-Racist Practice Within Probation: A Resource Pack for Action*, Merseyside: Merseyside Probation Service.

Khan, K. (2002), 'Does "Crack" Cocaine Discriminate? Deconstruing the Stereotypes', paper presented at Bristol University's Conference on Crack Cocaine, April 24-25.

King J. (1958), *The Probation Service*, Butterworths.

King, M. *et al.* (1994),'Incidence of Psychotic Illness in London: Comparison of Ethnic Groups', *British Medical Journal*, 309, 1115-1119.

Kolvin, I. *et al.* (1990), 'Social and Parenting Factors Affecting Criminal Offence Rates: Findings from the Newcastle 1,000 Family Study, (1947-1980)', *British Journal of Psychiatry*, vol. 152, pp. 80-90.

Kolvin, I. *et al.* (1990), *Continuing of Deprivation? The Newcastle 1,000 Family Study*, Avebury.

Langan M. and Day L. (1992), *Women Oppression and Social Work: Issues in Anti-Discriminatory Practice*, London: Routledge.

Lawrence, D. (1995), 'Race, Culture and the Probation Service' in McIvor, G. (ed.), *Working with Offenders*, London: Jessica Kingsley Publishers.

Lea, J. (1987), 'Police Racism: Some Theories and their Policy Implications' in R. Mathews and J. Young (eds.), *Confronting Crime*, London: Sage.

Lea, J. and Young, J. (1984), *What Is to be Done about Law and Order?*, Harmondsworth: Penguin.

Lee, M. and O'Brien, R. (1995), *The Game's Up: Redefining Child Prostitution*, London: The Childrens Society.

Leonard E. (1982), *Women, Crime and Society*, London: Longman.

Lewis D, *Black Women Offenders and Criminal Justice: Some Theoretical Considerations in Comparing Female and Male offenders*, Warren M (Ed), Sage, 1981, pp.89-105.

Lewis, G. (1996), 'Situated Voices: Black Women's Experience and Social Work', *Feminist Review*, 53:24-54.

Littlewood R. and Lipsedge M. (1979), *Transcultural Psychiatry*, Churchill-Livingstone.

Loeber, R. and Farrington, D. (eds.) (1998), *Serious and Violent Juvenile Offenders: Risk Factors and Successful interventions*, London: Sage Publications.

Loucks, N. (2002), *Just Visiting? The Role of Prison Visitors' Centres*, London: Action For Prisoners' Families/Prison Reform Trust.

MacKinnon, C. A. (1989), *Toward a Feminist Theory of the State*, Cambridge Mass: Harvard University Press.

Maden, Swinton and Gunn (1994), 'A Criminological and Psychiatric Survey of Women Serving a Prison Sentence', *British Journal of Criminology*, 34, (2).

The Magazine of the Prison Reform Trust, (October 2002), London.

Mair, G. (1986), 'Ethnic Minorities, Probation and the Magistrates Courts', *British Journal of Criminology*.

Mair G. and Brockington N. (1988), 'Female Offenders and the Probation Service', *Howard Journal*, 27, (2) May.

Mair, G. and May C. (1997), *Offenders on Probation*, Home Office Research Study 167, London: HMSO.

Mama, A. (1989), 'Violence Against Black Women: Gender, Race and State Responses', *Feminist Review*, 32: 30-49.

Mama, A (1993) 'Black Women and the Police: A Place where the Law is not Upheld', in W. James and C. Harris (eds.), *Inside Babylon: The Caribbean Diaspora in Britain*, London: Verso.

McGuire, J. (ed.), (1995), *What Works? Reducing Re-offending: Guidelines from Research and Practice*, Chichester: John Wiley and Sons.

McQuillan T, (1992), *Pre-sentence Reports: An Anti-Discriminatory Perspective*, Association of Black Probation Officers.

Mercer, K. and Julien, I. (1988), 'Race, Sexual Politics and Black Masculinity: A Dossier', in R. Chapman and J. Rutherford (eds.), *Male Order: Unwrapping Masculinity*, London: Lawrence and Wishart.

Mirrlees-Black, C. (1999), *Domestic Violence: Findings From A New British Crime Survey Self-Completion Questionnaire*, Home Office Research Study 191, London: Home Office.

Mistry, T. (1993), 'Establishing a Feminist Model of Groupwork in the Probation Service' in Brown, A. and Caddick, B. (eds.), *Groupwork with Offenders*, London: Whiting and Birch.

Moodley, P. and Perkins, R. (1991), 'Routes to Psychiatric Inpatient Care in an Inner London Borough', *Social Psychiatry and Psychiatric Epidemiology*, 26,47-51.

Morris A. (1988), 'Sex and Sentencing', *Criminal Law Review*.

Morris A. (1987), *Women, Crime and Criminal Justice*, Oxford: Basil Blackwell.

Morris, A. *et al.* (1995), *Managing the Needs of Female Prisoners*, London: Home Office

Moxon, D. (1988), *Sentencing Practice in the Crown Court*, Research Study No. 103, London: Home Office

Mtezuka, M. (1996), 'Issues of Race and Culture in Child Abuse', in B. Fawcett, *et al.* (eds.), *Violence and Gender Relations: Theories and Interventions*, London: Sage.

Munice, J. (1999), *Youth and Crime*, London: Sage.

Munice, J. (2000), 'Pragmatic Realism? Searching for Criminology in the New Youth Justice' in B. Goldson (ed.), *The New Youth Justice*, Lyme Regis: Russell House Publishing.

Munice, J. and MacLaughlin, E. (1998), *Criminological Perspectives: A Reader*, London: Sage.

NAAPS (1997), *The National Association of Asian Probation Service: Working Together for Change*, London: NAAPS.

Nacro (1989), *Race and Criminal Justice*, London: Nacro.

Nacro (1991a), *Black Communities and the Probation Service: Working Together for Change*, A Report of the Sub-committee of the Nacro Race Issues Advisory Committee, London: Nacro.

Nacro (1991b), *Black People's Experience Of Criminal Justice*, London: Nacro.

Nacro (1991c), *A Fresh Start for Women Prisoners*, London: Nacro.

Nacro (1993), *Women Leaving Prison*, London: Nacro.

Nacro (1996), *Women Prisoners: Towards A New Millennium*, London: Nacro.

Nacro (1997), *Policing Local Communities: The Tottenham Experiment*, London.

Nacro (2000a), Prisoner Resettlement Surveys, (unpublished), London.

Nacro (2000b), *Race and Prisons: A Snapshot Survey*, London: Nacro.

Nacro (2001), *Women Beyond Bars*, London: Nacro.

Nacro (2002), *Resettling Prisoners from Black and Minority Ethnic Groups*, London: Nacro.

Naffine, N. (1990), *Law and the Sexes*, London: Allen and Unwin.

Naffine, N. (1997), *Feminism and Criminology*, Cambridge: Polity Press.

NAPO (1988), *Racism, Representation and the Criminal Justice System*, London: NAPO.

NAPO and ABPO (1996), *Race, Discrimination and the Criminal Justice System*, London: NAPO and ABPO.

Ndetei, D. M. and Vadher, A. (1984), 'A Cross-cultural Study of the Frequencies of Schneider's First Rank Symptoms of Schizophrenia', *Acta Psychiatrica Scandinivia*, 70, 540-544.

Nelken, D. (1989), 'Discipline and Punish: Some Notes on the Margin', *Howard Journal*, 28.

Neustatter, A. (2002), *Locked In, Locked Out: The Experience of Young Offenders Out of Society and In Prison*, Gulbenkian Foundation: London.

O'Dwyer, J. and Carlen, P. (1985), 'Josie: Surviving Holloway and Other Women's Prisons' in P. Carlen *et al.*, (1985), *Criminal Women*, Cambridge: Polity Press.

Offences Against Prison Discipline and Punishments 1991 (1992), London: Home Office.

Office for National Statistics (2001), *Social Trends 31*, London: Stationery Office .

Whitfield, D (2002), Introduction to the Probation Service, Waterside Press.

Padel U. and Stevenson P. (1988), *Insiders: Women's Experience of Prisons*, Virago.

Parkman, S. *et al.* (1997), 'Ethnic Differences in Satisfaction with Mental Health Services among Representative People with Psychosis in South London: PRISM Study 4', *British Journal of Psychiatry*, 171, 260-264.

Pathak, S. (2000), *Race Research for the Future: Ethnicity in Education, Training and the Labour Market*, Research Topic Paper, London: DfEE.

Phillips, C. *et al.* (2000), *A Review of Audits and Strategies Produced by Crime and Disorder Partnerships in 1999*, Home Office Briefing Note 8/00, London: Home Office.

Pinder R. (1984), *Probation Work in a Multi-Racial Society*, University of Leeds Applied Anthropology Group.

Platt S. (1986), 'Return of Broadwater Farm', *New Socialist*, April.

Player E. (1988), *Women Lifers: Assessing the Experience*, Cropwood Series, No 19.

Player E. (1989), *Women and Crime in the City*, Basingstoke: Macmillan.

Policing London (1985), Greater London Council, 3,16:17-32.

Pollak O. (1950), *The Criminality of Women*, Philadelphia: University of Pennsylvania Press.

Poverty in Black and White: Deprivation and Ethnic Minorities (1992), Child Poverty Action Group with the Runnymede Trust.

Prison Reform Trust (1991), *The Identikit Prisoner*, London: Prison Reform Trust.

Prison Reform Trust (2000), *Justice for Women: The Need for Reform*, Report of the Committee on Women's Imprisonment chaired by Professor Dorothy Wedderburn, London: Prison Reform Trust

Probation Studies Unit (2000), *Draft Report on the Retrospective Study of the Hereford and Worcester Probation Service Women's Programme*, (unpublished), Oxford University Centre for Criminological Research.

Race and Criminal Justice, Penal Affairs Consortium, September 1996.

Race and Sentencing: A Study in the Crown Court (1992), Clarendon Press.

Race and Criminal Justice, Penal Affairs Consortium, September 1996.

Radelet M. and Pierce G. (1985), Race and Prosecution Discretion in Homicide Cases, *Law and Society Review.*

Raynor, P. *et al.* (1994), *Effective Probation Practice,* London: Macmillan.

Reiner, R. (1992a), *The Politics of the Police* (edn 2), London: Harvester Wheatsheaf.

Reiner R. (1992b), 'Race, Crime and Justice: Models of Interpretation' in L. Gelsthorpe (ed.), *Minority Ethnic Groups in the Criminal Justice System',* Cambridge: Cambridge Institute of Criminology.

Rex, J. and Moore, R. (1967), *Race, Community and Conflict,* London: Oxford University Press.

Rex, S. (2000), 'Beyond Cognitive Behaviourism? Reflections on the Effectiveness Literature'. Paper Presented at the 24th Cropwood Conference, 'Future Directions for Community Penalties', University of Cambridge

Rice, M (1990), 'Challenging Orthodoxies in Feminist Theory: A Black Feminist Critique', in L. Gelsthorpe and A. Morris, *Feminist Perspectives in Criminology*, Milton Keynes: Open University Press.

Roberts, C. (1989), *Women and Rape,* Harvester Wheatsheaf.

Roberts, Y., 'To the Slaughter', *New Statesman and Society,* 13 October 1989.

Rock, P. (1996), *Reconstructing Women's Prison: The Holloway Redevelopment Project 1968-88,* Oxford: Clarendon Press.

Rumgay, J. (1996), 'Women Offenders: Towards a Needs Based Policy', *Vista,* September, 104-15.

Runnymede Trust (2000), *The Future of Multi-Ethnic Britain: The Parekh Report,* London: Profile Books.

Scarman, L. (1981), *The Scarman Report,* London: Home Office.

Scraton, P. (1987), *Law, Order and the Authoritarian State: Reading in Critical Criminology,* Milton Keynes: Open University Press.

Senior, P. (1993), 'Groupwork in the Probation Service: Care or Control in the 1990s' in Brown, A. and Caddick, B. (eds.), *Groupwork with Offenders,* London: Whiting and Birch.

Shah, R. and Pease, K. (1992), 'Crime, Race and Reporting to the Police', *Howard Journal.*

Shaw, M. (1993), 'Reforming Federal Women's Imprisonment' in E. Adelberg and C. Curtis (eds.), *In Conflict With The Law: Women and The Canadian Justice System,* Vancouver: Press Gang Publishers.

Sherman Gottfredson, D. *et al.* (1997), 'Preventing Crime: What Works and What Doesn't, What's Promising', Report to the United States Congress at http//www.ncjrs.org.

Simon R. J. (1975), *Women and Crime,* Massachusetts: Lexington.

Simourd, L. and Andrews, D. (1996), 'Correlates of Delinquency: a Look at Gender Differences' @ Microsoft Internet Explorer, Vol. 6, No. 1, pp. 1-7.

Sivanandan, A. (1983), 'Challenging Racism: Strategies for the Eighties', *Race and Class.*

Skogan, W. G. (1990), 'The Police and the Public in England and Wales: A British Crime Survey', Home Office Research Study 117, London: Home Office.

Sly, F. *et al.* (1999), 'Trends in the Labour Market Participation of Ethnic Groups', *Labour Market Trends,* December 1999, 631-639.

Smart, C. (1989), *Feminism and the Power of Law,* London: Routledge.

Smart, C. (1992), *Regulating Womanhood,* London: Routledge.

Smith, D. J. (1994), *Race, Crime and Criminal Justice,* in M. Maguire, *et al.* (eds), *The Oxford Handbook of Criminology,* (edn. 2) Oxford: Clarendon.

Smith, D. J. (1997), 'Ethnic Origins, Crime and Criminal Justice,' in Maguire, M. *et al.* (eds.), *The Oxford Handbook of Criminology,* (Edn. 2), Oxford: Clarendon.

Smith, D. and Stewart J. (1998), 'Probation and Social Exclusion', in C. Jones Finer and M. Nellis (eds.), *Crime and Social Exclusion,* pp. 96-115, Oxford: Blackwell.

Social Exclusion Unit (2002), *Reducing Re-offending by Ex-prisoners,* London: HMSO.

Social Work Services and Prisons. Inspectorates for Scotland (1998), *Women Offenders: A Safer Way,* Edinburgh: HMSO.

Southall Black Sisters (1989), 'Two Struggles: Challenging Male Violence and the Police', in C. Dunhill (ed.), *The Boys in Blue: Women's Challenge to the Police,* London: Virago.

Spelman, E. (1988), *Inessential Women,* Boston: Beacon Press.

Stafford Law Review (1990), Cited in Marlee Kline.

Steele, J (2002), 'Police Fear Crime Explosion as School-Age Muggers Graduate to Guns', *Daily Telegraph*, January 3.

Steffensmeier, D. and Haynie, D. (2000), Gender, Structural Disadvantage and Urban Crime: Do Macrosocial Variables Also Explain Female Offending Rates?', *Criminology*, vol. 38, no. 2, pp. 403-38.

Stevens, P. and Willis, C. F. (1981), 'Ethnic Minorities and Complaints against the Police', Research and Planning Unit Paper No. 5, London: Home Office.

Swigert, V. L. and Farrel R. A. (1977), *Glenview, Deviance and Social Control*, University of Illinois Press.

'The Women of Broadwater Farm' (1989), Local Pamphlet.

Tarzi, A. (1993), *Victims of Freedom*, University of Cambridge Institute of Criminology.

Taylor, W. (1981), *Probation and After-Care in a Multi-Racial Society*, London: Commission for Racial Equality.

Thomas, D. (1998), *R. v. Ollerenshaw*, Commentary, *Criminal Law Review*, July: 515-16.

Tuck, M. and Southgate, P. (1981), *Ethnic Minorities, Crime and Policing: A Survey of the Experiences of West Indians and Whites*, Home Office Research Study 70. London: Home Office.

Tuklo Orenda Associates (1999), *Making a Difference, A Positive and Practical Guide to Working with Black Offenders*, Tuklo Orenda Associates for the South West Probation Training Consortium, with support from the Home Office Probation Unit.

Vennard, J. and Hedderman, C. (1998), 'Effective Interventions with Offenders', in P. Goldblatt and C. Lewis (eds.), *Reducing Offending: An Assessment of Research Evidence on Ways of Dealing with Offending Behaviour*, Home Office Research Study, 187, London: HMSO.

Villarosa, L. (1994), *Body and Soul: The Black Woman's Guide to Physical Health and Emotional Well-Being*, New York: Harper Perennial.

Visher, C. (1983), 'Gender, Police Arrest Decisions and Notions of Chivalry', *Criminology*, 21:5-2.

Voakes, R. and Fowler, Q. (1989), *Sentencing, Race and Social Enquiry Reports*, West Yorkshire Probation Service.

Walker, M. A. (1989), 'The Court Disposal and Remands of White, Afro-Caribbean, and Asian Men (London, 1983)', *British Journal of Criminology*.

Wedderburn, Professor Dorothy (2000), *Justice for Women: The Need for Reform*, Report of the Committee on Women's Imprisonment, London: Prison Reform Trust.

Wessely, S. *et al.* (1991), 'Schizophrenia and Afro-Caribbeans: A Case Control Study', *British Journal of Psychiatry*, 159, 795-801.

Whitehouse, P. (1983), 'Race, Bias and Social Enquiry Reports', *Probation Journal*.

Wilkinson, C. (1988), *Post-Release Experience of Female Prisoners*, Cropwood Series, No 19.

Williams, P. (2001), *Evaluation of the Black Offender Groupwork Programme*, Greater Manchester Probation Service.

Willis, C. F. (1983), 'The Use, Effectiveness and Impact of Police Stop and Search Powers', Research and Planning Unit Paper Jno. 15, London: Home Office.

Wilson, M. (1993), *Crossing the Boundaries; Black Women and Incest*, London: Virago.

Women in Custody (1989), NAPO, May.

Woolner, C. (2000), 'Guns and Violent Crime in America', MA Criminology Dissertation, Middlesex University.

Worrall, A. (1990), *Offending Women: Female Lawbreakers and the Criminal Justice System*, London: Routledge.

Worrall, A. (1997), *Punishment in the Community*, Harlow: Longman.

Young, J. (1986), 'The Failure of Radial Criminology: The Need for a Radical Realism', in R. Matthews and J. Young (eds.), *Confronting Crime*, London: Sage

Young, J. (1999), *The Exclusive Society: Social Exclusion in Crime and Difference in Late Modernity*, London: Sage.

Yung, B. R. and Hammond, W.R. (1997), 'Anti-social Behaviour in Minority Groups: Epidemiological and Cultural Perspectives' in M. Stoff and J. Breiling (eds.), *Handbook of Anti-social Behaviour*, New York: John Wiley.

Zedner, L. (1991), *Women, Crime and Custody in Victorian England*, Oxford: Clarendon Press.

Zimring F. E. (1976), *Making the Punishment Fit the Crime*, Hastings Centre, Report No. 6.

INDEX

AN OPEN INVITATION

The Waterside A to Z of Criminal Justice and Penal Affairs is scheduled for publication towards the end of 2003.

The work—which is currently in progress—already contains some 15,000 entries comprising words, phrases, acronyms, abbreviations, explanations and items of interest about criminal justice and penal affairs.

The entries are both current and historical covering important landmarks, key developments, trials, cases, events, issues, publications and people who have made a significant contribution to the system as it is today.

Each entry consists of one or more paragraphs (entries are sometimes longer depending on the subject matter). The work is cross-referenced so that connections can be made between related (and sometimes not so obviously-related) subjects.

The work builds on experience of writing, editing and publishing in this field over many years—including some 200 Waterside Press projects alone. The aim is for the *A to Z* to be a comprehensive, interesting, useful, educational and functional collection of concise explanations.

No matter how extensive the research, there is always 'yet another' area to explore. If you think that you have a topic, issue or information which might be included—perhaps something that you felt could, or should, have been explained to you, or which still puzzles or perplexes you—you are invited to email a brief note to editorial@watersidepress.co.uk (or you can write to Bryan Gibson, Waterside Press, Domum Road, Winchester SO23 9NN) when a corresponding item can be considered for inclusion (if too late for the first edition, then in subsequent ones).

For further details of the *A to Z* and information about the publication schedule please visit our web-site: www.watersidepress.co.uk or telephone 01962 855567.

Information about **Angela Devlin's** work *Invisible Women: What's Wrong with Women's Prisons?* and **Penny Green's** book *Drugs, Trafficking and Criminal Policy: The Scapegoat Strategy* (both mentioned by **Ruth Chigwada-Bailey** in *Black Women's Experiences of Criminal Justice* can also be viewed at the web-site—along with other titles of interest to readers of this work.